PENGUIN LIFE

Parent Talk

Dr Wendy Mogel is a clinical psychologist, parenting expert, a *New York Times* bestselling author and international keynote speaker. Her mission is the protection and promotion of self-reliance, resilience, accountability and exuberance in children. She was once on a programme with President Barack Obama, once with His Holiness the Dalai Lama, and once with the circus.

ALSO BY WENDY MOGEL

The Blessing of a Skinned Knee
The Blessing of a B Minus

Parent Talk

*Transform Your Relationship
with Your Child by Learning
What to Say, How to Say
It and When to Listen*

Wendy Mogel

PENGUIN LIFE

AN IMPRINT OF

PENGUIN BOOKS

PENGUIN LIFE

UK | USA | Canada | Ireland | Australia
India | New Zealand | South Africa

Penguin Life is part of the Penguin Random House group of companies
whose addresses can be found at global.penguinrandomhouse.com.

First published in the United States of America by Scribner, an imprint of Simon and Schuster, Inc. 2018
First published in Great Britain by Penguin Life 2018
001

Printed and bound in Great Britain by Clays Ltd, Elcograf S.p.A.

A CIP catalogue record for this book is available from the British Library

ISBN: 978–0–241–27658–7

www.greenpenguin.co.uk

Penguin Random House is committed to a
sustainable future for our business, our readers
and our planet. This book is made from Forest
Stewardship Council® certified paper.

To Ann and Leonard Mogel

It was as though she had stepped into a boat and was swept off by a strong current. She did not know what all the words meant, and she could not pronounce a good many of the names, but nobody interrupted to correct her, and she read on and on, steadied by the strongly marked rhythm, drawn forward swiftly from one clanging, sonorous rhyme to another.

—Dorothy Canfield Fisher,
from *Understood Betsy*, 1916

Contents

Contents

Author's Note

When I was a psychology student in the 1970s, some awful fictions were sold as fact: schizophrenia was caused by "schizophrenogenic" (overprotective yet rejecting) mothers; autism by "refrigerator" mothers; male homosexuality by weak dads, helpless to control their overbearing wives. During the same era, the women's movement aimed to banish the concept of biology as destiny. Girls and boys came into the world as equals. What mattered was nurture. Provide girls with blocks and boys with dolls, and the differences would evaporate. While well-intentioned, this approach to protecting rights and allowing for growth and unlimited opportunity was too narrow and didn't withstand scientific scrutiny.

Yet the 1970s also yielded some awesome truths that hold today. One was the theory of psychological androgyny developed by social psychologist Sandra Bem. Her robust research revealed that girls who exhibited some traits traditionally considered "masculine" and boys who displayed some that were considered "feminine" were emotionally healthier than children whose range of attitudes and behaviors fell at the extremes of gender norms. Bem found that narrowly defined, restrictive gender roles had a negative effect on individuals and on society as a whole.

Bem began a movement that shifted from fixed definitions of gender expression to today's more nuanced understanding of the rich and complex variations of human identity and sexuality. In the late 1980s, I had an experience that helped me deepen my insight into this topic. The parents of four-and-a-half-year-old Ash came to see me about their son's perplexing behavior. His mom said, "At least once a day, Ash suddenly turns his head and looks upward with a concerned expression on his face. Then he lifts his arms, bends both elbows, scrunches up his fists, and dashes across the room on his toes. I asked him why he was doing this and he explained in a matter-of-fact tone, 'When Cinderella sees the clock is about to chime midnight, she has to gather up the skirts of her ball gown so she can fly over to the pumpkin coach really, really fast.' Dr. Mogel, we're worried he's suffering from gender identity disorder."

At that time, "GID" was considered a mental disorder and was much in the news. To determine an appropriate diagnosis and treatment plan, I consulted with two senior psychiatrist colleagues who specialized in working with young boys who had this "condition." One held a philosophy of rigid rules akin to those employed by gay conversion therapists: "Tell those parents to immediately purge the boy's room of any dolls and feminine costumes, not to permit any playdates with girls, and that Dad has to start playing sports with him every day. They should also enroll him in at least one peewee team."

The other colleague said, "Tell the parents to let him be. To celebrate his imagination and even join in the fun. Mom might ask, 'Do the seats in a pumpkin coach have cushions? Or are they more like benches?'"

When I met with Ash's parents I told them not to worry over his present behavior or forecast his future. "All we know *now* is that sometimes he's Cinderella and we love him. And that your respect for his creativity and self-expression is vital for his growth."

The 1990s brought advanced technological tools in neuroscience, providing a flood of data about gender differences in rates of cognitive, emotional, and physical development; sensory perceptions like hearing and sight; anatomy and brain architecture; the effect of hormones on emotions; and other attributes that are subtle but significant when communicating with children and teenagers. We don't yet have a substantial body of research on whether transgendered people have brains more similar to their "experienced gender" than to their "assigned gender" (the one checked off on the box on their birth certificate) but the work has begun. Today most mental health professionals (and young people) understand that gender falls on a spectrum rather than into neat binary categories, and that each person's experience of who they are, how they want to dress, what name they prefer to be called, and who they are drawn to for companionship, romance, and sexual involvement don't fit into pre-determined or fixed classifications.

With technology and social media, parents must be lifelong learners in order to make and enforce sensible and protective rules for their children. The same is true of understanding gender expression. If you want your child to see you as a trusted traveler, you have to do your homework. I know of no better starting place than the website genderspectrum.org. It's a jargon-free, non-polemical, sober, and thorough resource for educators, parents, and teenagers.

In reading the *Parent Talk* chapters about boys and girls and my statements about attitudes and behaviors of mothers and fathers, please insert mental quotation marks as needed around the references to gender differences. The same applies if you are a single parent, a same-sex couple, or belong to any of the new family configurations that now coexist alongside the more traditional nuclear family.

A sensitive understanding of biological differences provides insight into how we can help girls become the confident and creative scientists, engineers, and mathematicians we'll need in the twenty-first century while at the same time protecting them from pressure to be perfect and overly accommodating of others in every aspect of their lives. It allows us to find the best ways to promote the pride and capabilities of boys in a changing economy and in classrooms where their high energy and delight in "finding the funny" are too often seen as symptoms of a problem. Boys need adult mentors to raise them to be men who are emotionally expressive, deeply connected to and concerned about others, and capable of regulating their strong impulses.

My main goal in *Parent Talk* is to teach readers how to learn the dialect needed to converse with their daughters and sons at every stage and in every phase of the child's life. Some lessons are based on the new understanding of neuroscience and biology, some on my decades of clinical practice with all types of families, some on recent and unfolding cultural insights. None are meant to stereotype or generalize. Always, I rely on parents to adapt strategies to suit their own values and the evolving spirit, personality, and needs of their unique child.

In order to protect the privacy of the individuals and institutions described in this book, I've changed names, identifying characteristics, and locations of events as appropriate.

Introduction

This is a book for parents who want to find their voice.

Some of you are new mothers or fathers, just beginning the life-long conversation that will redefine you and shape the tiny being you have conjured into the world.

Some of you have been parents for a few years or for many. You may be hoarse from saying the same things over and over, whether reminding, pleading, or screaming, and still you aren't heard: your child forgets to flush the toilet, tells his little sister she's stupid, says he can't fall asleep ever, and dawdles in the morning always. Or despite your nightly appeals or threats, your daughter does her homework while socializing online and speaks to you in a manner so rough and rude, your own mother would have grounded you for it. Your words are weightless but you don't give up, you just lose faith in yourself and lose hope for your child.

Some of you are mute. You *have* given up. You have lost inspiration, confidence, and the energy to keep trying to connect with your child. You've mastered the perfect angle from which to take a selfie with your fourteen-year-old, but the two of you seem to have nothing in common. So you default to nagging about schoolwork or retreat to the easy companionship of screens or the demands of your job.

Hoarse or mute, new parents or seasoned, you wonder if there's a magic formula that will make everything easier, everything better.

1

Introduction

There's no magic formula. All you have is your voice. But if you know how to use it, your voice is all you need.

Parent Talk is about talking to children and teenagers and teaching them to express themselves in spoken language. It's about using words and tone, cadence and timing, setting and demeanor, to deepen your relationship with your child. It's not a formula but a practice.

Humans are wired to communicate. The baby looks you in the eye, your mirror neurons fire away, she coos and babbles. You instinctively repeat her sounds, gestures, and expressions. Soon the two of you are exchanging words, then sentences. But although it is the most natural of skills, talking to a child requires devotion, forethought, and patience. It involves the serve and return volley of vocalizations, the restraint required for good listening, and a welcoming attitude toward breezy, rib-tickling, gross-out, deep, heartbreaking, heartfelt, awkward-but-worthy, and illuminating talk. All these conversations enrich family life by building bonds of love and trust, enhancing children's understanding of their own passions and preferences, and helping them see their parents and other adults as complete people.

I've been working with parents and children for more than three decades. My focus has been on educating parents about child development, family dynamics, and unrealistic cultural expectations. This understanding helped them relate to their children in a more sensitive and authoritative way. But a few years ago I began to change my approach.

I had always encouraged parents to reenact with me the arguments or impasses they were experiencing with their children. As we drilled down during these sessions, I started noticing *how* they were saying things as much as *what* they were saying. These women and men were normally excellent communicators. With other adults they spoke in strong, clear, direct tones. But when role-playing the fights with their children, I watched an often dramatic transformation. They shrank and froze. They sounded weak, wounded, indignant, exasperated. Some talked in baby voices. Some whispered. All sounded high-pitched and pinched. Their shoulders would hunch up, and they'd start jabbing their fingers accusingly.

At that point I would ask, "And then did you start shouting?" Heads bowed, they would nod. I'd say, "How loud? Do it now." They would try. I'd smile. "Wow, she really won that round, huh?" We'd laugh. Sharing this frustration and shame had a dual purpose: it lightened their load and helped them see that even if their words were psychologically spot-on, the children weren't listening because of the way the message was being delivered.

I decided to flip my usual process with a few clients and begin our work together by coaching them on vocal techniques. I would introduce the concepts of speaking in a lower register and with more warmth, slowing their tempo, and displaying relaxed but confident body language. Then we'd practice, and I would encourage them to use their new skills starting that night.

The children's transformations were surprisingly swift. Parents reported that even small changes in their tone and demeanor shifted the entire metabolism of the relationship. When the parents trained themselves to listen attentively and have child-sized conversations with their young sons and daughters, the children cooperated and became more obliging and expansive. The same thing happened when parents learned to find openings for respectful, agenda-free conversations with teenagers.

The art of conversation with children rests not only on content but also on learning to speak in an ever-changing dialect that evolves as the child matures. Nearly any idea can be communicated if the adult's style and form matches the cognitive development, interests, and temperament of the child listener. These factors, along with typical gender differences in how children learn, influence what a boy or girl hears and comprehends. Your seven-year-old son is doomed if you expect him to listen and respond the way his older sister did at that age. But tune in to *his* channel and you'll have an easier time getting through.

The lessons in this book are designed to elevate the atmosphere in your home, bring you closer to your children, and act as a counterbalance to our nervous and distracted culture. But to take full advantage of these strategies, there's one more voice you may need to adjust. It's the voice in your head whispering, *There's not enough.* Not enough resources, spots in the best schools, teacher's attention, opportunities, friends who'll provide the right type of influence. Not enough hours in the day, funds in the account, time to protect the planet, chances to do things over. Fear of scarcity is alive and blooming inside the minds of most parents. That's what sends their voice into the pinched and panicky zone. Fear is behind the rushing, hovering, chiding, and pleading that sours our conversations with our children.

For as long as I've practiced therapy with families, parents have been worried about scarcity. Now, as technology pulls us toward a thrilling but unfathomable future, they are even more frightened. The children must cultivate twenty-first-century skills! But what are those? Coding or welding? Robotics or foraging? Fluency in Mandarin, or the social and emotional finesse to be both a leader and a team player? Or all of the above? Well-meaning parents swing between frantic overplanning and hopeless paralysis. Meanwhile their children suffer from anxiety, depression, nightmares, eating disorders, and dwindling motivation.

The pace of our world will keep speeding up. Although this feels terrifying, as if you can't do the one thing you're programmed to do—*protect your child*—it is also liberating. Worry and plan as you might, you can't predict which skills will be rewarded, which degrees will lead to the most fulfilling careers, which jobs will be the most lucrative, or which cities will be safe for your child twenty years from now. The way to protect your child is not by trying to outmaneuver the future. It's by focusing on what is timeless and providing the basics children have always needed: stability, consistency, tenderness, and acceptance.

Relinquish the fear and you open a door to enchantment. One of the great pleasures of being a parent is getting to grow up a second time, in another era, led by a small person with a sensibility that is quite different from yours. Children's fresh perspective, playfulness, and innocence, their ardent desire to know, adds color to your life. Being a parent can reduce rather than increase your stress if you recognize that it's a chance to explore majestic and mysterious places alongside your son or daughter. No matter how much jeopardy our planet is in, it's still green and watery and full of beauty and magic, and children are filled with wonder. They will lead you on an incredible journey if they trust you, if you take the time, and if you're willing to follow.

CHAPTER 1

The Audience Is Listening

From Infancy through Toddlerhood

A mother's first words to her newborn are soft and musical, sweet and high. Social scientists call this instinctive language Parentese. It used to be known as Motherese, until researchers noticed that when speaking to babies, men also emphasize key words, simplify their syntax, and slow their delivery to match the child's attention span and comprehension level. Children as young as three spontaneously speak Parentese to babies and toddlers.

What are the hallmarks of Parentese? A lilting cadence with enough variation to draw baby's focus. A raised pitch that is gentle rather than squeaky. Drawn-out vowels and clear, exaggerated consonants. A simple but appealing vocabulary with alliteration and repetition: "That's a big bubble! It's bedtime for baby. Bedtime for a sweet, sleepy baby." While infants can't understand the meaning of individual words, they are alert to diverse aspects of your presentation—volume and rhythm, emphasis and repetition, eye contact, facial expressions, and gestures.

Perhaps most important is the constant feedback between parent and child. The baby points and smiles or cries, and the parent describes what the child is seeing: "That's a BIG DOGGIE! A big doggie on our street!" As the child learns to form words, the parent offers gentle encouragement, using proper pronunciation and expanding on the topic:

"Twuck!"

"That's right, it's a yellow truck."

Parent Talk

As early as 1977, Harvard psychologist and linguist Catherine E. Snow wrote that "language acquisition is the result of a process of *interaction* between mother and child, which begins early in infancy, to which the child makes as important a contribution as the mother, and which is crucial to cognitive and *emotional* development as well as language acquisition." She was ahead of her time: for two decades there were no experimental studies to back up her claim. But scientific advances now suggest that brain development is indeed linked to social interaction. Parentese, baby's bridge to verbal communication, is more than a way to teach language. It helps shape and support a child's ability to think.

WHAT TO SAY TO A BABY

From the first days of life, your baby is learning about tone and rhythm and how sentences are constructed. Enjoy this fleeting phase of parenthood. Take the liberty to indulge in uncensored monologues that would bore, offend, or irk those with more developed comprehension. Soon enough your toddler will be able to repeat verbatim that which you did not intend to share with other adults. Your child will have the verbal skill to command, "Don't talk! No singing!" At bedtime your imperious four-year-old will decree, "No. Not that story! I want the one about how I fall into a magical hole and meet two princesses named Mariella and Marietta and one night they go swimming in the moat and they meet a fish who can speak French. Tell a story exactly like that, but this time it's not a fish. And it's not French. OK?" This is what awaits you, but for now your baby will cheerfully tolerate your aimless thinking out loud.

In addition to chatting about your thoughts, feelings, and plans, get in the habit of narrating your baby's daily routines. Pulling a shirt off baby without warning can surprise her; wiping a tender bottom might sting; water poured on the head without explanation can startle. Previewing the action helps baby learn trust and acclimates her to her world. Turn off the radio or television when you're talking so she can hear your words easily. Use vivid, simple, but detailed descriptions:

"Now I'm going to wash you with this slippery soap. See the bubbles? You can pop them!"

"These pointy spikes on your comb are called teeth, like teeth in your mouth. All in a row."

Don't worry about introducing unfamiliar words. This is how baby expands her vocabulary, and new sounds and combinations of syllables will hold her interest as much as your lively narration. Use words that come prepackaged with sensory delights:

"The WATER SPLASHES when we slap our hands down!"

"This peach is really ripe! The juice SQUIRTS out when I bite it!"

"I hear Mittens PURRING. Do you hear him?"

Prepare your baby for specific sensations she will experience:

"Our new rug is here. Let's see how it feels to touch it. It's SOFT and FUZZY!"

"This is your red sweater. Let's put it on so you'll be WARM."

Orient her to her surroundings:

"Listen. Do you hear that loud whirring sound? There might be a HELICOPTER in the SKY above the house. Let's go see if we can find it!"

"Now we're going out the door and down the steps. One, two, three! Here's our car in the driveway."

Of course there will be plenty of times when your loving voice will not please or comfort. Don't take it personally if your tired or cranky baby rejects you or ignores your tender tone. Sometimes a good cry is the exercise she needs most.

SINGING AWAY THE BABY BLUES

In every culture mothers sing lullabies to soothe both their babies and themselves. The songs follow a consistent pattern. Their meter mimics the rocking motion the fetus experienced in the womb, and the melodies are simple, often composed of only five notes. The tempo is steady and hypnotic. These attributes align with the newborn's limited ability to process sound and movement. When mother sings, baby feels the familiar vibration of her vocal cords, the rhythmic movement of her breath, and is soothed by the swaying of her body.

Lullabies serve a deeper purpose than merely quieting a fussy child. Just as their musical form is consistent across the globe, so is the startling nature of their lyrics. Some are plaintive incantations to "hush, go to sleep," but often the words slide into a darker realm of uncertainty, fear, and loneliness.

> Twelve weary months have crept away
> Since he, upon thy natal day
> Left thee and me, to seek afar
> A bloody fate in doubtful war.
> Baloo, my boy, lie still and sleep.
> It grieves me sore to hear thee weep.
>
> —"Lady Anne Bothwell's Lament,"
> Scotland

> Hush, little baby, don't you cry.
> You know your mama was born to die.
>
> —"All My Trials," Bahamas

Lullabies are a weary parent's chance to express raw truths. When dark feelings are transposed into music, the day's buildup of frustration, fear, and resentment is given wings. Instead of hardening into bitterness, it evaporates, refreshing your view of the loveliness of your sleeping child.

The healing properties of lullabies have been confirmed by science. Studies of infants in intensive care units show that hearing a lullaby steadies babies' heart rate and breathing, helps them eat and sleep better, and reduces their perception of pain during medical tests. And as baby listens to your lullaby, she's learning to communicate. She takes in your words and facial expressions, and she coos back. She watches your lips and mimics the shapes they make. Babies absorb your song with all their senses.

BLOOMING AND PRUNING: LANGUAGE AND BABY'S BRAIN

Technology allows us to peek inside the human brain and see how spoken language impacts children's development even before birth. Picture an incubator, its wee inhabitant a preemie delivered eight to fifteen weeks early. Inside the incubator, a small speaker plays the sound of mother's voice and heartbeat. Forty incubators are equipped with speakers; twenty preemies receive an extra three hours each day of the sounds of Mom. After one month, researchers use neuroimaging to measure each preemie's auditory cortex, the hearing center of the brain. Those with the extra hours of Mom have significantly larger auditory centers in the temporal lobe. Her voice and heartbeat have literally caused the baby's brain to grow larger.

The prenatal connection between mother's voice and baby's brain development has been proven in several studies of newborns. One day after birth, a newborn will suck on a pacifier faster for the reward of hearing a recording of his own mother's voice. Newborns can discriminate between their parents' language and one that is unfamiliar, and show a preference for the text of a book that was often read out loud before their birth.

How can babies know so much so soon? They are well-stocked packages. Just as female infants are born with all the eggs they'll need in later life to make babies of their own, the newborn's brain comes equipped with one hundred billion neurons and the ability to learn and reproduce the sounds and tones of any language. In the womb the sense of hearing is highly developed, which is why babies are born with some auditory neural pathways already well established.

After birth the brain is flooded with unfamiliar sounds as well as sights, smells, flavors, and textures. From this sensory soup the baby shapes a predictable world. The child could need *anything* to survive: the ability to identify rain clouds, or bicycle horns, or the smell of the family horse. The purr of Portuguese, the click of Khoekhoe, or the five tones required to speak Mandarin. The brain says, *Bring it on!*

and creates trillions of extra synapses by the time the child is three, twice the number an adult will possess.

Scientists call this *synaptic blooming*, and it makes the brains of young children extremely responsive to new input. For instance, with all those extra synapses, young children can easily absorb more than one language. As learning occurs, some synapses get eliminated, or pruned. Which ones? Those that are not used. The synapses that enable a child to click in Khoekhoe will shrivel if he is not raised in Namibia. The synapses that help a child discern the brightness of stars will diminish if she is not born to a seafaring tribe that navigates by the night sky. And if a child hears too few words in his native language, some of the unused synapses—such as those that support grammar and pronunciation—will wither. This doesn't mean it's impossible for the child to eventually master these skills, it means it will require more effort. Ideally, a child should get plenty of grammatically correct, properly pronounced, vocabulary-rich verbal input between birth and age five.

The brain of the child who hears a generous variety of words and sounds in a consistent context is etched with a rich map of neural pathways, and as he begins to mimic what he hears, the pathways are embedded more deeply. Numerous studies have documented the effect of the "word gap"—the difference in social and academic prowess among children who hear a plentiful assortment of words and those who don't. Watching television or playing with educational "language enrichment" apps does not support language learning in children under the age of two. Just as bodies need nutrients to grow, the brains of babies and young children thrive best in an atmosphere of abundant human-to-human verbal exchange.

WHY TALKING WITH DAD MAKES BABIES SMARTER

A toddler and his dad are ambling along my neighborhood's main street on Sunday morning when the boy sees something he wants. He smiles, releases his father's hand, and runs ahead to a bookstore. He bangs on the glass door with a small fist.

Dad: That's right, Jeb. That's the bookstore. It's closed today.

Jeb stops smiling and starts pounding.

Dad: I know. It's fun in there. That's where we go for story
time. Let's look inside. See? No one's there today, but we'll
come back again tomorrow when it's open.

The settings, posture, pace, social expectations, and language of
mothers and fathers teach different, equally valuable skills. Mothers'
style promotes social learning and bonding, while fathers provide a
bridge to the outside world by using a more adult tone, a different
lexicon, and more open-ended dialogue. Studies show that when
fathers hold a baby in their lap or wear a versatile carrier, they more
frequently choose to face the baby outward toward the passing scene
than do mothers, who face the baby toward their own body. It's a
fitting metaphor for the way time spent with Dad broadens and
enriches children's experience throughout their lives.

Again in my neighborhood: A dad kneels at eye level next to a
two-year-old in a stroller. They watch as workmen use a jackhammer
to break up a driveway across the street. Dirt and chunks of concrete
fly. The pair are mesmerized, equally appreciative of the noisy, dusty
spectacle.

Fathers bring to child-rearing a sense of adventure and taste for
risk that is often at odds with mothers' natural urge to protect and
plan. Dads take kids on buses and trains not only with the goal of
reaching a destination but also to share the thrill of traveling in large
vehicles with lots of people. They follow impulses to explore, to seek,
to be on the move and be in the moment even without packing extra
binkies, wipes, and snacks. When they encounter a challenge, the
children learn how to deal with the unexpected by watching Dad.

Lynne Vernon-Feagans studies the psychology of literacy and early
language development at the University of North Carolina. Her work
reveals that when fathers use a diverse vocabulary in interactions with

their infants, the children have more advanced communication skills at fifteen months and more advanced expressive language development at thirty-six months. Even if Mom and Dad have equivalent vocabularies, the children learn words more readily if Dad has been regularly interacting with them.

The researchers believe this might be because mothers generally still tend to spend more time with their children than do fathers. Mom can recite *Busy Penguins* in her sleep, so her commentary on the text may become a bit rote. The mother may also anticipate her child's wishes, unintentionally short-circuiting the conversation. If a brief whimper will produce lunch, why bother formulating a sentence? Out of habit, Mom may use words she knows the child already understands. When Dad isn't as attuned, it's natural for him to use new words, thus expanding the child's vocabulary. The novelty of spending time with Dad may also account for baby paying closer attention. It's not that dads are better playmates, just that they are different from Mom.

THE GIGGLES START HERE

Just as babies welcome your off-key lullaby, they find a well-timed joke endlessly funny. "Well-timed" means understanding how much sensory input they can tolerate. Your first bits will use physical sensations and sound. By two months your baby will smile back at you and mimic you if you stick out your tongue. But as with all stimulation for baby, there is a fragile boundary between fear and delight. Any rough handling—including tickling—can cause protest or tears, and the same silly snort that causes giggles when delivered gently will be alarming if it gets too loud.

Blow a raspberry on the belly of your four- or five-month-old and you can hear his laugh followed by passionate communication with his eyes, facial expression, feet, and legs: *Do it again! And now do it again, again!* As baby grows into toddlerhood, both physical and verbal antics amuse him. An adult crawls on the floor, barks, sniffs the air, and curls up like the dog. Or simply pokes her head from behind the door and says, "Boo!" Hilarious! And now baby starts to try his own material. Mom asks, "Where's your nose?" and he points to his foot, grinning madly. Will Mom chuckle if he puts a colander on his head like a hat? How about if he pours his milk from the high chair onto the floor? Oops, Mom looks peeved. Maybe she'll get a kick out of seeing the cereal bowl fly across the room. Jeez, tough crowd.

Some children are naturals. During a diaper change, my friend's eighteen-month-old son got some poop on his finger. He pointed at his mom and gleefully commanded, "Taste it!"

One two-year-old cracks herself up by mispronouncing names: her brother Jack is "Mack" and Daddy is "Paddy." Another tells her mom, "Amy Russell, you're a pretzel!" Eventually many toddlers get cagey. Two-year-old Flora says to her dad:

"Knock knock."
Dad: "Who's there?"
Flora: "Tickle."
Dad: "Tickle who?"
Flora: "Tickle Chloe [her big sister]!"

All through the very early years, children are deeply appreciative of adults who take the time to clown around, pretend to fall and bump into things, affect cartoon voices and silly walks, or indulge in over-the-top reactions like crying, "Oh, noooooo!" when a stuffed bear falls to the carpet. What an easy audience! You get to play on the main stage, kill with your lamest stand-up shtick, and develop the chops to coax a stubborn child to the table.

THE CONNECTION BETWEEN SOLID FOOD
AND SPEECH DEVELOPMENT

When I asked a friend with decades of experience as a preschool teacher if her students were showing more speech and articulation delays than in the past, she responded with an emphatic "Yes!" She said that people blame electronic gadgets but don't realize that part of the problem is the popularity of food pouches (plastic squeeze tubes of pureed fruits and vegetables). "The kids come into school sucking on their breakfast and then have another pouch filled with plum puree and quinoa for lunch. They get in a little baby-like trance, and there's definitely less conversation around the table."

There's a mechanical aspect to learning to speak that develops in tandem with baby's cognitive readiness. It's nature's way of making sure everything syncs up: the movements of the jaw, tongue, cheeks, mouth, and lips that allow baby to eat solid food are the same ones that facilitate speech. The muscles that allow us to talk are strengthened when we chew and swallow. As baby progresses from rooting for a nipple at birth, to more robust sucking, to eating her first mushy solids at age four to six months, she is preparing to utter her first words.

Certain speech milestones correlate directly to baby's eating milestones, for example, taking single sips from an open cup (not a sippy cup or bottle) correlates with advanced lip-movement sounds such as *"w,"* and being able to move food around inside the mouth enables baby to properly enunciate her words. As convenient as food pouches may be—and there's nothing wrong with occasionally using them as snacks—studies of children in day-care centers confirm what my colleague observed. Overuse of the pouches is affecting children's speech development.

Food pouches are a sorry substitute for the glorious world of cuisine. As a general guideline, babies older than one year should be able to sit in their high chairs and eat what the family is eating, with minimal modifications. The family dinner is a classic occasion for building conversational artistry, but mealtime with a toddler and one adult is also filled with opportunity. Here you can identify flavors, textures, and colors; describe why something is yummy or yucky; and experience the seasons through a bowl of fresh strawberries or pumpkin soup.

LOOK WHO'S NOT TALKING

The musical quality of Parentese may come naturally to everyone, but the amount of time parents spend talking to their babies varies widely. Many parents may consider songs, stories, and narration to be less important than keeping their child warm, fed, and well rested. Sometimes it's not a matter of priorities but of temperament. Maybe Mom is quiet by nature, or Dad feels shy about talking out loud to a baby who can only gurgle in response. Other parents, seeing how alert their baby is to facial expressions and how happily she responds to gentle physical play, consider the quality of that interaction both rich and sufficient.

Or maybe parents are distracted by a more predictably agreeable or urgently demanding companion: their phone. The impulse to respond to a beckoning ping diverts you from your baby's often subtle invitation to engage. Nothing on a screen provides such a personal and fleeting experience—fleeting because while your small child loves your singing and jokes today, she will not feel that way at fourteen.

Limiting your phone use while in the presence of your child is a healthy habit because babies learn language by having people talk to them and by overhearing conversations. For this to work, the child needs to hear both sides of the exchange. When a baby hears one half of a phone conversation, she can't fill in the gestalt—the context, meaning, back-and-forth rhythm of spoken words, and pauses that occur while listening. Instead she hears exclamations, random phrases, partial sentences. Meanwhile, the baby's own attempts to communicate by yelping, pointing, or kicking go unnoticed by the otherwise occupied parent.

Observed at a Starbucks in San Francisco: A dad holds a toddler in his arms as they approach the counter. I overhear him say, "Can you do me a favor?" The question strikes me as odd but polite, sweet, kind of cool. This man is confident that his tiny child can lend him a hand. Next I hear: "Look through the papers on my desk and find the unsigned contract. Then scan and send it now."

Whaaat? Idiot me. He's talking to his office on Bluetooth.

Still on the phone he says, "Hang on a second, OK?" He speaks to the barista and then resumes his conversation. His daughter is now excited by something she sees outside the window. She points her finger repeatedly and emits a few "ooh-oohs." I look outside and see . . . a cable car! Filled with people hanging onto straps! Passing right by us! Dad is still talking into the air. The little girl slumps and goes quiet. I soothe the pain of watching this with a revenge fantasy. *Just wait until that SAT verbal prep bill comes in the mail, my friend.*

I wish that scene were unusual. Nearly every time I'm out in public, I see children trying to get their parents' attention, but when parents are preoccupied on phones, the children quickly give up. Even sadder are the children who take one glance at the parent with the phone and don't even attempt to interrupt. One study found that adult behavior toward children during mealtime changes when phones or tablets are at the table: "Caregivers absorbed in devices frequently ignored the child's behavior for a while and then reacted with a scolding tone of voice, gave repeated instructions in a some-what robotic manner . . . seemed insensitive to the child's expressed needs, or used physical responses (e.g., one female adult kicked a child's foot under the table; another female caregiver pushed a young boy's hands away when he was trying to repeatedly lift her face up from looking at a tablet screen)."

The study reminds us that not just parents but all caretakers owe it to children to use devices judiciously. Talk to your babysitter or nanny about how babies' emotional and language development is delayed when the adults who are caring for them talk on their phones or focus on screens. Emphasize her vital role as your baby's teacher and conversational companion.

Children's reactions to phone-using caretakers or parents remind me of the famous "still face experiment" conducted in 1975 by develop-mental psychologist Ed Tronick. You can find it on YouTube; it's one of the most powerful and disturbing videos I've seen. The experiment begins with a mother talking to and playing with her infant. Mom is then instructed to turn her head away briefly and turn back with a blank look on her face. The camera stays on the infant's face as his expression changes from a recognition that something is a little off, to *Hey, Mom, seriously, what's up with you?* to increasingly intense efforts to re-engage Mom, to pure distress. It's painful to watch, and a relief when the mother is encouraged to follow her natural impulse to comfort her child.

The toddler at Starbucks who tried to get her distracted father's attention and then slumped in resignation reminded me of the babies in Dr. Tronick's lab. She wasn't frantic or frightened, as the child in the still-face experiment was, but her dejection reflected a tragic lesson learned.

TRANSPARENT DELIGHTS, OR WHY PRINT BEATS SCREEN

Babies can be boring and frustrating, toddlers irritating and relentless. The mother of a three-month-old once called me to ask, "OK, I've been lying on the floor with her for twenty minutes. Now what?" Another mom confessed, "Having a third baby was a huge mistake. I hate him. He doesn't sleep at all during the day and he's ugly. He looks like an old, bald man. And he cries all the time."

"We all want to cry all the time," I replied. "We just learn to control it."

"No one told me it would be like this! The girls were much easier."

Whether it's your first child or your fifth, the moment will come when you're either delirious from lack of sleep or bored beyond toleration. So why shouldn't you sneak a peek at your phone? Are you supposed to just stare at your baby until the two of you cry or nod off?

Not at all. But consider diverting yourself by looking at something that is not on a screen, like a book or magazine. When you do, the focus of your attention is more public, more accessible. Devices demand a different kind of engagement. Their pull on your emotions and cognition is more private, and your vision is tightly focused on a smaller space. Your peripheral awareness diminishes. If you're texting, it's interactive. If you're surfing the web or watching videos, it's moving and changing. The printed page is static. Nothing will change if you look up from it, which means you have more free-floating attention available to your environment. The parent who is reading a book in the park is more likely to notice his child's cry than a parent who is using his phone.

There is another, more subtle reason to choose print over electronic devices. If your child can see a cover, the heft of a book, the way you flip the pages of a magazine, she's absorbing useful information about you and learning more about your world and hers. The toddler can look over your shoulder with ease, comment on the cover or the images or ask whether the book is a good one. What is it about? Why do you want to read it? Your activity can serve as a catalyst for a conversation. In contrast, phones are not transparent, as Susan Dominus pointed out in a wistful essay entitled "Motherhood, Screened Off." She writes that whenever she grabs her phone, her children know she is also "holding a portal, as magical as the one in Narnia's wardrobe and with the same potential to transport me to another world or infinite worlds . . . How far am I going, they might reasonably worry, and how soon will I be back?"

In addition to the vagueness and inaccessibility of what you are doing on-screen, the fact that you can instantly swipe and hide it further closes you off to your child. It's true that grown-ups enjoy many diversions to which children should not be privy. This is part of the allure and mystery of adulthood. But texting is not mysterious, it's covert. Mysterious would be where Mom and Dad go on date night. Covert is exclusionary. A barrier.

Your baby—and later your toddler, child, and teenager—can get to know you by the books and magazines you read, the music you love, the teams you root for. When you're with your child, would you wear headphones to listen to music or follow a game? That would shut her out of the action. In the same way, letting her see what you're reading is a way to invite her into your world. Considering how much of her inner life you'll hope she will reveal to you in the years to come, sharing your own experiences now seems the comradely thing to do.

GADGETS AS BABYSITTERS

A young mom sits at a restaurant with a curly-haired boy snuggled in her lap, feeding him forkfuls of rice and vegetables. He squeaks, and she murmurs something in his ear. Then I see what he's squeaking at: a phone propped sideways where a teensy cartoon is playing. You may be thinking, *What's wrong with that? They're both happy, it's just a bit of entertainment! Relax already.*

I choose this scene to introduce the topic of iPads or phones as babysitters precisely because it's such a loving and innocent vignette. The trouble is, it is very likely occurring not once a week but multiple times a day. The research on young children using devices is ongoing, but as far as language development is concerned, the findings are not favorable.

Adults admit they are "addicted" to their devices, and there is science that supports the use of that word. Smartphones activate several parts of the brain that lead to compulsive behavior. From an evolutionary standpoint, we are driven to "seek." The neurotransmitter dopamine compels us to seek information, new experiences, and basics such as food and sex. Previously it was believed that dopamine controlled the brain's pleasure systems, but new studies reveal a more complex process: we feel pleasure when we seek and then find. "Finding" activates the opioid pleasure response. Neurologically speaking, we crave seeking as much as finding. Our phones allow us to seek information endlessly.

The seek-and-find pleasure is intensified if you don't know what you'll find or when you'll find it. Psychologists call this phenomenon "variable reinforcement." Text messages, tweets, and e-mail arrive at unpredictable, or "variable," times, prodding us to look and see the new information. The chimes that announce them tick another box on the compulsion list: the Pavlovian response.

21

None of this is coincidental. As longtime tech executive Bill Davidow reported in 2012, "Many Internet companies are learning what the tobacco industry has long known—addiction is good for business. There is little doubt that by applying current neuroscience techniques we will be able to create ever-more-compelling obsessions in the virtual world."

So parents are correct when they say they're addicted. Research is ongoing, but the spongelike brains of babies and toddlers should be protected from exposure to the addictive power of screens.

Parents who defend their babies' use of devices may claim that "it's educational" or "my child loves it!" Linda Stone, a tech executive, theorist, and coiner of the phrase "continuous partial attention," disagrees. "We may think that kids have a natural fascination with phones. Really, children have a fascination with whatever Mom and Dad find fascinating. If they are fascinated by the flowers coming up in the yard, that's what the children are going to find fascinating. And if Mom and Dad can't put down the device with the screen, the child is going to think, *That's where it's all at, that's where I need to be!*"

The American Academy of Pediatrics (AAP) has long advised parents not to allow any child under two to use a smartphone or tablet because of the potential delays in language development that are linked to such usage: "Neuroscience research shows that very young children learn best via two-way communication. 'Talk time' between caregiver and child remains critical for language development." In 2016 the AAP tweaked their position, saying that "some media can have educational value for children starting at around 18 months of age, but it's critically important that this be high-quality programming, such as the content offered by Sesame Workshop and PBS. . . . Problems begin when media use displaces physical activity, hands-on exploration and face-to-face social interaction in the real world, which is critical to learning. Too much screen time can also harm the amount and quality of sleep."

Currently there are no studies that link speech and language delays in elementary and high school students *exclusively* to the amount of time they spent on devices when they were very young. But a nation-wide study of students in the UK found that between 2007 and 2011 "the number of schoolchildren needing expert help for speech and language difficulties rose 71 per cent." iPhones first became available in January 2007.

SLEEP, NOISE, AND THE MUSIC OF THE TRIBE

There are times when you don't need to entertain your child with a device or anything else. Babies do occasionally sleep, and "getting them down" soon becomes the parents' passionate fixation. That's the reason for all the lullabies, the electronic vibrating crib-rocker, and the endless replays of Hawaiian slack-string guitar tunes or whatever random music baby has glommed onto as a sedative. Once he's nodded off, there's a tendency to tiptoe around and keep the house as silent as possible lest a raised voice wake him again.

The soundscape of your child's world is vital to his development. Yet just as an immaculate, germ-free environment reduces immunity to infection, there's no need to shush everyone up and create an unnaturally quiet zone at home just because baby is sleeping. While nothing soothes a newborn as powerfully as his mother's voice, he's also calmed by the other sounds of your tribe, which sifted through while he was in utero. The vacuum cleaner down the hall, the dog barking at the doorbell, big sister's rhythmic spring as she jumps on the couch—these are an old familiar soundtrack. He's more comfortable with your family's nearby rumble than with the lonely silence of an isolated nursery. The baby monitor calms your nerves, but not his.

Besides, almost any infant under the age of one is capable of falling asleep in a train wreck. You've seen them snoozing on Dad's shoulder in the midst of a boisterous birthday party. That said, babies should not be exposed to *excessive* noise outside the home. Their hearing is very sensitive, so you'll want to protect your little one from harsh, jarring, or high-decibel sounds. He'll look like a sweet lamb in the busy restaurant or at the outdoor festival, staring at the lights or dozing off, but you'll pay with an overstimulated, sleepless baby at two a.m.

More important, the noise could damage his hearing. Amplified music, revving car engines, the roar of large crowds (such as at sporting events), and other loud noises may cause permanent hearing loss in babies and young children. Because their skulls are thinner than those of adults, the inner ear is more vulnerable. Noise-canceling headphones for babies and children are inexpensive and easy to find online. If you think you might be in situations where your baby could be exposed to very loud noises, these are must-have accessories.

SILENT STEWARDSHIP: WHEN TO BE YOUR BABY'S QUIET COMPANION

Human beings have always used silence as a balm for the soul: the meditation room, the mountain hike, the secluded corner of a library. Silence is invaluable to babies as well, not as a precursor to nap time but as a gateway to the self. There are two powerful reasons for cultivating companionable silence with your baby. The first is practical and educational, the second more profound.

When babies are trying to solve problems at newly emerging edges of their competency, it's best for parents to refrain from jumping in too quickly with help, including verbal guidance. This is different from narrating daily rituals, and it requires some attentiveness on the part of the parent. Deborah Carlisle Solomon, an enlightened and experienced educator, told me that teaching mothers "not to talk, not to point, not even to ask questions directed toward solutions" is at the core of her infant-toddler curriculum.

Sitting in on a Mommy and Me class, I saw the parents' anxiety around this seemingly simple edict. Parents and babies were seated on a large flannel sheet strewn with toys. Eight-month-old Wyatt was stretching his arm toward a soft fabric ball that rested on a fold in the sheet, just beyond his grasp. Wyatt eyed the ball, grunting softly. His mother, seeing his effort, automatically reached out to slide it closer to him while describing her perception of his desire: "You want the ball!"

"Wait," the group facilitator softly coached her. "Let's watch and see what happens."

Young Wyatt was intent, determined, but not distressed. His grunting continued. Now mother was suffering more than child. It would be so easy to help! Suddenly Wyatt changed his strategy. Instead of reaching for the ball, he grabbed the sheet in his fist and pulled it with just enough force to release the ball from its fold, causing it to slide straight toward his waiting hand. The baby beamed! His mother exhaled.

"I know that was hard to watch at first, but look at Wyatt now," said Lisa. "That ball is gold! If you had made it easy for him to reach, it would still be a ball. Sit on your hands, imagine you have duct tape on your mouth, wait a few seconds before offering aid, use any trick to stop yourself from interfering with Wyatt's opportunity to talk himself through a problem."

Not long after observing Wyatt, I spent the morning at the beach. There I befriended Jenny, mother of two-year-old Theo. We watched as Theo filled his bucket with sand, poured the sand through a sieve, and did it all over again. And again. Sometimes he narrated the action by naming his equipment: "Buckeck . . . shovel." Other times he softly chanted, "Sand oh, sand oh, sand oh." But most of his moves required such deep concentration that he worked in silence. Jenny told me he had been at it for twenty minutes. "I keep reminding myself not to interrupt with a lesson. To let him be."

By controlling herself, Jenny granted Theo the opportunity to keep himself company. This is the second reason for practicing silent stewardship. The comfort of quiet camaraderie enables a child to begin to learn self-talk, the habit of positive internal dialogue. As he grows, self-talk will act as a powerful protectant against insecurity, anxious rumination, and frantic avoidance of boredom.

Solitary play is critically different from the way a small child interacts with an electronic device. Psychologist and sociologist Sherry

Turkle teaches and studies the impact of technology on human relationships at MIT. She warns, "Learning about solitude and being alone is the bedrock of early development, and you don't want your kids to miss out on that because you're pacifying them with a device. . . . They need to be able to explore their imagination. To be able to gather themselves and know who they are. So someday they can form a relationship with another person without a panic of being alone. If you don't teach your children to be alone, they'll only know how to be lonely."

Patient, silent stewardship, like any spiritual practice, takes self-discipline, conviction, and courage. In a world of anxious ambition, intruding on your child's relationship with himself can feel like enrichment. Not getting involved at every turn can feel like neglect. I'm ever more impressed when I see parents who recognize that often when adults do less, children can do more.

As children leave the toddler stage, their language acquisition picks up steam and their personalities blossom. We're entering full-blown childhood, land of long-winded stories, far-fetched excuses, outrageous misinterpretations, and future family legends. Keep your eyes and ears open.

CHAPTER 2

The Great Cathedral Space of Childhood

Learning the Language of Your Child's World

Boys and Girls Ages Three to Eleven

Is childhood the same in all eras, or is it defined by the adults who stand at its gates? Our modern experience of child-rearing is often tense and apprehensive. We listen to our children on the fly, or half-listen. Hurry causes us to try to maximize every interaction, hence spelling words threaded into bedtime stories and forced debriefings on the drive from school to practice. In our rush, we make careless assumptions or act on emotion rather than taking time to reflect.

Instead of unfiltered and meandering conversations, much adult-to-child communication is heavy on suggestions, reminders, and warnings. Just sitting with a child and listening—offering occasional observations or questions, not checking a phone—may seem like a lost art. But you can start with five uninterrupted minutes. Or even two. Those minutes with your one-of-a-kind-yet-changed-today-from-yesterday little person will yield surprising treasure and lead you to want more.

The world has changed dramatically in recent decades, but the conditions for a happy childhood remain simple. Food, shelter, security. A healthy amount of unstructured time, and a parent eager to hear about the day's adventures. Virginia Woolf wrote of her mother, "There she was, in the very centre of that great cathedral space which was childhood." A parent defines childhood not only by supplying a warm home but also by being at its center, ready to listen and willing to talk.

THREE FUNDAMENTAL TRUTHS ABOUT CHILDREN

Although children may beckon you to realms of enchantment, life can be hell when you're deep in the trenches of a typical day with them. And unlike any other social activity, it is not optional. When the ancient Jewish sages referred to *"tzar giddul banim,"* Hebrew for "the pain of raising children," they were acknowledging both the urgency and the seeming futility of getting your message across to distracted, contrary, ignorant, self-centered little fools. But a portion of the rough spots encountered each day may be smoothed by understanding three fundamental truths. If these seem self-evident and therefore easy to incorporate into your heart, worldview, and child-rearing routine, you are probably new to parenting.

1. *Boys and girls are different.*

They see and hear differently, learn differently, progress at different rates, find different situations and sounds amusing, and respond to different styles of verbal and nonverbal interactions. It's true that blunt or old-fashioned stereotypes can cause harm by narrowing or distorting our view of individual children, and there are many characteristics that boys and girls have in common. But parents and other adults need to appreciate the distinctive traits of each child while also accepting the existence of typical gender differences.

2. *Your child's bad behavior doesn't make you a bad parent.*

You can't take children's bad behavior personally. With few exceptions, their willfulness, petulance, resistance to reason, and otherwise crabby or insulting behavior is not a reflection of how much they love you or a barometer of your skill as a parent. There are many other influences in their lives: daily struggles, humiliations, unfulfilled longings, frustrations, and disappointment. Just like the mess at the bottom of their backpacks, they lug it all home. If they didn't feel you could take it, they wouldn't hurl their emotional junk your way.

3. *Today is a snapshot, not the epic movie of your child's life.*

Children are constantly evolving. Today is not predictive of much—not tomorrow, not the middle school years, not their eventual career, not what your relationship with them will be like when they've matured. In a world of constant ranking and rating, it's wildly countercultural to take a wait-and-see approach, but it is essential.

One final suggestion before we start our study of conversation. When talking with children, pretend you're an armchair traveler or cultural anthropologist. What are the ways of these people? What are their traditions, their beliefs? Whom do they admire, and why? What are they striving for? As you enter their land, let an open mind, curiosity, and courage be your guide.

VOCAL COACHING, LESSON ONE:
THE TUNE MATTERS AS MUCH AS THE LYRICS

Artists, musicians, and writers are always urged to "find their voice," meaning the truest expression of who they are. In everyday life our voice transmits not just literal information but also clues to the soul bubbling beneath. Your rhythm, tone, warmth or aloof distance, breathlessness or drawl matter to your child as much or more than the words you say. When your daughter reflects on her childhood, she'll recall the delight in your greetings and the irritation in your shouted commands, the lilt of your pet names for her, your chuckle or disapproving snort. Your son will remember the zest with which you cheered him, your repetitious cautionary speeches, the rage-propelled threats, the gentleness of your songs at bedtime. A great portion of what we appreciate, desire, and fear for our children comes through in the quality of our voice. And most of the time, we have no idea how we sound to them.

My voice lessons with parents often begin with a call like the one I received from a distraught mother. "We have an emergency with our daughter, Ruby! She's awful in every way. It's a nightmare!" The woman was speaking in a pressured whisper. I envisioned her hiding out in a bathroom. "We need to see you as soon as possible. We'll cancel anything."

"How old is Ruby?"

"Four."

Four? From her mother's panic, I would have guessed fifteen. But four-year-old girls can blindside their parents, transforming in weeks from grinning toddlers into glittery pink despots. She's so sweet, a charming sidekick, and then one day Bellatrix Lestrange shows up and won't leave. And the parents' confidence begins to falter.

I met with Ruby's mom and inquired about the composition of the family, Ruby's general physical health, her eating and sleeping patterns, and any difficult experiences she had weathered. I then invited the mom to give me a play-by-play account of some typical recent "nightmare" scenarios. After hearing a few examples, I smiled and interrupted: "Whoa! I wish I had filmed you just now. You'd be able to hear how much your tone changed. Your voice got really high. You narrowed your eyes, tensed your jaw and your shoulders, started flapping your arms and pointing. Do you think that happens when you're talking to Ruby?"

"Probably. Because I'm furious! She's so mean to me."

"At four, 'mean' words come from frustration, anxiety, or fatigue. Ruby melts down with the people she loves and trusts the most. And that's you."

"But she does it at birthday parties and even with my parents! It's so embarrassing."

"Let's try a new approach here. Instead of attempting to figure out the where, when, and why of Ruby's provocative behavior, or what kind of consequences might help her exercise more self-control, let's work on one simple change. Let's try a little vocal coaching."

The basic voice lesson I teach involves pitch, speed, tone, and body language.

1. When you start to feel tense while talking to a child of any age, relax your facial muscles and shoulders. Rest your hands in your lap. No pointing.
2. Take a deep breath. Consciously lower your pitch and slow your rate of speech.
3. Don't use a patronizing or babyish tone.

I conduct a similar exercise with all my new clients: I ask them to describe in detail a situation that led to an argument or meltdown with their child. Where were they in the house? What time of day was it? When had they last eaten? Inevitably, as the parent tells the story, she gets exasperated and her voice rises just as it did at the time of the incident. This high-pitched, strained voice communicates indignation, fear, and lack of authority. It's nearly as common among fathers as mothers.

As soon as the parent's voice goes up, roles shift. The child may now view the parent as a taunting older sibling or a whimpering younger one. As the child fights back or signals that he's stopped listening, the parents' frustration increases: the weak vocal message is now accompanied by alarmed or submissive nonverbal cues (hunched shoulders, open mouth, those gesticulating hands). When a strong parent shrinks and withers, the child rises up. He sees and hears (not in words but in pitch and tone) that he's winning the round. This child does not feel the thrill of victory. Although it's not conscious, he feels afraid—afraid and powerful, a bad combination. The parent's behavior signals: *I can't handle it when you act like a child.*

In subsequent sessions with parents, we explore the feelings that are reflected in their stressed voice, pointless repetition, and panicked behavior. At the same time, we practice more voice lessons. If you have a calmer voice, you're going to feel calmer. If you intentionally

31

lower your pitch, your child sees that you can control your feelings and that the situation is not unsettling or even unusual. Children respond by becoming calmer themselves and by ceding power, often gratefully (although they're not aware of it). This in turn lets you shift from trying to maintain control, or feeling shame over losing it, to figuring out why the trouble may have started. A changed vocal tone leads naturally to changed behavior and perspective.

You don't have to *feel* calm to act as if you are and reap all the benefits. Performers, public speakers, and teachers depend on acting "as if" to make their living. You can learn to do it, too.

FIELD TERMS OF THE SPOKEN WORD

I've done lots of talking in my time. I've spent thirty-five years doing therapy and delivered more than five hundred lectures and conference keynotes. As a researcher, I've conducted formal interviews with hundreds of adults and students. But when I began to appreciate the startling improvement in parent-child relationships made possible by small yet specific adjustments to voice and body language, I tapped some new resources: acting coaches and voice teachers. These professionals know which approaches hold listeners' attention or lose it, which inspire engagement and goodwill or irritate and alienate people. Like all disciplines, vocal coaching has its own lexicon. Here are the most common terms.

> **Pitch** is the register of your voice. A high pitch is pleasing to infants and pets but signals loss of power with children older than two or three. A lower pitch demonstrates self-control and authority.

> **Volume** is a formidable tool that is frequently abused. Shouting conveys weakness or inspires willed deafness in the listener, while speaking at a medium volume commands respect and serves as a compelling invitation to pay attention.

Tempo is the rate of speech. Speaking quickly can convey excitement or enthusiasm but also nervousness, displeasure, or agitation. Speaking slowly gives you time to emphasize specific points and gives a child time to process your message.

Pausing signals a transition to a new point or gives your child the chance to absorb an idea. For parents, pausing also means listening and keeping quiet, not immediately jumping in or correcting.

Tone or **timbre** is the emotional quality of your voice. It conveys your attitude, for example, preachy, pleased, condescending, curious, bored, nervous, or impressed.

Cadence is the rhythm of your speech. While babies love lullabies and a singsong cadence, older children find it annoying or insulting. Rehearsed speeches have a telltale flat cadence, while rote proclamations or paeans of praise—"That's *so* awesome!"—can come across as shallow and insincere.

Lexicon is the vocabulary you use with your child. You can expand your children's vocabulary by intentionally using words that are slightly more complex than the ones they currently know, delivered in context so it's easier for them to grasp the meaning.

Facial expressions should match your voice and words, but children will inevitably read things into your expression that you don't intend to display. They may demand "Why are your lips like that?" when you attempt to conceal frustration. My own daughters would accuse me of making "disgust face." It's impossible to maintain absolute control over your expressions, but you can train yourself to become more aware of the movements of your lips, mouth, jaw, and eyebrows. If you're feeling really tense but would prefer not to telegraph it, try a trick used by public speakers: squeeze your toes. It inconspicuously releases some of the stress.

A FEW WORDS ABOUT SILENCE

Quietly waiting for a child to finish his sentence is every bit as essential to a conversation as the way you express yourself. Most beneficial to parent-child exchanges: sitting at eye level with the child, hands folded in lap, making eye contact, and refraining from interruption. Stillness and resistance to distraction communicate your desire to hear the story because what your child has to say is captivating, important, and to be taken seriously. These moments provide children with relief and companionship on the scary shoals of their day.

No parent can do this every time their child speaks. But it's worth cultivating these skills because attentive and patient listening is an endangered form of communication despite its payoff: it fixes so many of the problems parents bring to my office, it's free, and like sleeping it comes naturally (or did, until we all got so busy we forgot how).

A TEMPLATE FOR CONVERSATIONS

By the age of four, children's conversational repertoire is abloom. They can now speak in full sentences, use complex grammar, and are increasingly able to pepper you with questions and engage in elaborate pretend play. Most young children are entertaining chatterboxes, but this is also the stage when they'll infuriate by ignoring you, dawdling, and arguing. Or they'll use empty patter to hold the floor, frustrating adults who think that reining them in will lower their self-esteem and joie de vivre.

With babies you bond by communicating through speech, touch, and animated gesture. With children, you get an able conversational partner who wants to tell you everything! True, they'll follow you around right up to the bathroom door and not pause for breath while you're inside. They're stubborn and demanding, exuberant and inquisitive. Your mission? Decrease the potential for tedium or exasperation, and increase the possibility of delight.

Treat young children with dignity by encouraging them to ponder aloud, inquire about topics that puzzle or frighten them, and tell tall tales. Ask for clarification and elaboration but tread lightly, not in legal deposition mode, not assuming that the end point will be unearthing a problem or transmitting an essential life lesson. Do lots of listening, and remember that children are not looking for downloads of information but for warm conversational companionship.

You're talking to someone whose attention span is limited, so keep requests and instructions brief and deliver them loudly and clearly enough to be heard by a child who might be daydreaming. Busy parents often flip commands over their shoulder as they leave a room. When they don't get an immediate response, they repeat themselves from a farther distance using a testier tone. From the child's perspective, it's like listening to a gruff giant without seeing his expression. *His voice sounds mad, but hey, I can't see his face, so I'll take a chance and just ignore him.*

Watch masterful teachers of young children in the classroom. When they want to communicate important information to a student, they drop to their knees, look the child in the eyes, speak in a low tone, wait a moment, and then ask the child to repeat the message. It's what I call "full-frontal listening": giving a child your complete attention, at eye level, with a hand gently resting on the child's shoulder.

As soon as children can speak, they begin to sleuth out hypocrisy. They sense the phony public relations pitch: "You are going to *love* science sleepaway camp!" They smell the hidden agenda: "So . . . did you raise your hand in class today?" (*Is your teacher giving you enough attention? Are you trying hard or spacing out?*) They bristle at fake praise, fake pride, and fake interest, because they can tell the difference between authentic appreciation of something they've said or done and an absent-minded "Good job!" This is where treating children with respect comes into play.

I've asked children which parental phrases annoy them the most (as in strikes them as manipulative, passive-aggressive, phony, or wishful thinking). Here are the winners.

"Just wanted to let you know . . ."
"You know what?"
"It'll be great!"
"You don't mean that."
"You know he didn't mean to."
"Can I talk to you for a sec?" (Child knows to translate to "for fifteen miserable minutes.")
"Who did you sit with at lunch?"
"OK?" (The tentative, pleading nature of ending a sentence with "OK?" undercuts your authority and irritates your child. It implies that they can say, "No, it's not OK," which is either not true or the bad kind of power that no child really wants.)
. . . and finally, "Be careful!"

Your tense (yet trite and predictable) bleat of "Be careful!" in the direction of your child riding a tricycle near a driveway is not likely to be helpful. Helpful would be "Madeleine, wait please. I want to tell you about the rules of the road [grown-up term inserted in context]. There's a good way to navigate [big word, in context]. If you see a driveway, always stop. While you're stopped, look at the street in front of the driveway to see if a car is about to pull in. Also look inside a car that's in a driveway to see if someone is about to back up."

An automatic "Be careful!" called out multiple times each day is a lazy incantation. It is understood by the child as *"I have generalized fear" (so don't pay me much mind)* or *"I don't trust your judgment" (so you don't have to develop any—just outsource it to me).*

When chatting with children, especially younger ones, you'll be treated to a display of often comical verbal blunders. Rather than reflexively correcting the mispronunciations, misuse of words, or misinformation about a topic, realize that doing so might limit your child's enthusiasm and make him wary of expressing himself. Instead, you can adopt a "pause and reflect before you correct" approach: let some mistakes pass, and repeat some words or ideas correctly but without pointing out the error.

Now let's take a look at constructive ways to open conversations and explore topics.

CONVERSATION OPENERS

Specific observations that show the depth of your attention are a solid way to begin. "I'm interested in the way you drew the cloud formation and the people standing over there. I think I see markers *and* paint. Looks like there's a story going on in this scene?" Close observation of the tools and intentions of your emerging artist is a more compelling way to open a conversation than asking yes or no questions or saying, "Cool picture! Great job!"

By the time children are four or five, they're already suspicious of the open-ended questions parents use when they're fishing for intel, for instance, "What did you do today?" or "How was lunch?" By remembering what they have already told you and then asking for more information, you signal that you're genuinely interested in *them*, not their achievements or popularity: "Did those tadpoles you're growing in the classroom turn into frogs yet?"

Open-ended questions like "Did you have fun?" are not necessarily anxious or prying, and your child may respond enthusiastically. But if you want to increase the odds of getting more than a one-syllable reply, try fleshing out the details: "Does Dion's family still have that trampoline in the backyard? Did his dad spray the hose on you while you jumped around, like he did last time?" If you're chatty and specific, your child will be more likely to respond in kind.

One engaging conversational approach is to uncover opportunities for your child to act as a valued consultant. Note: pose these kinds of questions only if you mean it and your child's input will be taken into serious consideration.

"Who would you like to join us at the beach?"
"What should we serve for lunch when Addie comes over?"
"Any ideas about how we can make your cousins feel welcome?"
"I'd like to hear the music you pick for the drive."
"Which do you think is a better choice, parking close to the entrance or the exit of the lot?"
"What do you have in mind for your birthday party?"
"What trick could we teach the puppy next?"

This style of questioning dignifies the child by giving her a true mission. It also provides a counterpoint to the routine parent-to-child inquiries necessary to get through the day:

"Do you remember what day we have to bring the turtle back to school?"
"Everybody have their seat belts on?"
"How did this mud get on the couch?"

Children's curiosity is often all that's needed to ignite a dialogue. An acquaintance told me how much he enjoyed the company of his seven-year-old nephew: "We ride our bikes every afternoon. Jack is brilliant at conversation openers. He'll ask me, 'Uncle Ryan, who's your favorite Marvel superhero? What made you laugh the longest? Did you ever get your heart broken?'"

EXPANDING THE CONVERSATION

There are several strategies for making the conversation more engaging to both you and your child. The easiest is to repeat the child's news and ask follow-up questions. Try to include a specific reference to what the child has told you. It's perfectly fine to say, "I never knew that! Tell me more." But you could also say, "I never knew that about the ancient Egyptians. *Everybody* shaved their heads? Why?" Repeating it means you were really impressed with the information.

Affinity is another approach. "What you're saying reminds me of something that happened when I was in fifth grade. Two girls from my class completely bailed on the field trip to the museum! They never came back to the school bus and later got into big trouble for it. Why do you think they did that?" Slightly scandalous topics intrigue young kids. And because it is *your* history, not their life, they are safe to express their own imaginative hypotheses about what the girls might have been thinking—or not thinking!

Rephrasing a child's comments with a request for clarification will also take you to enlightening places.

"Let's see. I think I know what you mean. One part of you wants to sleep at Jasper's and another part isn't sure. Do I have it right?"

"Tell me if this is what you're trying to figure out . . ."

Be a willing fellow traveler into the darker realms. Ask for details about their dreams, drawings, and the tragedies and consequences of decisions made by characters in books. Like the silent stewardship that gives babies a chance to keep themselves company, emotional companionship is one of your goals.

Child: In my dream a big monster was chasing me.
Mother: Wow! How big? As big as a giraffe? Or a house? Or a big mountain?
Child: Bigger, Mom! Just his mouth was as big as a mountain!
Mother: Whoa, that's HUGE. I think it's the biggest monster I've ever heard of. I can see why you felt really scared. Did it look like any kind of animal you've seen? Was it one solid color, or did its coat have a pattern like dots or stripes?
Child: It was purple with giant green spots. [Likely not true, but instead a post hoc elaboration, which is fine and good since accuracy is not the purpose of this kind of dialogue.]

39

Through this relaxed and intimate exchange, your child is shifting from the role of persecuted victim to playful storyteller. Now it's just Noah and Mom and the polka-dot monster sitting in the family room in the soft light of morning. The next time a predator shows up in Noah's dreamscape, the playful embellishments he's invented and the homey memory of sharing with Mom can help shape the narrative.

Ask your child if he'd like you to type up his dreams or stories or write them down in a journal. Even if he's old enough to do this himself, you want to make it easy and avoid turning the enterprise into a homework-style assignment. If he accepts your offer to be his scribe, you can follow with: "Would you like to illustrate the text?" Your curiosity and respect turns fear into creativity and forges a further bridge between scary images and a calm, protective parent. You can also read the story back to him—children love it when Mom or Dad gives a dramatic interpretation of their creation.

CONVERSATION CLOSERS

A nice way to end a chat is "I have to go make a call for work/start dinner/get dressed to go out, but this has been a very interesting conversation. Thank you!" This might feel formal, but it conveys how valuable the exchange was to you and also teaches your child how to express appreciation.

When the dialogue is not as pleasurable—for example, when you and your child hold different points of view—watch out for the trap of thinking you have to keep plowing ahead until you reach consensus. Once child or parent runs out of emotional fuel, it's hard to see the other person's side. Instead of hammering away with reason and logic, stretching to come up with a creative solution that pleases everyone, or giving in, you can defer decisions and further discussion. Phrases that don't bow to or dismiss your child's passion, desperation, or urgency have the additional value of modeling techniques she can use when faced with peer pressure as she enters the middle school years.

"I hear you. I see your point. But I need some time to think this over."

"I need to talk with your mother about that."

"We'll revisit this after I've slept on it."

"This is new for me. I haven't put my mind to it yet."

"I don't know the answer, but I can find out more and we'll talk about it tomorrow."

And it's sometimes appropriate to simply say, "No." A fancy version of "no" that's easy to remember uses the acronym ACE:

Acknowledge what the child wishes: "I realize you don't want to come home now because you and Sophia haven't finished decorating the tree house and Sophia's mom invited you to sleep over."

Provide **C**ontext: "I have to say no this time because you have a game starting at nine tomorrow and you need to sleep in your own bed so you'll be rested and ready to play."

Offer genuine **E**mpathy: "I know it's hard to leave when you're having so much fun. Still, we need to get back home. It's time to say our good-byes."

You're the authority, and even if your child wishes she could have the sleepover, it's ultimately more reassuring to her that you are reliably in charge.

CLEARING SPACE FOR CONVERSATIONS

When parents come to see me about a child who is uncooperative or unhappy at home, I ask about the source of the friction: "What percentage of your communication with your child consists of nagging, reminding, or chastising?" The parents' answers are consistently rueful, exaggerated, pure mea culpa: "Uh . . . 90 percent, 100?"

This is never true. These parents have all sorts of interesting, unscripted conversations with their kids, but their confession tells me they're often in "Be careful!" mode. They don't trust the child to manage ordinary daily responsibilities, so they compulsively nag and chastise.

I then ask how much time their child spends absorbed in screen-based activities. Typical verbal response: "Too much." Nonverbal: sad facial expression, lowered head shaking back and forth, hands raised with open palms in gesture of resigned helplessness.

The reason I ask about nagging and screen time is to raise the parents' awareness about the cost of these entrenched habits. Squabbling with parents and playing with devices too often consumes much of a child's day outside of school. This leaves little room for intimate, free-range dialogue.

Every conversation is waiting in the wings for its cue: the child's sense that a parent is both ready to listen and devoted to offering a generous "yes and" to expand the discussion. Rich parent-child discourse flows from spontaneous moments protected by an unspoken set of rules. The parent is:

- Trustworthy. What's said to you stays with you.
- Respectful. You don't act mocking or dismissive.
- Curious. You ask questions and are eager to hear more.
- Genuinely interested. You don't nod reflexively but ask for clarification when you don't understand.
- Attuned. When your child telegraphs seriousness, excitement, or puzzlement, you aren't too preoccupied to notice; further, you can be relied upon to actively fend off distractions, to listen and respond thoughtfully.
- Patient. You often let the conversation continue until its natural conclusion.

The frequency of this sort of interchange? Daily, but not every time your child utters any string of words or displays a facial expression unaccompanied by its backstory. Length of conversation? To be determined moment by moment, as circumstances permit. You still need to run a reasonably efficient household and personal life.

Many parents rely on drive time, bath time, or bedtime as built-in opportunities for extended conversations about the day's highlights. Certainly these routines provide dependable windows for connection, but they are also limited. By evening adults and children are tired, or the grown-ups still have work to do and the rituals get rushed. That's why a parent's attentive presence needs to be flexible and accessible.

Once I've talked with parents about how nagging, chastising, and too much screen time can inhibit a child's desire to communicate, they become more attuned to openings for impromptu chats. Instead of a child's demands or excuses, they are treated to observations both hilarious and profound, while their child grows more confident and eloquent.

Making room for your child begins in the morning. If you're like most adults, your first encounter upon awakening is with your cell phone. It's a stupendously reliable and pleasing alarm clock. But . . . take a peek at texts or e-mail or the news, and your mind shifts into a complex prioritizing mode: this request, that information; *Do I store it, act on it, or ignore it?* If you dive into your phone before you've gazed on the face of your child, he's likely to find you preoccupied and churning. But if you can resist the impulse to check your in-box, you get the opportunity to ponder what lies ahead for your child on this particular day. What happened in his world yesterday? Anything he's been looking forward to? Worried about? This brief, loving assessment gives you the best odds of entering his freshly unfolding story with words that will provide a little bolt of encouragement before he leaves the house.

Digital distractions present the biggest obstacle to conversation as the day progresses. To protect the boundaries that enable families to bond, experts agree there should be no phones or devices:

- During shared meals at home or in restaurants.
- While driving.

43

- At bath time.
- At bedtime.

Beyond that, you can't go wrong by muting your phone when you're around your child and leaving it in your purse or otherwise out of view.

Your child will mimic your phone habits just as she mirrors your manners and opinions. But technology is different from table manners—it's a radical cultural shift, and its unintended consequences will only become clear over time. We don't know how, twenty years from now, devices will have affected a young person's ability to form relationships or artfully engage in conversation. We do know that these skills are acquired in childhood and depend on parents' ongoing cultivation.

SEVEN ATE NINE!
WHY HUMOR MATTERS MORE THAN JUST ABOUT ANYTHING

The first time you make your baby laugh is a delight. But the first time your young child makes you laugh out loud is cosmic: a reward for your years of toil and a reliable bellwether of the quality of his life ahead.

When parents come to see me about their child, I always make time in the consultation to shift away from the troubles and look at the child with a different lens. I ask about his sense of humor. Does he intentionally do things to amuse others? You? His teacher? His friends? The friends' parents? Taking your child's funny bone seriously means providing a venue for far-fetched stories, contorted nicknames, and vintage groaners ("Dad! Why is six afraid of seven?"). In the "anything-goes" shelter of your presence, your kid can entertain you with his wicked impersonations of his classmates or request that you belt out "We Are the Champions" together with all the operatic trills. No one in your life will ever appreciate your performance as much as a four- or five-year-old.

You'll discover there are certain things you both find hilarious (an easy one if you have a pet). And now you're building a storehouse of in-jokes. A cranky cereal bowl! Her fake haughty English accent! Mispronunciations so charming they get a permanent place of honor on the family playlist.

Car in the shop for repairs.

Four-year-old girl: I love the lentil car!
Dad: I like the rental car, too.

Pulling up to a restaurant.

Girl: Look, look, they have ballet parking here!

Shared mirth has the power to bond us and elevate our moods; enjoying slapstick comedy and deftly executed pratfalls allows us to experience violent fantasies without the pain of real-world consequences. Fish stories and breathless accounts of derring-do take the narrator out of jeopardy or disappointment and put her in control of the outcome. Exaggeration and heroics are understood to be part of the fun.

These royal modes of communication are often squeezed out by the weightier agenda of our world: lessons about fair play, explanations about online safety, lectures on the dangers of peer pressure. The devaluation of levity can be seen in many preschool classrooms, where the curriculum has shifted away from the bountiful lessons of play and socializing to grim seriousness about reading readiness and test preparation. Which brings us to a paradox: while developing children's sense of humor is often deemed too fluffy, its actual value is beyond measure.

Throughout your child's life, her friends, romantic partners, colleagues, and employers will be drawn to her not only because of her impressive skill set (lots of people have that) but also because of how much they enjoy her company. Will she be fun to play with, agreeable to work with? Her ability to see the comical aspects of our human predicament will greatly influence the sort of life she leads and the people in it. Laughter is our consolation prize for the indignities and cruel plot twists we all endure, beginning in childhood. And a good sense of humor is a playground superpower: a ticket into the social life of a new school or out of the tense hold of a class bully. It's as important as any other aspect of a child's health and development.

Adults tend to have a fatalistic attitude about humor—you're either born funny or you're not. Yet like with painting a landscape or cooking a gourmet meal, a little bit of talent can be nurtured. What is parenting, really, but a form of motivational speaking? And who are the stars in that field? Those who deliver a serious message in a humorous package. So make your home a venue for finding the funny, and try to refine your own comic delivery and storytelling skills.

Laughter is the best relief valve for our culture of relentless striving, and children learn how to use it by watching you. So on the night before your child faces a daunting spelling bee or tae kwon do belt test, pivot away from last-minute preparation and instead relax together with a book of jokes and riddles. Ask her to show you her current favorite YouTube video or GIF, or read a funny story together at bedtime. And before you go to sleep, you pivot, too, by making a quick visit to theonion.com, where the headlines reliably put parenting worries in perspective. Here are a few I've used in lectures:

- "Parents Seize Creative Control of 3rd Grade Art Project"
- "Daily Spin Class Only Thing Keeping Mom from Driving Car Full of Kids into the Ocean"
- "Parents of Crying Child Must Not Be Any Good"

And one I haven't:

- "Parenting Expert Has Nerve to Tell You How to Raise Your Own Goddamn Kids"

MISUSES OF HUMOR: WHEN GOOD INTENTIONS CREATE MISTRUST

Humor is a supremely effective way to help your child process difficult experiences and see them in a new light. But heed the wisdom of professional comedians: tragedy *plus time* equals comedy.

Consideration of your child's temperament will guide you in your timing. A flubbed performance, a friend who moved on to the cool crowd, a camping trip with nonstop rain are richer in the telling than in the moment. If your child comes to expect you to quickly reframe her sadness, hurt, or disappointment (no matter how seemingly trivial) by reacting in a playful manner, she may feel belittled or betrayed, or develop meta-emotions like shame over sadness or guilt over anger. And she may learn not to turn to you when life triggers strong feelings and she's in need of a thoughtful listener with a compassionate heart.

Kids often apply a double standard to parent-generated humor. A jokey comment from Mom may cause a child to cringe or even cry, but when Dad makes *the exact same wisecrack*, he's met with admiration and howls. This reaction isn't 100 percent guaranteed, however. I sometimes have to remind fathers that even the most sophisticated-seeming young children take words literally, care deeply about their dad's opinions, and model their own behavior on his. When the irony and sarcasm so pervasive in the media is casually deployed at home, it can have an unintended effect on children, causing them to hide tender feelings and act like cool little cynics.

WHEN CHILDREN REVERT TO BABY TALK

The mother of five-year-old Antonia was worried: her normally articulate child had suddenly started talking like a two-year-old. "Is it because I'm pregnant? Does she feel pressure to be a big girl now? It's pretty annoying, and it's embarrassing when she does it in front of strangers."

Probing a bit, I learned that Antonia was about to start kindergarten in a few weeks and also that her grandma had just sold her cozy house and moved to a more manageable apartment. It was a lot of change for the little girl.

"I'd say that the baby talk is a healthy reaction to the changes Antonia is anticipating: the wonders or horrors of the new baby, the wonders or horrors of kindergarten. And no more familiar Grandma haven."

Tiny people have large-sized existential concerns, but there's no need to unpack them or dig for details unless a child asks questions. To deal with her anxiety, Antonia was employing a mild and safe form of regression rather than bed-wetting, thumb-sucking, biting or hitting classmates, or public tantrums. How to handle? I advised this mother:

1. Consider the baby talk a heavy accent. Tell Antonia you can't understand her *but only when you actually can't*. If she says: "Mama, wannah nuhver bwankie," don't tell her to use her "big girl" voice (which has the potential to humiliate and cause her to use that even more babyish mode of communication, tears). Instead look directly at her (without a critical stare), speak slowly, and using a polite but appropriately perplexed tone ask her to repeat her request or comment. Then try to interpret. No need to make this a drawn-out tête-à-tête, or it will teach her that baby talk is a magic trick for getting Mom's attention.
2. When she is not addressing you, ignore the baby talk entirely. Even when you feel mortified in front of your mother or the waitress.
3. Don't weigh in when she talks baby talk to her father. That's between them.
4. Connect with her in a "loving my big girl" way. "It's Grandma's birthday next week. What kind of cake do you think she'd like?"

Baby talk is a low-cost way for a child to give herself an emotional pressure-release valve at times of transition. It's temporary and will fade once the child gets used to her new routine or environment.

The Great Cathedral Space of Childhood

FAIRY TALES WON'T COME TRUE, THEY WON'T HAPPEN TO YOU

> Fairy tales do not tell children that dragons exist. Children
> already know that dragons exist. Fairy tales tell children
> that the dragon can be killed.
>
> —G. K. Chesterton

Incredibly, even as a harried family agenda feels normal because it's the norm, age-old bedtime rituals remain sacrosanct. The stagecraft and script: a softly lit room, pillow, blanket, a teddy or shredded lovie, parent fully focused on child, a private time for reading and talking that concludes with the exchange of loving sentiments. How best to turn on the spigot of conversational flow during this slow and gentle interlude between daytime and dreamtime?

For very young children, rhythm, rhyme, and talking animals fascinate and charm. Together you pat the bunny, say "Goodnight, moon," and look for Spot. As children's attention span and comprehension of words and ideas mature, you join them in commiserating with glum Eeyore, visiting lands filled with friendly but wild things, night kitchens, giant peaches, and chocolate factories. But then what? Having exhausted the canon of beloved classics, many children (particularly those with older siblings) request more thrilling fare: "Let's read *Harry Potter*!" Don't be too quick to agree, because if you skip from Pooh to Dumbledore, you'll miss out on fairy tales.

Fairy tales! Super gory, sexist, classist, unjust, harsh. Why end your child's short-lived innocence by introducing him to abandonment, abduction, and attempted cannibalism (*Hansel and Gretel*); child slavery and being orphaned (*Cinderella*); vicious wild animal predation (*Little Red Riding Hood*)? Because when you venture together into the dark woods from the safety of a warm bedroom, you offer your child a sturdy container for intense but inchoate thoughts and feelings that pile up during the day.

In his classic book *The Uses of Enchantment: The Meaning and Importance of Fairy Tales*, psychologist Bruno Bettelheim describes how these strange and wild tales enthrall the young child by offering acceptance and approval of the chaotic emotional states churning within him. By introducing him to villains, you give him characters on which to project his own violent feelings—for example, the normal human admixture of love and hate he feels, but can't name or express, toward his family and friends. By seeing how clever, resilient, resourceful children triumph over evil, he learns that actions have consequences and is offered hope and examples of heroism. "The fairy tale is suggestive," Bettelheim writes. "Its messages may imply solutions, but it never spells them out. Fairy tales leave to the child's fantasizing whether and how to apply to himself what the story reveals about life and human nature."

At any point in the story, a parent can stop and ask the child what she thinks of the main character's predicament. What would she do if it were her? Why? Can she guess what will happen next? What does she think *should* happen to the character?

The fantastical nature of fairy tales provides an opening for your child to ask about whatever may be haunting or perplexing her. Don't hold back frank answers. Simplicity and candor relieve a young child's fretful mind. Whatever path your child is eager to explore, shine your flashlight there. One seven-year-old boy was fixated on the age of the characters in the stories: "Little kids like Hansel and Gretel could never beat a witch in real life. She'd eat them." Sensing his anxiety, his parents gave him books from a series of true stories about children who faced frightening situations in real life. Titles included *I Survived the Sinking of the Titanic* and *I Survived Hurricane Katrina*. This boy's outlook changed from apprehensive to adventurous, to the point that the following summer he strategized with his dad: "Let's not swim near the lifeguard station or he might tell us not to go in."

THE BANK OF GOODWILL

Teaching children to be courteous, helpful, and considerate regardless of their mood or immediate desires is a conversation that will last for roughly two and a half decades. But there's a way to tip the scales in your favor. A concept coined by psychologist and author Bob Ditter describes it well: "the bank of goodwill." Mutual respect between parent and child depends upon a parent's deposits in this bank. This is where small gestures of trust and tolerance directed toward the child build up and accrue interest: letting the Lego construction stay where it is for an entire week may be more valuable than a trip to Disneyland.

Raising children is often cast as a matter of picking your battles. There is much wisdom in that, but it's a defensive tactic. The bank of goodwill is proactive. Rather than waiting for a battle to brew and then deciding whether it's worth fighting, you consciously look for ways to let your child feel independent and appreciated. When you've consistently made deposits in the bank of goodwill, children are more likely to tolerate strict rules or those they perceive as irrational or unfair.

What guarantees a high return on investment? Being enthusiastic and captivated by your child's stories, his cache of esoteric (to you, not him) information, and his breathless but hard-to-follow narratives containing lots of sentences connected by "and then . . . and then . . . and then . . ." Ask your son for *more* details about tornadoes or drones or professional sports brackets. Display a good-natured tolerance for your daughter's clothing choices, however flamboyant or strange, as long as they don't violate the school dress code. Resist making reference to how carefully the two of you shopped for her wardrobe. Remind yourself that respect begets respect.

Mom: You've worn those leggings to school every single day for a week now.
Daughter: I love them, Mom. They're soft.
Mom: Ah, yes, soft is comfortable.

Honor your son's desire to keep his room off-limits to his younger sister when he isn't home, and he'll be more willing to help her with her homework when you're too busy. Honor your daughter's wish not to be forced to kiss a family friend hello and good-bye, and she'll be more likely to answer his clumsy, well-intended questions with a smile: "No, Uncle Jeff, I don't have a boyfriend yet 'cause I'm only in third grade!"

Minor indulgences make a big impression. One girl said, "In the checkout line at the market, sometimes my mom lets me get a few Lindor chocolate balls with different color shiny wrappers. She lets me pick my favorites." When I heard this, I could tell that the few seconds Mom was willing to wait while her daughter chose from among the colors was a high-value currency in the bank of goodwill.

When I conduct interviews with groups of students around the country, one question always gets an instantly enthusiastic response: "What do you like to do with your parents?" The children's eagerness to speak reveals how much pleasure they get out of their parent's company and points to the many ways parents accrue goodwill, possibly without being aware of it. Below, a tiny sample:

"Dad's my buddy. We ride our bikes and play cards."
"My mom and dad pull out their record collection and we all dance."
"I cook with my mom. She taught me how to grill hamburgers with the cheese on the inside!"
"My mom and I watch *The Great British Bake Off* and talk the whole time. It's so fun."
"I like praying with my mom."
"We ride dirt bikes every weekend."
"Dad and I jump off a cliff into the lake. Mom can't watch."
"My parents were born in India. We watch Bollywood movies together."
"When I get into the car, my mom looks at me, pats my arm, and says, 'Hi, sweets' before we drive off. I really like that."

The Great Cathedral Space of Childhood

The bank of goodwill is more than just a strategy for encouraging good behavior. It's a philosophy that will lighten the atmosphere in your home throughout the years your children are living there. At every age, children will bring you the worst problems you can imagine and also the most dazzling moments. The more you know what gladdens your child's heart, the more of those moments you'll get to see.

CHAPTER 3

The Biggest, Strongest, Fastest

Connecting with Young Boys

Ages Three to Eleven

I'm fond of children. Except boys.

—Lewis Carroll

Mom, Mom, did you know there are four hundred and fifty kinds of sharks? The biggest is the great white. It's SIXTY FEET LONG! But sharks kill only one person a year. Dogs kill two hundred people a year! You know what country has the fastest Wi-Fi? South Korea. We are so slow! We're behind Lithuania and Latvia and Portugal. Did you know that baby bumblebees are called drones? THAT'S WHERE THE WORD COMES FROM! You know, the word drone! *I'm not kidding. Look it up.*

Conversing with little boys requires a surprisingly delicate touch. Seeking to make their mark, to exercise power and prowess, boys holler, snort, hoot, and recite facts in ways that can be irritating to adults. A reflexive response to a boy's oddly intense monologue delivered without concern for his listener's diminishing level of interest might be an impatient "OK, OK, I get it." Or, "Enough now, it's time to get in the car." As he burbles on, your lizard brain generates queasy concern: *There is something wrong with this boy.* But if you resist shushing him in order to move along to the next activity, you get a reward: the poetry in a soliloquy containing the words *great white, Lithuania,* and *baby bumblebee.* Where else will you hear them in a single paragraph?

In this chapter you'll learn why boys express themselves in a style that often strikes girls and women as peculiar or offensive; how exciting new findings in brain science reveal the adaptive functions of young males' selective listening, shouting, and crudeness; and the dramatic impact of cultural shifts on boys' development. Using this information as a map, you can reframe his words and actions as a gift. It's not as neatly wrapped as the one presented by his sister, but it springs from the way his lively mind connects to the passions of his heart. Speak back to him in "boy," and he'll listen. Whatever you aim to communicate—compassion, appreciation, or acceptable codes of conduct—he'll hear it.

WHAT ARE LITTLE BOYS MADE OF?

As school demands and safety concerns have grown, boys' rambunctious ways have come to be seen as problems rather than natural characteristics to be appreciated. These changes affect both how parents size up their sons and how the boys feel about themselves. Until about ten years ago, most parents of young boys came to see me at the recommendation of their sons' schools. The student was behind in reading and writing, or restless, devilish, or puzzlingly out of sorts. Today, the parents call me on their own. The most common reason? Their sons' worrisome worries. These anguished parents use such similar phrases that I feel as if I'm listening to actors reading lines for a casting agent. Here's the mother of six-and-a-half-year-old Spencer:

> Spencer insists that one of us stay in his room with him while he gets dressed for school. Even if he wants something badly after he gets home—a Lego part or his flip-flops—he refuses to go upstairs

by himself. He asks so many questions about his homework that I usually just sit with him the whole time.

He's miserable if he knows we're going out for the evening. If we leave before he's asleep, he begs the babysitter to let him call us. He has bad dreams and wants to get in our bed; if we say no, he gets into bed with his little sister. And he'll only consent to sleepovers if they're at our house.

Other parents come to me because their sons seem persistently rude, crass, and uncaring. Eight-year-old Hugo's mother relates her daily frustrations:

Hugo thinks he's hilarious when he says stuff like, "Hey, Mom, looks like you're pregnant. Why didn't you tell anyone?" Or when he calls his little brother the Amazing Hairy-Footed Booby, which starts a fight every time. He says other people's food looks gross when I've repeatedly told him not to, and then chews with his mouth open just to disgust us.

Spencer's parents worry that he'll never be self-sufficient and that his wimpiness will make him a target for bullies. Hugo's parents fret that his insensitivity to others is evidence of their son's emerging poor character and a grim forecast of the troubles they'll face as he enters his teenage years. Yet as heartbreaking, pathetic, or annoying as their parents find them to be at home, the boys' teachers usually think they're terrific. When I ask what transpired at the last parent-teacher conference, the responses are again remarkably consistent: "Oh, the teachers love him! They say he's a great addition to the class. That he jumps right in and is kind to the younger kids on the play yard. They really enjoy his sense of humor." Often the parents tell me that upon hearing these observations they look at each other and think, *OUR son? Maybe she's describing another kid.*

After the teacher's enthusiastic report of the boy's admirable traits, she will move on, as every teacher must, to "areas in need of improvement." Perhaps he has a tendency to brag a bit, go for the laugh, blurt out rather than filter his thoughts. Maybe he asks to visit the nurse for one vague symptom or another a bit too frequently. I tell the parents that I'm struck by how quickly after the conference their sons' strengths have evaporated from memory while "areas in need of improvement" remain vivid, supporting their concerns about the helpless or rude behavior they see in their boy at home.

I've seen a pattern emerge over the past decade that in many cases explains Spencer's helplessness and, at least partially, Hugo's "immature" acting out. Most children valiantly hold it together during the school day and then soldier through their extracurriculars or practices. But once boys hit the soft landing of home and drop their backpack by the front door, these sturdy young males regress into needy, irritating puddles of babyishness. (Girls have a different way of handling this touchdown, as we'll see in the next chapter.) The boys are not good-tired, like they might be after a few hours of running around and playing with friends. No, they are weary. And anxious. This anxiety is their energy, imagination, and lust for adventure turned inward, against the self.

Parents fear their sons will end up being social pariahs or unemployable slackers unless they learn to contain themselves, so they focus on teaching them how. But if most of our conversations with boys consist of chiding, correcting, or warning them, we're doing damage regardless of our careful phrasing. We say, "I'm not mad at you, Caleb, I'm unhappy with your behavior." But that's not true, and Caleb knows it. He *is* his behavior, so you *are* mad at him. What he can't figure out is, why?

THE WEIRD WAYS OF WEIRD SOCIETIES

In his brilliant book *The Anthropology of Childhood*, David Lancy describes how the current norms and expectations of parents in Western, Educated, Industrialized, Rich, Democratic (WEIRD) societies contrast with those of other cultures around the globe and with an

America of generations past. The boys in non-WEIRD societies are given tasks that raise their social standing and also meet their natural need to move. Boys long to patrol distant territory and hunt for needed provisions, Lancy writes. If denied the opportunity, trouble awaits.

Parents often complain that their sons are too rowdy, too squirmy, too loud—but compared to whom? Compared to girls. Throughout most of human history (and in some cultures today), rowdiness wasn't a problem because there were many aspects of daily life that required some members of the community to be physically powerful, aggressive, full of energy, and possessed of a booming voice that could scare away predators. The roles of men and women were narrow and distinct, but both types of characteristics—the wild and the mild—were necessary to the survival of the clan.

Not anymore. In modern societies, the shift to a technological economy has deflated the value of testosterone except on the football field or in action movies. Our culture reveres those who can sit for long periods of time focusing on mental tasks. This is reflected in the way our children are taught, beginning in preschool. And although awareness is growing about best practices for raising boys, our concern about sexual coercion and the media's focus on acts of male violence make it hard to relax into appreciation of boys' many endearing characteristics: frankness, ease in getting over emotional slights, high energy, and high-spirited ways. It's easy to perceive these traits as rudeness and use them to predict troubles ahead. Or to merely endure boys' "antics" until they evolve into a more acceptable (girl-like) state. Horsing around with friends or Dad can take some of the pressure off young boys, but occasional male bonding can't be expected to counterbalance an entire sociological shift.

The most loving and supportive parents may find it hard to tolerate their son's physicality, excitability, and the space consumed by his constructions, games, weaponry, and gear. Often the boys who have it the toughest are those with older sisters, because it's difficult for parents not to compare the siblings' behavior and abilities. This is reinforced by the many books and websites with unisex milestones:

"Most babies will probably be able to . . . Some babies will be able to . . . A few babies will be able to . . ." While parents may be reassured by measuring their infants against a normal range, the fact is that the brains of girls and boys develop differently from before birth and throughout their childhood and teenage years.

If you have a basic understanding of how boys' brains develop, you'll be able to speak your son's language: words and sentences he can grasp delivered at a length, rate, and volume he can easily hear. You'll recognize your son's behavior as part of the broad sweep of boyhood rather than judging him from within the narrow context of your family or his classroom. By familiarizing yourself with common male behaviors, you can add them to what you already know about your son's personality and have a deeper understanding of what might be driving his moods, words, and actions. And if you're the parent of a girl, learning about the brain development of boys will make you a little more appreciative of (or patient with) the yelling, jumping, gun-slinging, stat-loving sons of your friends and relatives.

THE BRAINS OF BOYS

Male and female brains interpret the world differently. New techniques in neuroscience, such as brain mapping, allow us to get closer to understanding this complex organ, even if a complete grasp of it remains tantalizingly out of reach. For instance, using functional magnetic resonance imagery, researchers can watch neuronal activity in real time. They've learned that different areas of the brain light up when girls and boys speak, do puzzles, or are presented with visual distractions. We know that the brains of boys and girls develop at different rates and times, and in a different order in the areas that affect language, spatial memory, and motor coordination. The neurochemicals serotonin and oxytocin occur in different quantities in boys and girls, affecting their responses to stimuli, and the levels of hormones such as testosterone, estrogen, and progesterone have an impact on the mood and behavior of boys and girls prior to puberty.

Over recent decades we've also learned a great deal about neural plasticity: experience affects every aspect of brain functioning. While inborn differences in brain anatomy may explain why boys get squirmy in class or show loyalty to their friend by shouting "Race ya up the hill!" and why girls tenderly rock their dolls to sleep, we also know that every child is unique and evolving. Stereotypes are dangerous; their history is littered with prejudice and false assumptions. We adults have a responsibility to appreciate sensitivity and chattiness in boys so inclined, and to teach those who aren't how to be empathic and articulate. It's also our duty to encourage daring and technical aptitude in girls. We can do this by raising our awareness of typical gender tendencies while at the same time staying alert to the individual traits and temperament of each child.

No one has more experience with this than classroom teachers. Their desire to meet the needs of all students has fueled much of the research into children's brain development and how it affects learning and communication. It takes some finesse to get the best out of boys in an environment like the classroom, with its heavy emphasis on verbal expression, listening, and impulse control.

Leonard Sax, psychologist, family physician, and author of *Boys Adrift* and *Why Gender Matters*, studies the impact classroom noise has on boys and girls. He found that in mixed-gender classrooms, the teachers who were most successful in capturing the attention of boys spoke six to eight decibels louder than other teachers. This empirical observation is supported by biological research showing that boys' sense of hearing is not as acute as girls'. At the same time, Sax observed that boys were able to tolerate a higher level of background noise. "The hum of a buzzing fan, or the sound of fingers tapping on a desk, may be quite annoying to a girl or to the (female) teacher, but is less likely to annoy a boy."

If underperforming boys were sitting at the back of the classroom, Sax reasoned, it would make sense to move them to the front, where they could hear the teacher better. But social and emotional gender differences came into play: for the boys, saving face among friends was more important than getting the teacher's approval or improving their grades. In classrooms where children are allowed to sit wherever they like, rowdy boys tend to sit in the back. If a teacher moves one of them to the front, "that boy's first priority often may be to prove to his buddies in the back row that he is not a teacher's pet, that he remains 'one of the guys.' As a result, he may become more disruptive and inattentive in the front row than he was in the back row."

That is exactly the type of conundrum parents of boys face as they try to encourage their sons to listen, follow directions, express themselves verbally, articulate feelings, and think before blurting things out. The more you know about the set of tools with which your son is equipped, the easier it will be to engage him. If you're having trouble, you can run through a mental checklist of typical male traits to determine which ones might be at play. This exercise in linking communication obstacles to hardwired biological differences is equally helpful for parents of girls, as we'll see in the next chapter.

In the chart below you'll find brain, neurochemical, and hormonally based attributes that affect communication with boys and girls. (It isn't a list of *all* the developmental differences, hence no mention of things like boys' better mastery of spatial and mathematical reasoning.) These traits are generally accepted by the scientific community as of this writing. A more expansive chart can be found in the Appendix.

RELATIVE DIFFERENCES BETWEEN BOYS AND GIRLS IN BRAIN DEVELOPMENT AND FUNCTION	
Boys	**Girls**
Develop language skills more slowly than girls.	Develop language skills earlier than boys.
Nearly all of boys' speech is comprehensible by age four and a half. On average, they say fewer words per day than girls and speak more slowly.	Nearly all of girls' speech is comprehensible by age three. On average, they say two to three times as many words per day as boys and speak twice as fast.

Boys	Girls
Learn to read at a slower rate than girls.	Learn to read one year to eighteen months earlier than boys.
Quicker to act on impulse, more frequent need for motor release (physical activity).	Find it easier to sit for longer periods of time.
Less likely to perceive signs of pain or distress in others.	Respond more frequently and rapidly to signs of pain or distress.
To comfortably hear a speaker, boys require the person's voice to be six to eight decibels louder than girls require. They have a higher tolerance for background noise.	Can discern voices at lower decibels and also can discriminate nuances of tone better than boys. Hear better at higher frequencies. Are more easily annoyed or distracted by background noise.
Process visual cues differently than girls; are drawn to motion and see best in bright light.	Attuned to the meaning of facial expressions and body language; are better at seeing in low light.
Experience greater separation anxiety and cry more easily before age three. Later react to moderate challenge or confrontation with excitement or exhilaration.	Ability to read social cues helps them adjust to new environments. React to extreme stress by withdrawing or with psychosomatic symptoms.
Have higher levels of testosterone; however, levels vary widely among boys. Testosterone leads boys to express social energy through attempts at physical and social dominance.	Have higher levels of estrogen and progesterone, the "bonding" hormones. Girls use social energy to form attachments to peers and adults.

YOUR SON: FRAGILE YET CLUELESS

Two aspects of brain development are especially significant when talking to boys between the ages of three or four and puberty. One is that boys and girls process emotions differently. Because boys have fewer verbal and cognitive tools to make sense of their feelings or sleuth out what caused them, they take longer to heal. A family argument that a girl might witness, discuss with a friend, and emotionally file away by the next morning can take your son longer to process. If he's glum when you pick him up from school, the reason could lie in something that happened two days ago, not that afternoon.

The second noteworthy difference between boys and girls is the amounts of serotonin and oxytocin their brains secrete. Boys have less. The smaller amount of serotonin makes them more impulsive and fidgety than girls, while the lower level of oxytocin makes them slower to respond to the emotional or physical pain of others. When you're worrying about your son's callous behavior, bear in mind that it's not necessarily a character flaw but more likely just a standard-issue boy trait that will change as he grows. (And think how quickly he would race over to help his grandmother if she fell!)

Obviously, there are limits. Even if he's well behaved in school, a pattern of purposely hurting animals, other kids, adults, or himself; setting fires; or exhibiting behavior distinct from the usual playful boy-to-boy tussling should lead you to seek the guidance of a professional.

SPEAK LOUDLY, CALMLY, SIMPLY. REPEAT.

The universal complaints of parents about their sons are the boys' fickle listening skills, rowdiness, and tactlessness. As it happens, these traits are fueled by the same juice that gives little boys their freewheeling, openhearted lust for life. Your task is to manage your own reactions to your son's behavior and teach him some socially astute work-arounds.

It begins with how the adults speak to each other. In families where angry shouting is commonplace, the parents are inadvertently training their sons to respond only to insults or screaming. The boys often conclude that the problem isn't their own behavior but their parents' bad mood or stupid rules. Why else would Mom or Dad become so enraged by seemingly minor infractions? "You never hang up your towel! You always forget!" He's a boy. This task is not high on his agenda. He's not thinking about hanging up the towel so it's dry for his next bath because he doesn't care if it's dry for his next bath.

It's normal for a boy not to respond to his parents' words the first time or even the second. When that happens, there's a good possibility that he *literally did not hear you*, especially if he was fully absorbed in an activity. This is the way their brains work. Understanding this can prevent or preempt feelings of outrage or indignation. So prepare to repeat yourself, and maximize your impact by observing the following voice lessons.

Volume and Pitch

Boys of all ages respond best to short sentences that are spoken fairly loudly but not at a high pitch: "Taylor. Look at me. It's five thirty. It's time to go to the kitchen to feed Snowball." Don't give more than two instructions at once. Expect to be ignored. Instead of asking "What did I say?" followed by a threat, repeat your request at the same loud-but-not-yelling volume. If he *has* heard you and is hoping you'll give up, calmly repeating the request lets him know you're not going away. Avoid escalating to, "For the THIRD time, THE POOR DOG IS HUNGRY AND AS FAR AS I KNOW HE CAN'T FEED HIMSELF."

Clapping out a simple rhythm (clap clap CLAP, clap clap CLAP) is a teacher's trick for getting children's attention. It's a useful tactic for boys because they respond to loud noises and get a kick out of the gamelike aspect of it. This is a good alternative to yelling. If the situation is urgent, use the full-frontal listening technique: get down to the boy's level, place a hand on his shoulder, look him in the eye, and ask him to repeat what you've said.

Because boys process both sensory data and emotions more slowly than girls, they may not only take longer to respond but also be more easily wounded if you shout at them. And while they may tolerate a certain amount of bellowing from Dad, similar treatment from Mom can really sting.

Tone

Boys *do not hear* subtle differences in tone, so your sighs or sarcastic hinting may be lost on your son. If he does happen to notice, it will likely confuse and hurt him rather than serve as a motivator. A sorrow-ful tone may go entirely over his head, leading you to feel insulted or ignored even though he honestly didn't grasp the undercurrents. When boys reach adolescence, this changes and they become ultrasensitive to their parents' tone, at which point you'll have to train yourself to sound chipper and nonjudgmental. You might as well start now.

Tempo

Although he may be chattering away at quite a clip, keep your own tempo moderate. Boys' language skills develop more slowly than girls', and this includes their ability to listen as well as speak. Talk at a relaxed pace, but try not to taunt him, as in robotically announcing, "Please. Put. Bowl. In. Sink." (Although, given how tone-deaf boys can be, he might just think it's funny, which is one of the endearing things about sons.)

Pausing

Speech and language pathologist Ariela Schmidt Shandling attributes increased stuttering in boys to the tension created when parents demand that their sons "Hurry up! Get to the point!" When talking with boys, train yourself to allow for their pauses, "ummmms," and false starts as they work to articulate their thoughts. Be aware that there might not be a recognizable point; they may simply be offering you a tasty bit of information. If you're asking them to repeat what you've just told them, allow them enough time to do it, even if they have to stop and struggle to remember. Go gently.

Body Language

Face your son when talking to him. Sit on the floor if that's where he's playing. Although he is not as adept as a girl would be at read-ing expressions, he needs to see your face because it helps focus his attention. Don't get angry with him if he ignores a stern glance or tiny head-shake of disapproval. He probably didn't register it. Keep your shoulders down and your arms relaxed—no waving your hands or pointing and jabbing in the air.

THE WORK-AROUNDS

You can't force a boy to care about hanging up his wet towel, empathize when a friend trips and falls, or want to sit quietly when his biology is screaming at him to leap up and race across an open field. But there are ways to help your son adjust his behavior so he isn't always on the receiving end of other people's wrath and disappointment.

What *not* to say: "Your behavior is inappropriate. You need to focus in class and stop being so disruptive. Then you'll have more success." Abstract words like *inappropriate, focus, disruptive*, and *success* mean little to a small boy. When delivered in a stern, preachy tone, they sound like the *wah-wuh-wah-wah* of the adults in the *Peanuts* cartoons.

Rather than hoping your logic will convince your son to change, approach him as a co-conspirator. Act as if you're a cultural anthropologist familiarizing him with the odd but predictable ways of members of different tribes. Your tone should be collegial as you confide:

> Listen, Jesse, all the people you're having trouble with—girls, your grandparents, the older boys at school, teachers, even your mom and me—we all have similar reactions to certain things you (and all kids) do. It may not make much sense. But the secret to getting into less trouble is to learn the patterns. It's like a code. If you can memorize how these people will react, you'll be able to predict what will make them mad or disappointed. You won't have to wonder, "What did I do this time?"

The mischief and mouthing-off that adults find so irritating are normal expressions of boys' verve, swagger, and desire to entertain or provoke in what they see as a fair and playful fashion. I've listed the most common of these behaviors below, along with an example of how you might present them to your son. As you read, you may find yourself thinking, *My son is very bright. Surely he knows this already. He's just choosing not to act civilized.* But certain social norms can strike boys as ridiculous or baffling, which is why it's helpful to spell things out. Then it's his choice: maybe pulling his sister's hair and hearing her shriek is worth a time-out. Maybe not. Don't get into an argument about whether this is right or wrong or she's being a wimp. And don't soft pedal information with qualifiers like "I know you like to make the kids in class laugh, and you're so funny! But you have to pay attention, OK?" You are delivering vital secret codes, and you need to be straightforward.

Rather than loading your son up with a preprogrammed rule book, wait until some choice he's made has led to a bit of trouble. Boys are rarely remorseful about their transgressions because they don't think they've done anything wrong. Instead, he'll likely be indignant or puzzled. Treat this reaction not as stupidity or willful rudeness but as simple ignorance. Then step in with the secret knowledge, using the same matter-of-fact tone you did when he was a toddler and you taught him not to pull the puppy's ears. With your guidance he'll be able to start practicing self-control.

Note: In the examples below, I use terms such as "get mad at you" and "yell at you" because your son will instantly understand what you mean. Children typically use the phrase "yelled at me" to describe any type of reprimand, even the mildest.

Teasing Others about Their Appearance

"If you make fun of the way someone looks or the clothes they're wearing, even if they know you like them, sometimes they may insult you back. Sometimes they may feel embarrassed or get mad at you. It may hurt their feelings. This is usually more true for girls and adults, but lots of boys are sensitive, too."

If your son is getting into trouble for teasing or insulting other kids, you can also say some version of "If you insult someone's appearance and they tell their parent or the teacher, a grown-up may lecture you, punish you, or call me. Some kids don't mind being teased, others mind it a lot. Pay attention and see how different people react."

Teasing Others about Their Performance

The rules for teasing about appearance also apply to performance, with an extra caveat: Today's parents are particularly thin-skinned about doubts cast on their child's abilities, even by another child. So try to raise your son's consciousness about offering what he sees as constructive criticism along the lines of "Your pitching SUCKS!" He may shrug and say, "Just telling the truth, Mom. And everybody knows it." Maybe so, but learning how to give subtle yet useful critiques—and knowing when to keep quiet—is a social skill best acquired early.

Try telling your son, "When someone makes a mistake, they usually know it and already feel bad. Before saying anything, wait to see what happens. If someone else criticizes them, see how they react and how the adults react. Saying something mean may get you into trouble even if it's true. And it may hurt the other person's feelings."

Or: "Rather than insulting someone who messed up, think about an observation you made that might help them improve. For example, 'I have an idea about a different way to stand that might help your pitch.' If they want to know what it is, they'll ask you."

Blurting Out a Negative Opinion

"When a thought pops into your head—let's say you think the show your sister is watching is dumb, or the homework your teacher assigned is boring, or your friend chose the wrong brand of skateboard—stop first and think about what might happen if you tell them. The person may feel annoyed with you or they may not want to be your friend anymore, even if you're right or your comment made everybody laugh. Some people are more touchy than others.

If you watch how they react in different situations, it's not too hard to figure out. When you're meeting someone for the first time, it's always better not to criticize them."

Interrupting

"If you cut people off when they're talking, they may lose their train of thought or think you don't care about what they're saying. Wait until there's a pause in their story and then respond to what they've said or jump in with a story of your own that's on the same topic."

Touching, Pulling, Shoving

"I'm sure you've already noticed that girls and boys play in different ways. Most girls will get angry, hurt, cry, or tell a grown-up if you poke, shove, hit, pull their hair, yank on their clothes, or punch them, even playfully. Your guy friends may react differently, but some boys do mind. Your best bet is to start out by being gentle and not touch people unless you're friends and you know they won't care. And never be rough with grown-ups unless they invite you to, like when you and Dad play Pirate Blackbeard or Ninja Warrior."

Clowning Around in Class

"Sometimes a teacher will laugh at your joke, and sometimes she'll get mad. Usually you'll figure out her sense of humor as you get to know her. Before you make a funny comment, consider that you might get yelled at or labeled a troublemaker. Think about your track record with that particular teacher and ask yourself if it's worth the risk."

Distracting Other Students

"It's hard for teachers to hold the attention of a class, especially if there are a lot of students and no aide or co-teacher. Distracting other kids by whispering or gesturing or passing notes makes the teacher's job harder. Even if you're helping them! Teachers don't like it. Of course, when you're working in groups or teams, it's fine to talk to other students."

Grossing People Out

"Many people have a different reaction to gross things than you and your friends do. Although you may think it's funny to gross them out, kids may call you stupid or a baby, tell other kids, or yell. An adult might punish you."

Being Too Loud: Inside and Outside Voices

Tell the boy, "Let me show you what adults consider to be an inside voice compared to an outside voice. Starting with the softest possible whisper, say, 'I love big red balloons.' OK, now a little louder . . ." Continue until you hit the "outside voice" level, and call that Level 7. Then go past it until you're both screaming and laughing. Label that Level 10. Then say, "Inside you always want to aim for four or five. That goes for when you're inside a car, too, because any extra big noise can distract the person who's driving. Outside, if you talk louder than a level seven, even if you're in our backyard or on the playground, if there are adults nearby, someone's going to tell you to be quiet or a stranger might worry that you're having a problem."

ACTING ON IMPULSE: TEACHING BOYS HOW
TO RECOGNIZE AND NAME BIG FEELINGS

Boys take longer than girls to recognize the thoughts and physical signs that mean *A big uncomfortable feeling is happening right now! Let's see which one, and what might have caused it, and what I can do to make myself feel better without getting into trouble.* A boy hears Mom rebuking him for grabbing a toy from his baby sister, or the teacher calling him out for kicking the chair in front of him, or Dad accusing him of lying about being pushed by another kid, and he can't explain why he did it because he honestly doesn't know.

Adults can help young boys connect the dots between their impulsive actions and their feelings by introducing them to concepts expressed in words like being *jealous* of the baby (grab!), *frustrated* and *discouraged* when the teacher explains fractions again and you still don't understand (kick!), and *embarrassed* when you trip and tear your new jeans and get dirt and pebbles in your knee (lie!). What often differentiates boys from girls, as we'll see when we discuss this topic in the next chapter, is that the girls are aware they're feeling something, they just don't have the exact word for it. They might say they "hate" somebody when what they actually feel is envy. Boys don't necessarily make that much of a connection. They have no idea why they grabbed the toy or kicked the chair; they just felt like it.

Listening while your son tells his side of the tale, you might have some success in guiding him to acknowledge feelings of which he was unaware, which led to reactions or choices that led to trouble. If he's open to it, you can point him to specific physical reactions that help him realize he's upset, like a tummy ache, a strong reaction to a minor injury, a pounding heart, or feeling sweaty. But this method won't be effective if he's still feeling stung or resentful or humiliated. Sending him to his room to "think about it!" can be helpful by giving *you* a chance to calm down, but from his perspective, what is there to think about besides the unfairness of the world or how often he has bad luck or is just plain misunderstood?

Sometimes the best way to help young boys gain insight about their actions and feelings is to use an indirect approach. For boys (and men), saving face is of utmost importance, so pick a feeling your son needs to understand and insert the concept into a setting that does not involve him. For example, while reading a bedtime story, gently stop the action to pose a question. Ask him what he thinks the character feels or how he would feel if he were in that situation. Then repeat what he's said, agree ("So true! So sad!"), and deepen the landscape of emotions. "If that happened to me, I might feel a little excited AND a little worried." This way your son doesn't have to acknowledge his own hurt, fear, or anger, but hearing a parent name it models and teaches empathy. It also reinforces the neural pathways for compassion toward himself and others.

Certainly every one of us, even after years of therapy, is still learning to recognize the relationship between triggering events or thoughts and our own feelings. Offering young boys options besides fight, flee, stew, and pretend it never happened saves them from unnecessary anguish and gives them tools they can use to reflect before reacting to the next emotional challenge.

A HERO NEEDS A QUEST

All young boys face the same three existential questions:

> *How can I be myself without getting into trouble?*
> *Does anyone consider me a hero?*
> *What do I contribute to this family that someone else doesn't already contribute better?*

The strategies we've looked at so far should help your son with the first question. As you spend less time arguing over his behavior, the nuances of his personality will come into focus and you can steer him toward activities that will let him be a hero and nurture his unique contributions.

Your son's quirks and passions will become clear bit by bit. Observe and listen. Let him talk in the dark, in the car, while moving, while waiting for the bus or sitting on the subway. In general he's more comfortable chatting side by side than face-to-face (the "full-frontal" technique is for important requests or reprimands, not casual chats). Your role is to be attentive and receptive to the commentary. Some boys prefer to write down a big thought, confession, or heartfelt sentiment and slip a note under your door rather than say it in person. If *you* leave little notes every so often on his desk, night table, or pillow, you've opened up an avenue of communication he hadn't realized was available and he'll be more likely to do the same.

As for your contribution to conversations with your son, shooting hoops is a good metaphor: you say a little something, and then another little something, and sometimes it goes through—you get a basket. With young boys this approach works much better than long, serious discussions and explanations.

Much will be revealed on the walk or drive to school if you stay curious, which means resisting the urge to use the time to remind or instruct. Instead, ask easygoing questions or make comments with interesting content:

"I noticed that the Melmans got a new dog. A really big one. Have *you* seen any new developments on our block lately?"

A dialogue can unfold:

"On Halloween the people who live in the house next to the Melmans gave out super gross candy!"

"Eww. Gross-looking or gross-tasting?"

"Both! [Pause.] Mom, am I weird? I think I don't really like most Halloween candy."

"I would call that having a discerning palate. [This comment uses a new term in context, great for vocabulary building.] You know what you like. It's interesting because you get really excited to go trick-or-treating."

"'Cause I want to get a lot of candy, the most candy, but I don't want to eat it. I want to have the candy to trade. Especially when other kids run out."

"That makes sense. You've figured out your strategy."

During a twenty-minute stroll around the neighborhood you can pursue a goal such as finding a really good stick, one that's thick and long and straight. Boys seek bounty—a rotting bird corpse, a pile of shattered car-window glass—and they need a good stick to prod their discoveries. If you have alleys in your neighborhood, try wandering down them. Inspect the abandoned furniture, peer through a hole in the fence to someone's backyard, gaze at the contents of an open garage crammed with junk. It's like going on a treasure hunt or brazenly ignoring a "No Trespassing" sign, which little boys (and plenty of girls) love to do.

A physician friend of mine, always working long hours, used to take her young son on fake errands up to an hour away to give them uninterrupted time alone together in the car. She had an older daughter as well, but finding time to talk with her wasn't a challenge and didn't require choreography. Now when this twenty-four-year-old son comes home to visit, he always asks his mom if she'd like to accompany him on some errands. Sweet!

Fine conversations may take place while you're ambling alongside your son, but equally fun are the tales of derring-do he'll bring home from solo treks or those with friends. Find opportunities for him to play outdoors in the least restricted environment you can abide. Free time, no structure, no parents, and room to roam creates fertile soil for his budding narrative technique. Like the synchronicity between learning to eat solid food and learning to speak, boys' desire to venture into wild places supports their verbal development. Their emotional wiring makes it difficult for them to articulate feelings, but they'll be bursting to tell you about the squirrel trap they built in your backyard and to explain in detail how it works. (Don't worry. It probably won't.)

Where can your children—both girls and boys—run around and have pretend sword fights with branches? What can they climb on, and what can they hide under? Where can they make a clubhouse and have friends over and make up their own rules? Where can they get away from you? Family camp, the dock at Grandpa's house, your backyard? Exploring the perimeter of a pond at the park? These are the places your boy can practice his heroic moves and gather a trove of stories to bring home.

Free time and unstructured play does much more than cultivate children's facility with language. It also has a positive effect on their mood and spirit. Peter Gray, research professor of psychology at Boston College, studies the relationship between psychopathology and a sense of "agency" (developmentally appropriate control over the quality and quantity of one's daily activities). He writes, "By depriving children of opportunities to play on their own, away from direct adult supervision and control, we are depriving them of opportunities to learn how to take control of their own lives. We may think we are protecting them, but in fact we are diminishing their joy, diminishing their sense of self-control, preventing them from discovering and exploring the endeavors they would most love, and increasing the odds that they will suffer from anxiety, depression, and other disorders."

In other words, a hero needs—really *needs*—a quest. And an adult he can tell all about it.

AMAZING FACTS, WORLD RECORDS, AND OTHER BELIEVE-IT-OR-NOTS

The third part of a boy's predicament—*What do I contribute to this family that someone else doesn't already contribute better?*—is a trick question because you and your son may have different definitions of *contribute.* You may consider it to be performance-based and an element of family citizenship: help siblings, do chores, cooperate with parents. It's true that those are vital to your son's sense of place and purpose within your family. But they are not worth as much to an imaginative little boy as the true coin of his realm: information. The four hundred kinds of sharks, the tallest building in the world, the smallest video camera used by the CIA, the most baskets ever shot in a single game . . . How would you know about these astounding facts if he didn't tell you?

Try to be enchanted with his enchantment, even when his preferred topics fall far outside the range of subject matter you normally find compelling. How? One tactic is to act a bit ignorant, seeking his expert knowledge no matter how meager. Your enthusiasm is a deposit in the bank of goodwill. Say, "Interesting!" "What else do you know about microrobots?" "Are there other tricks spies use?"

Of course, he may be reciting the same roster of dinosaurs you've already heard fifty times—the stale inventory that makes you want to steer your car to a liquor store. The reason he's repeating himself is that he's run out of material. Little boys need more information not only to sate their curiosity but also to keep you captivated. The surest way to refresh the monologue is to feed him some new facts and experiences via books, videos, or outings: a trip to the library, harbor, pier, or train station; a ride up the elevator in a tall building; a morning at the flea market or farmer's market; or a big-ticket excursion to the museum, aquarium, or zoo. You can get your son to change the channel by exposing him to more channels.

Boys want to prove themselves, to be masters of a universe. Collecting information is a way of getting their arms all the way around a topic. If that information involves superlatives—the biggest, strongest, fastest—even better. Extremes are good. What's the fastest animal? The cheetah. How fast? Seventy-five miles per hour. What animal kills its prey the fastest? The alligator snapping turtle! Its prey dies instantly!

Some parents and sons naturally share affinities, and some get to introduce each other to novel realms. If either parent feels ignorant or unmoved by their boy's passions, they can try switching the channel to a different interest or studying up. It can be as simple as Googling a few facts and saying, "Yesterday I found out that . . ." Listen to your son's response and you'll learn what enthralls him. Among the topics and concepts to consider for their fascination potential:

Superlatives. The biggest, fastest, tallest, smallest, heaviest, longest, loudest, deepest, oldest, strongest.

Superpowers. Magic: you can fool the eye and trick people. Spies: you have a different identity; you can wear a disguise. Codes: you have special secret knowledge. Detectives. Ninjas. Athletes. Astronauts.

Extreme terrain. Space, deserts, oceans, the jungle. The distance between Mars and Jupiter; the number of Earths that would fit into the Sun; the Mariana Trench and the strange creatures that dwell there; Death Valley, the lowest and hottest place on Earth; the Amazon River, longest on Earth, home to the anaconda, the longest snake. They eat goats!

Giant creatures. Dinosaurs, whales, giant squid, elephants, grizzly bears, woolly mammoths.

Predators. Kill times; methods of killing; how do they consume their prey?

Deadliest Warrior. This television series aired from 2009 to 2011 and covered a topic about which boys love to speculate. Who would have won, a samurai or a Viking? A pirate or a Mongol? Watch a few episodes with your son and you'll have plenty to discuss.

Monster Bug Wars. The same thing as *Deadliest Warrior*, but with insects! Find them on YouTube.

Modes of transportation. Big: eighteen-wheelers, super-stretch limos, the *Titanic*. Exotic: submarines, blimps. Future: hover boards that really hover, driverless cars, jet packs.

Scores, game averages, player stats. For nonsporty parents this can be a tough one, but give it a try if your son is so inclined. You may discover your inner fan.

If you accept that listening and talking to a young boy is different from the familiar back-and-forth between adults (or between adults and girls), you can flow along with his densely packed recitation of facts, stats, and world records. His aim is not to charm or bond but to share the mind-blowing discoveries he's made with the ones he loves the most.

The Biggest, Strongest, Fastest

RESPECTING YOUR SON'S BOYISHNESS
WHILE RESPECTING HIS SCHOOL

Today's boys must deal with confounding expectations: be a combatant on the playing field, a gentleman in the lunch line, and a scholar in the classroom. The parents' challenge is to acknowledge this high-wire act without undermining the legitimacy of institutions where a boy needs to thrive, especially school.

Even as our insight into the neuroscience of gender differences has grown, and as child development experts (and parents) are questioning the frequent prescribing of attention-deficit medications to young children, the fact remains that boys must sit quietly and perform to "girl" standards at school and sometimes even at summer camps that emphasize high-level skill building. What are you, as a parent, to do, aside from homeschooling or enrolling your son in an institution with more boy-savvy teaching strategies—if one exists near your home, your son is eligible, and you can afford it?

If you sense that your son is frustrated and feels like he doesn't measure up and never will—a frequent concern among the families I counsel—validate his struggle and offer empathy, but beware of employing a tone or message that signals pity. Children interpret sympathy as permission to take a pass: "Dad, you know it's unfair! It's not my fault I didn't remember the assignment."

Resist the impulse to team up with him to fight the school. When parents challenge the teacher on every perceived injustice and middling grade, the effort backfires. Rather than empowering the child, it increases his sense of inadequacy, leading to apathy, anger, and bitterness. And blaming the school and teacher drives experienced teachers nuts. They remember how effective it was when parents and teachers were united and children understood that they couldn't play one against the other. Despite the built-in disadvantages boys today face in many schools, solidarity among adults is usually better for children. It's consistent, and the occasional lapse in fairness is excellent practice for how the world works. Parents who side with their kids against the "system" are setting a dangerous and unrealistic precedent by teaching them that they are above the rules.

The positive way to acknowledge the school conundrum is a bit subversive. It involves regular celebration of boyishness while subtly comparing his day at school to aspects of your adult day that are difficult and dull. For instance, you could take him to the do-it-yourself car wash and say, "I spent most of the afternoon in a long meeting and this is really fun. Let's blast this sucker clean!"

You're showing him that you enjoy the chance to get a little wet and kind of dirty, to let off some steam and have a good time—and washing the car is a handy way to accomplish all that. What you're demonstrating is balance. The implication is, *Yes, parts of the workday and school day are hard and boring, but we're both good soldiers when we're on duty. And when we're off duty, we both appreciate using a giant water hose that sprays twenty feet!* Washing the car together lets your boy know that you crave the physical, unstructured, nonacademic side of life just as much as he does. And you consistently look for ways to enjoy that side.

Very rarely, there are situations where a particular school or teacher is causing real harm to a child. That's when you get to model diplomacy and courage, requesting a change of workload or teacher.* If your efforts fail, you may need to enroll your son in a different school. But for the great majority of parents, seeing their sons through elementary school does not require battling teachers or switching institutions. It just takes patience and an awareness of how boys develop.

When my father was young, his big brother would lightly slap him on his face each morning and say, "This is to remind you to listen to the teacher today." It sounds harsh (and I'm not recommending it!), but it was an acknowledgment of how hard it is for boys to sit still, a rudimentary lesson in self-control, and a reminder of the importance of taking advantage of the opportunity to learn. Then again, my

* In Chapter 10, "The Trustees," you'll find more information about handling situations where a teacher is clearly unfit for the job.

dad lived in Brighton Beach, where he got to jump into the ocean and swim around the rocks or sneak into the beach club to hear the bands play live music. No adult was geotracking his every move. Today's boys are prisoners unless their parents make sure they have an escape hatch. It's one more reason to set your son loose where the wild(ish) things are.

GAMING: THIEF OF TIME AND BAND OF BROTHERS

A long, long time ago—actually about thirty years—children had little homework and had a posse of neighborhood friends right outside the front door. They set their own agenda and used all five senses in the three-dimensional world: riding bikes; climbing trees; throwing a baseball, snowball, or water balloon. Look down your block. No kid in sight. Look at your son. The one sitting safe and warm in his room. Controller in hand, he can shoot weapons, scramble through war zones, throttle the enemy, and shout at the screen, satisfying some of his natural impulses.

So many aspects of technology are in flux, so many questions unresolved. Are we overly concerned about gaming and social media the way parents in the 1950s were about television? Or are we dangerously oblivious, like the doctors in cigarette ads of the same era who urged people to "give your throat a vacation . . . smoke a FRESH cigarette!" Each family and every child is different, so how can we thoughtfully decide on proper rules for gaming?

It isn't easy. But gaming has been studied so extensively over the past twenty years that it is a parent's duty to set some limits. The research is disturbing enough that in 2013 the *Diagnostic and Statistical Manual of Mental Disorders (DSM-5)* identified Internet Gaming Disorder as a new condition warranting intensive investigation: "The 'gamers' play compulsively, to the exclusion of other interests, and their persistent and recurrent online activity results in clinically significant impairment or distress. . . . They experience symptoms of withdrawal when kept from gaming."

The likelihood is remote that your child will become addicted to video gaming in the clinical sense of being dysfunctional in multiple areas of life. Only about 8 percent of gamers between the ages of eight and eighteen meet that criteria. For most boys, friendship in the digital age includes playing networked games via voice, which leads to "collaboration, conversation, the fun of trash talking, and feelings of happy connection." A large, nationally representative study published in the journal *Pediatrics* showed that children aged ten to fifteen who play video games on any platform for an hour or less a day demonstrate better psychosocial adjustment compared with no play, whereas the opposite was true for those engaging in more than three hours of daily play.

Still, for many parents and their sons, daily wrangling over the extent of time spent gaming is a source of perpetual conflict. Although the boys may not hole up in their rooms for days without eating or bathing, their hours-long gaming sessions meet the nonclinical, popular definition of addiction.

Randy Kulman, PhD, founder of LearningWorks for Kids, a company that evaluates educational apps and videos, concurs: "In terms of psychological adjustment, playing for one hour a day seems to be the healthiest amount of time." To detach your child from a game, they suggest establishing a consistent routine. Give a ten-minute warning when the session is about to end and use a visual timer the child can see. When time's up, have a post-game tradition in place, such as eating a snack or discussing the recent session.

You can introduce your child to the concept of limits by drawing a comparison to yourself: "With lots of fun things, our cravings overpower judgment about what's good for us. Take chocolate cake. If I had it in the house all the time, I'd want to eat too much of it, even though I know that's not healthy. My desire would be stronger than my willpower. I can't let you play video games longer than is healthy for you, even though I understand that you disagree with me about it right now."

As boys get older, most demand games that immerse them in

combat, fantasy worlds, or criminal activities where success means chasing people, gunning them down, or otherwise vanquishing them. The most recent research findings don't show a correlation between playing violent video games and violent real-life behavior, but again, moderation and knowledge of your own child will guide you.

There is one other question worth pondering: What are boys *not* doing when they're playing video games? They're not interacting face-to-face with other children or adults in varied environments. Boys, much more than girls, need practice with person-to-person communication, real-life impulse control, articulating thoughts and feelings, compromising, and reading people's expressions. The more socially awkward the boy, the more he'll be negatively impacted by not getting to practice these interpersonal skills. A group of gaming buddies can definitely be a positive part of a young boy's life, but limits are needed and non-gaming playdates and outings are still essential.

With gaming, there's a healthy-to-unhealthy continuum that goes like this:

Interest → Pleasure and Skill Acquisition → Passion and Pride → Preoccupation → Obsession

How can you tell where your son falls? Look at the big picture of his life for guidance in setting rules about duration of play. Does he enjoy friends apart from gaming with them, for example, in sports, theater, hanging out in the neighborhood? Do his teachers describe him as a spirited person who participates in a range of activities at school? (Note: I'm not asking if he is a leader or outgoing or popular. Despite American ideals, these are not qualities essential to emotional health.) Does he enjoy spending time at family gatherings and on trips? Does he have a grandparent, uncle, cousin, friend of the family, or friend's parent with whom he enjoys talking and who enjoys talking to him? Does he have other passionate interests (collecting baseball cards or facts or stories) that provide him with special expertise and conversational fodder to use with new friends and acquaintances? If you can answer yes to most of these questions, you probably have your gaming timer calibrated just right. Keep an alert eye on the balance in his life and adjust as needed.

THE BANK OF GOODWILL FOR BOYS

We've seen how boys love to impress their parents with their knowledge, skills, jokes, and nerve. Your enthusiasm for your son's passions and tolerance for some of the jetsam he leaves in his wake are reliable sources of funding for the bank of goodwill. By demonstrating not only your love but also your respect, you earn your son's trust, smoothing the way for your larger agenda—all the instruction on language, manners, behavior, and empathy that are so vital to his growth. With that in mind, here are some more suggestions for adding to the bank of goodwill.

- Sign him up for a kids' cooking class. They're full of boys. Why? Fire, chopping, grilling, knife sharpening. The junior chefs learn how to use all sorts of tools that are usually off-limits and also how to prepare some meals.
- Let him completely take over a part of the backyard (or the weedy overgrown side yard, always a favorite boy haunt).
- Let him do whatever he wants in his bedroom as long as it does not include allowing food to rot, and with the caveat that he not leave his personal belongings—including shoes that could cause others to trip, drinking glasses, and plates he used—in other rooms of the house. He abides by the neatness level in the rest of the house but gets to do what he wants in his own room.
- If he shares a bedroom, search for a place in your home that can be his private domain and where he can be messy indefinitely, like a corner of the basement, attic, or garage.

- Take him to a big league athletic competition, a setting where hollering, booing, and jumping for joy is proper etiquette. Or out beyond where the waves break at the beach or on the fastest roller coaster.
- Let him pick a recorded book to listen to in the car. Speculate about the characters, with no topic off-limits. Enter the crannies of his world.
- Allow him to wear the same outfit to school many days in a row, even if it includes a cape and boots, as long as the items are clean (frayed or faded are fine).
- Let him have one free day off school each semester for an outing or adventure (unless he's missed school frequently due to illness or to dodge a test). He gets to choose the day and the agenda. This is not a reward for performance; it is a pure gift. It's a good idea for girls, too.

Although young boys enter childhood with fewer words than girls, speak less, and use simpler sentences, that doesn't mean they aren't deeply and actively connected to the people around them. Parents need only attempt to speak their son's language (or, in the case of fathers, remember it) and the boys will meet them halfway, absorbing a more nuanced vocabulary and, in the process, seeing their world fill in with detail and new levels of meaning.

And what of their sisters? Parents won't need to speak "girl" to connect with them. Girls speak "grown-up" beginning around age four. But there is still much parents can teach their daughters about communicating in our complex culture, as we'll see in the next chapter.

CHAPTER 4

The Boss, the Bestie, the High Priestess of Pretend

Conversing with Young Girls

Ages Three to Eleven

Four-year-old Mira runs into the preschool play yard, but instead of trotting toward her gaggle of friends, she stops short and heads over to her teacher. Eyes wide, left arm akimbo, right hand on her cheek with fingers splayed out, she sings, "Susanna! Is that a new skirt I see?"

"Good morning, Mira. Yes, I'm wearing a new skirt today."

"Where'd you get it?"

"I bought it at a store called Anthropologie."

"I LOVE THAT STORE! That's where they have glittering doorknobs in baskets."

This interchange highlights some remarkable elements at play. Without planning or effort, Mira used a gangbuster opening line. Her question was triggered by instant recognition of visual cues (the specific design, color, or fabric of a skirt) that were weighed against a large body of information (her teacher's entire work wardrobe) stored in Mira's memory. Her use of advanced vocabulary words (*glittering, doorknobs, baskets*) and complex sentence structure enlivened the exchange, and her expressive pose signaled her curiosity, surprise, and delight.

Mira's mastery of the art of conversation successfully charmed an adult listener. So successfully that now, many years later, I am able to relate word for word this dialogue between my daughter Susanna and her tiny student.

Little girls are able to engage adults by speaking their language. Their eloquence and ability to interpret subtle verbal and nonverbal cues allow them to flourish in a wide variety of social settings. Most girls can easily tolerate the regimen of the classroom in early grades, partly because of their ability to listen and respond and partly because they care deeply about pleasing the teacher. But the attributes that make for success in areas valued by our society also lead parents to have unrealistic expectations for their daughters.

A common pitfall for parents of girls is mistaking their daughter's verbal sophistication for emotional maturity and interpreting her meltdowns as regression or manipulation. They're indignant because she sounds so worldly yet acts so childish. Adding to the confusion is the fact that girls are entering puberty earlier than they used to: seven or eight is now considered normal by the American Academy of Pediatrics.* Although menstruation is a few years off, hormones make these girls susceptible to media messages about how females should look and act (flirty! pretty! provocative!). The girls' sassy words and alluring manner reflect those messages long before they understand what they mean. This is alarming to parents and supports their impression that the girls are "four going on forty." But they're not.

The spirited little fashionista isn't "acting" childish with her poutiness and demands, she *is* a child. And she is caught in a trap neither she nor her parents can see. Propelled by hormones, cultural pressures, and her proficiency with language, she comes across as experienced when in reality she's more a canny observer and agile mimic. Her parents' frustration and dismay with her behavior can

---

* Parents of young children are dismayed when I tell them that the age of the onset of puberty continues to drop. What the American Academy of Pediatrics once classified as an abnormality called "precocious puberty" (defined by onset at age eight in girls and nine in boys) is now considered within the normal range.

cause the girl to become doubly mad: mad at them for being angry at her *and* mad at herself because she wants to be their good girl.

Yet she can't help it. She keeps talking, arguing, and pleading her case because the words come so easily and her feelings are so intense. She has passionate preferences: *Not that dress! Not that yogurt! Not that shampoo, story, pair of socks! Not that crayon! Purple but not THAT purple.*

She has feverish desires: *I told you everyone has a trampoline! An American Girl doll! Gets to stay up later than I do! Has wedge shoes! And you said maybe. Right? So when? Mom? You said!*

If you're the parent of a girl you'll eventually come to realize that the arguments—about everyday injustice or clothes or her room or hair or friends or food—are not going to be resolved during a single earnest, logical discussion. You'll want to pace yourself, because raising a forthright, reasonable daughter means going over what feels like exactly the same gritty ground, in slightly altered forms, every day for years.

With ages and stages in mind and with practice, you can adjust your message and delivery so that you and your daughter are able to ride the rapids of her childhood with less friction and more mutual appreciation. You can teach yourself to view her pickiness as discernment, her hyperbole as an abundance of heart. Working below your daughter's radar, you can guide her in a way that protects her wild individuality and rapid cognitive and physical growth and at the same time teaches her good manners and family citizenship.

A MOTHER'S BURDEN

The relationship between daughters and mothers is significantly different from that between daughters and their dads. Before we tackle the best ways to converse with a young girl, let's examine how these differences play out within a family.

The anatomical brains of mothers and daughters share gender-specific design features: they are attuned to facial expressions, tone of voice, and body language, and they're programmed to sense and respond to the feelings and opinions of others. (For an overview of brain development in females, see page 62 or the more detailed chart in the appendix.) These perceptions and the concern they stimulate is increased in female-to-female connections. When both mother and daughter are scrutinizing each other's tone, furrowed brow, or sigh, it can lead to emotional static. They may misread each other's motivations because, despite their similarities, a young girl and an adult woman have different perspectives. Or they can stumble together into overtalking problems (what psychologists call co-rumination). These dynamics lie at the root of many of the blowups between mothers and daughters.

Added to the innate challenges of female-to-female communication are the specific pressures of our modern culture. Mothers today are extremely close to their children. Even when they work outside the home, moms are more often the ones involved on a microscopic level: organizing, scheduling, making sure the children arrive on time. This means that much of their communication with their children consists of questioning and prodding them.

Mothers also are under a relatively new pressure to get parenting right. Consider that the use of the word *parenting* has become pervasive only over the past twenty years; prior to that, the common term was *child rearing*. It went from "Your child is lovely" to "You're such a good mom"—with the spotlight now on Mom, not the child. Mothers worry about every choice, and there are so many choices to make. They feel as if they're being judged from every corner: the ghosts of their own family history, their parents and in-laws, the other moms, the school, the Web, the media, social media . . . With so many voices weighing in, getting it right feels impossible.

WHAT ABOUT DAD?

Today's fathers cherish their children and typically are far more involved in family life than their own dads were. And because men are not wired to detect social cues the way women are, the emotional static is turned down when they relate to their daughters. Dads don't sweat the small stuff (*When did she last wash that hair? What did she just mumble?*) and therefore they don't ask or criticize her about it. This makes for a more relaxed relationship.

Fathers don't fret over the nuances of parenting or what other parents think of their "fathering" skills. For women, being a good mom feels like a referendum on their worth as a human being. Their anxiety extends to making sure Dad is getting it right, too. This is true for mothers of sons as well as daughters, but in my work with families a clear pattern emerges: moms have a higher tolerance for a father's parenting approach if the child is a boy. Moms respect the father-son bond because a jostling "just-us-guys" relationship is part of getting it right. Dad's gruffness, teasing, and straight talk is just as essential for daughters as it is for sons, but many mothers show disdain for Dad's approach, with his daughter.

Time and again, mothers describe scenarios in which they've chastised the father in front of the children for what the mom considers less-than-ideal role modeling. They take issue with Dad's personal habits, such as his imperfect table manners, love of "bad" foods, leaving socks on the living room floor, occasional cursing. His parenting style also riles the moms, who cite things like the father's too-blunt criticism, roughhousing, or overly high standards for the girl's academic or athletic performance.

When I hear these concerns, I caution the mothers that their open criticism in the presence of the children is teaching them that a child's fragile sensibilities take precedence over a father's dignity and freedom in his own home. And I ask:

- Do the children whine and dawdle less and cooperate more when Dad is giving orders?
- Do they show affection toward him, for example by demonstrating signs of happiness when he comes home?
- Do they enjoy spending time with him?

- Do they appreciate his sense of humor? Spirit of adventure? Esoteric knowledge? Worldly wisdom? Capacity to play?

If the mothers answer, "Yes, but—" I say, "I know this doesn't seem fair, but there's a double standard of what is considered permissible behavior for moms and dads. Dads get away with more."

Not surprisingly, some fathers get tired of being chided and micromanaged. They lose confidence, so they back off. This is an immense loss to the little girl and the person she will become. Fathers (or, if Dad is not available, another mature and devoted male adult) fill a complex and crucial role in the upbringing of girls. I've seen in my practice what is confirmed in the literature: girls who have absent, uninvolved, addicted, or workaholic fathers—dads who are not engaged—are more likely to be prematurely sexually active. It's not the family experience a loving mother would consciously encourage.

Because of the roadblocks mothers unintentionally throw up between girls and their fathers, and because moms are supervising the daily routine, girls clock more hours with Mom than with Dad. All that proximity breeds friction and disputes. Meanwhile, time with Dad often is not only rarer but also associated with the more pleasant events of life, such as learning to ride a bike or driving to weekend soccer games. During those interludes the girls don't argue, whine, or complain as much as they do when they're with Mom. I'm not saying some dads don't get their children dressed for school or make dinner; of course they do. But in most households the mother manages the daily details, and communication between mother and daughter, while more in sync, is also more fractious. For these reasons I'll be addressing mothers directly throughout most of this chapter, but the strategies work equally well for either parent.

KEEP IT HONEST, SIMPLE, AND COLLEGIAL

The baseline rule for parents of girls is "Be straight with your daughter." Unlike little boys, girls notice stammers and silences. Not only do they hear the words, they easily detect a sales pitch or half-lie. If you deliver your message in a direct and honest manner, you create a relaxed conversational atmosphere with a foundation of trust. Aim for an attitude that is collegial rather than enmeshed. Enmeshment is defined by insufficient boundaries: your child's status is your status, her emotions are your emotions, her creativity and athletic prowess and inner life are yours. This is intrusive and unhealthy. Collegial is "I'm on your side, but I'm separate from you."

All young children respond best to brief, clear instructions: "Time to grab your books and your lunch box," "Please empty the dishwasher," "Could you tell Dad it's time to leave?" Girls will probably hear you the first time. They may ignore you but are more likely to fend you off with "In a minute!" Anything you request that does not align with what they wish to be doing at the moment is an invitation to argue or stall.

In an effort to avoid a fight, mothers will often say things like, "Do you really want to wear that to school? Do you think you've done this homework thoroughly enough?" These are passive-aggressive rhetorical questions that no girl is going to answer with "Oh, thank you, Mommy! I can't believe I was going to wear this dress. Why, I'd be so chilly!" Mom is trying to maneuver her daughter into thinking it's her idea, but it makes the mother seem weak and amounts to a challenge ("Yes, I want to wear this and I *will* wear it!").

Questions like these can be dispensed with if you stop trying to run ahead of your child with a shield to protect her from the natural consequences of her actions, such as being cold or getting a poor grade. Natural consequences and other outside forces, like the school dress code, can do a lot of the work for you, leaving fewer things to argue about. But there's no getting around it: with daughters, negotiation is going to be a way of life for a long time. The following voice lessons will help keep the debates civilized.

Parent Talk

Volume and Pitch

> **Daughter:** Why are you yelling?
> **Mom:** I'M NOT YELLING!

When children do not respond the way mothers desire, many moms find themselves shouting. They're shocked at how quickly it happens, and it often escalates to name-calling as well. Girls will match you decibel for decibel, which makes it even more crucial that you control yourself. An effective trick is an acronym courtesy of Alcoholics Anonymous: HALT. When you hear your voice start to rise, ask yourself if you are hungry, angry, lonely, or tired. Then ask yourself why. Often your loneliness or anger has nothing to do with your child; she just happens to be in your line of fire. At these moments candor is not only a wise strategic choice, it can also shift the focus of the conversation. If you say, "I'm really wiped out today, so I'm telling you in advance that I may sound cranky," lots of daughters will ask, "Why? What happened?" If it's a situation you don't mind sharing, this gives her a chance to sympathize, make you laugh, practice cheering and comforting another person.

Tone

Girls are acutely sensitive to tone that reveals scorn, mockery, or indignation. Sadly, these have become default attitudes for some adults as they speed through the traffic of their lives. Many parents aren't aware of how angry or dismissive their comments, snorts, and little barks of laughter sound. Your daughter may not seem to be listening—she's singing along to the song on the radio—yet between mother and daughter every emotional message is amplified. Shifting your focus can help. Try singing along with her for a few minutes before asking her to quiet down and listen to you. Get your mind off your agenda and allow yourself to groove in girl world for a while. It's much more fun there, and your tone will improve accordingly.

Tempo

Speaking slowly is effective with boys because they're preoccupied and they can't hear as well as girls. With daughters, talk quickly enough to hold their interest but not as quickly as *they* talk. Girls of all ages speak urgently and breathlessly, and mothers are prone to matching that tempo and escalating it. Matching is a normal mode of communication among females: a woman will tell a story, and then her friend will tell a similar one in empathy, and it strengthens their bond. They'll match each other's level of excitement and speech patterns, too.

Deborah Tannen, professor of linguistics at Georgetown University and author of several seminal books on communication, describes woman-to-woman speech patterns as having specific characteristics including "troubles talk," "cooperative overlapping," and "rapport talk." Sometimes the overlap and escalation between mother and daughter is positive and thrilling:

"Mom! My class is going to the museum and we get to spend the night there!"

"Wow, sleeping at the museum! I bet you'll come home with some great stories."

But other times mothers find themselves matching their daughters' anxious meltdowns. Mothers are in a leadership role with their daughters, not a sister or friend relationship, so it's best to retain your authority by holding to a slower tempo.

Pausing

When you pause to transition to a new point and give your child time to absorb an idea, a daughter may step right in with her counterarguments. That means "pausing" might be a one-way street: you are pausing and she is not. Take that time to really listen to what she's saying, realizing that you can't read her mind, no matter how close the two of you are. Exploring her point of view doesn't mean you agree with it.

Parent Talk

Body Language

Although daughters are primarily attuned to facial expressions and vocal tone, their awareness also extends to physical signs as subtle as the tilt of a parent's head or her grip on the steering wheel. Be particularly mindful of your body language when you're reacting to your daughter's choice of games, costumes, and other forms of play. Rolling your eyes, sighing, turning away, a baffled shrug or wince are felt by children as contempt. When little girls try on identities, not all of them will be architect, vet, or Wonder Woman. Bossy cop, YouTube star, and princess may also take center stage for a while. A parent's unspoken disapproval can throw cold water on this festival of self-expression and cause the young girl to doubt her instincts and playful impulses.

SHELTER FROM YOUR DAUGHTER'S PRYING EYES

Sometimes it can seem as if there's no escape from your little girl's laser stare. A typical dialogue:

"Mom, why are you mad?"

"I'm not mad."

"Well, what's wrong?"

"NOTHING!"

It's perfectly fine for your daughter to see a range of emotions in her mother. Otherwise you're a scary zombie mom. If she's done something to irritate you, you can say, "I didn't realize it, but I *am* mad and soon I'm going to be furious, so let's take this up again after I've had some time to think and am feeling calmer."

Or, "Yes, I'm mad because we had an agreement and you didn't stick to it. You'll need to help me understand what happened, because otherwise we're going to have to make this rule stricter, and I know that's not what you want."

Of course, there will be times when a mother's bad mood or jumpiness has nothing to do with the child, but she doesn't want to explain herself (nor should she have to). The daughter's probing makes Mom feel cornered, so she gets testy. But denying you are angry or upset leaves your daughter puzzled and wondering what she's done wrong. Instead, you can acknowledge her observation while also maintaining your privacy. When she asks, "Why are you making that face, Mom?" You can reply:

> "Some differences of opinion at the office, happens once in awhile. Nothing to do with you, sweetheart."
> "A mix-up with my schedule and Dad's. We'll figure it out. We always do."
> "I just realized that I said yes to too many things."

Verify what she sees, then give a general explanation you're comfortable with. Your daughter may sense there's more to the story, but unless there is serious trouble or illness within the family, children ages three to eleven are not terribly interested in your problems as long as they aren't the cause of them. It's not because they don't care about you; it's because they have only a modest concept of the pressures of adult life. Your daughter (or son) doesn't need all the facts; she just needs to know she's not imagining things and that you and she share the same reality.

RECOGNIZING AND NAMING BIG FEELINGS

Seven-year-old Ada rushes across the playground after school. Will she be smiling and crash into her parent's arms with a giant hug? Or will she be scowling and stomp past her mom or dad? Either way, the parent braces for an exaggerated outburst about the WORST thing that ever happened (or the BEST!), something that must be fixed RIGHT NOW, a decision that will be huge for her WHOLE FUTURE! Sobs, frantic explanations, pleading, and shouting may ensue. The dramatics are exhausting and a parent would be forgiven for thinking, *Can I just mainline some of that life force while you go fix yourself a martini and get a grip?*

Young girls can be so intense that it's frightening, leading parents to jump to conclusions: *Does this mean she's depressed? Bipolar?* If the daughter is gushing about a play that's going to be THE BEST ONE THEY EVER HAD AT THIS SCHOOL, parents fret, *Will she be disappointed? Sad when it's over?* They have an urge to get there first, to anticipate their child's reactions so they can protect her from big feelings. What she really needs is help understanding and naming those feelings.

As children reach age four and older, they spend more time in school and among larger groups of people. Those environments arouse emotions they haven't felt in a public arena, such as embarrassment, longing, betrayal, and jealousy. Reassuring a confused or distraught child that "it'll be OK" may soothe her for the time being but won't help her gain more understanding of herself. The more difficult and rewarding task is to stay calm and teach her to expand her emotional vocabulary.

For example, a first grader may feel envious of her classmate, Chloe, the one who has ("It's so not fair!") the prettiest hair, can climb to the top of the slide really fast, *and* has the neatest handwriting. Unable to recognize these feelings as envy or understand that this reaction is both common and normal, she may declare that she "hates school" or call herself "stupid" or claim she "hates Bailey," who is both "mean *and* stupid." Or your child may substitute complaints about pain ("My throat hurts") when what she (or he) is experiencing falls into what she believes is the category of "not nice" feelings. My interviews with school nurses confirm that *hurt* is often the new *hate.* Even the youngest children figure out that feeling "hurt" keeps their hands clean, character-wise, yet garners satisfying attention and empathy from parents.

There's a careful path to pick through an upset child's tangle of words and feelings. When she comes home with a tale of grief, injustice, or anger, rather than digging for the backstory, begin by listening without pity or panic. This is tricky, because if you're too concerned, she'll learn to play the victim card: *Every time I cry a lot,*

98

Mommy drops whatever she's doing and gives me love. So you're aiming for a somewhat detached compassion, as if you were a sympathetic school counselor rather than her parent. Again, collegial rather than enmeshed. When she sees that you're not panicking or matching her distraught tone and tempo, she's likely to tell you what's happened without much prodding. "Chloe is in Silver Cluster and I wanted to sit next to her but I can't because Ms. Healy put me in Blue Cluster and Ms. Healy doesn't even care."

Now you can be kind and curious. "What's bothering you the most about it?" Encourage her to try a few hypotheses. She will eventually come around to something you sense is at the heart of the matter, such as, "I think Ms. Healy won't like me because I was mad. And she always likes Chloe, and Silver Cluster is right near Ms. Healy's desk." What she might be feeling is envy and the anxiety that comes from feeling left out.

The parent has a couple of choices at this point. If you've been in a situation that seems similar, you can say: "I remember in first grade when I used to sit behind my friend Julia and braid her red hair. I was envious of it—I wished I had red hair. Well, the teacher separated us just because I was playing with Julia's ponytail! I was really embarrassed because I had to move my seat right then, in front of everyone." *Envy* and *embarrassment* now have real-life definitions for your daughter. And you can still soothe her: "The next day the teacher made me room monitor for the week, so I knew she wasn't mad. And now that I'm a grown-up. I know that teachers have a hundred little moments like this every day. I don't think you have to worry." You're helping your child look at the past (your history) and think about the future (what her teacher might do tomorrow, like your teacher did).

These personal anecdotes should always be true, not invented to make a point. If you trot out parallel stories too often, your child will figure out the gimmick and stop trusting you. So you can also take another tack and say, "As I listen to you, it sounds like you're sad to be sitting away from your friend and you're also a little scared about the teacher. And you're feeling like it's not fair that Chloe gets to sit near her. So maybe you're feeling a little worried and jealous or envious of Chloe. *Jealousy* or *envy* is what you feel when someone has something you wish you had." And you can add, "You know, everyone has those feelings sometimes."

This is delicate. You're introducing a higher order of emotional language, but you don't want your daughter to feel ashamed or humiliated. The goal of a conversation like this is to help her move just one step up in understanding the nuances of emotion, from *mad, hurt*, or *sad* to *envious, embarrassed*, or *anxious*.

If you need to ask your daughter for clarification about the event that upset her, use open-ended rather than yes-or-no or leading questions. Not, "Were you furious?," but instead, "What was that like? How did you feel at that moment? What about now?" By doing this, you'll be more likely to get honest, detailed, revealing answers.

We want to protect our children from pain, and emotions like envy, loneliness, embarrassment, and anxiety can be painful. But if we don't expose them, children won't get familiar with the wave pattern of emotion: *I feel this. Oh, it's because . . .* Or, *The last time this happened I helped myself feel better by . . .* Self-reflection leads to self-knowledge, the foundation of good judgment. It's risky not to expose children to the elements, be they physical, social, academic, or emotional.

TRICKED INTO A FIGHT (BUT NOT ALWAYS ON PURPOSE)

Even wise, compassionate parents sometimes yell at their kids. You could say that yelling is also exposing your child to emotional elements, but it's best not to go there too often and, if you do, to apologize for losing your temper. Little girls soon figure out what triggers a parent's irritation, but many times they'll push your buttons without meaning to or being able to help themselves. The following issues come up often with the mothers I counsel.

The Boss, the Bestie, the High Priestess of Pretend

Daughter Insults Mother

"You're so stupid, Mommy! I don't love you. I love Daddy. You're the meanest mommy. You're a bad mommy."

It's completely normal for young girls to insult their mothers (but rarely their fathers). At age four, you can respond the way you would to a two-year-old's tantrum, by acknowledging her frustration without taking her words at face value.

With an older child it's appropriate to say, "I know you're upset, but in this family we don't insult each other, we explain what happened that made us angry." One caveat: don't say, "In this family we don't . . ." unless it is true. And as always with children's behavior, put the insult into context. If your daughter is frequently angry and rude and such attitudes are not common in your family, consider one of two options: she's upset about something else and kicking the cat (Mom), or you're so invested in pleasing her that she's developed the habit of treating you in a demeaning manner. This is not a lesson you want to teach her about how any woman allows herself to be treated.

Daughter Insists on Having the Last Word

It is tempting, if you didn't get to have the last word as a child and don't get to have the last word with your partner, mother, or colleagues, to have the last word with your young daughter. Strategically it's smarter to let her have it and revisit the discussion at a later time if necessary. Let her save face. She has very little power or independence, and she's going to get it cheaply by yelling, "I will, too!" Let it go and see if she follows through on her threat. If so, you can deal with it then. Usually she's just aiming for dignity. If you protect her dignity now, you'll have more traction when she's a teenager because she'll know you respect her. It's a long-term investment in the bank of goodwill.

Parent Talk

Daughter Promotes Dubious Plan

When a daughter is lobbying for permission to do something that's risky or not on the family calendar, Mom may rush in trying to reason with her or lay down the law. The daughter's exhilaration is like a flame to the weary mother's fuse:

> "Mom, guess what? I'm going ice-skating with Celine and Nola on Saturday night!"
> "Not this weekend! You know your grandparents are coming."
> "But I told Nola's mom yes!"
> "This is family! End of discussion!"
> "NO! Not fair. I see Nonny and Poppa ALL THE TIME! Mom! Mom! Mom!"

Your agitation is only going to make her up her assault. Instead, you can press "pause" with a conversation closer:

> "We've already made a plan with Nonny and Poppa, so I'll need to get more details about the timing from Nola's mom."
> Or, "It's been a long day. I need to sleep on it. I'll give you my decision tomorrow when I pick you up from school."

This is excellent role modeling for a girl so that, when she gets to middle school, she doesn't feel pressured by her peers to respond right away. She learns to reflect first and can access the language that will buy her time. Always keep your word and get back to her. At that point you can revisit the discussion with a compromise or a calmly stated refusal. You'll be braced for her frustration, less likely to match it, and better able to suggest an alternative plan. It's also possible that in the heat of the moment you said no too quickly.

The Boss, the Bestie, the High Priestess of Pretend

Daughter Asks for Mom's Honest Opinion

Young daughters frequently invite your opinion—"Be honest!"—and after you give it accuse you of criticizing them. Let's say you're the mother of ten-year-old Daphne, who asks, "Do you think my thighs are fat? Be honest! I do. I think they're really fat, so I'm not wearing shorts anymore." What can you truthfully tell Daphne, given that her body is changing weekly and whatever negative response you utter might be hurtful and soon irrelevant? Unless Daphne is dangerously overweight, you could say, "I'm your mom so I may be biased, but I think you're gorgeous and your thighs are fine."

To which Daphne might reply, "Mom, really! I mean it! Are my thighs fat?"

"Not to me, Daphne. They look like perfect ten-year-old thighs. But you should wear clothes you feel comfortable in, so if you don't want to wear shorts, that's OK."

"You make me crazy!"

Daphne may be exasperated and think, *I can't trust Mom's opinion, she admits she loves me too much to see that my thighs are fat.* Good! Let someone else criticize her thighs. One of the perks of being her mother is that you don't have to make her feel bad even if she's luring you into it. When it comes to her physical appearance, "Mom's bias" is a card you can play today, ten years from now, and all her life. If she asks your honest opinion about an unflattering item of clothing or makeup (as opposed to her body or face), you can respond with, "That's not a style I like on anyone." It's the rare daughter who actually wants truthful critiques from her mother. She's looking for acceptance and approval.

Withholding your judgment is also the best policy when your daughter asks for your honest opinion about a new friend. Unless you suspect danger, let her learn for herself how to determine who is trustworthy and kind, who seeks out trouble, who is fickle. In the spirit of keeping your enemies close, arrange for a playdate. "Caitlyn?

I really don't know her yet, so I don't have an opinion. Would you like to invite her over here?"

DON'T SAY A WORD ABOUT HER WEIGHT

All the most recent studies of the impact of well-intentioned "room for improvement"–style comments about girls' weight come to the same conclusion: don't do it. Critical comments from parents magnify girls' natural tendency to doubt themselves as they leave childhood and enter the teenage years, the era of both comparisons and change (*What body will I wake up in this morning?*).

When parents make negative comments about a child's weight, the child is more likely to carry negative feelings about her body into adulthood. If you believe your daughter is indulging in excessive, uncontrolled "comfort eating," get a professional opinion. Otherwise stay mum on this highly charged topic. Model healthy habits for your daughter, remark on her strengths in any and every domain, and start teaching her media literacy. Go to medialiteracynow.org for a comprehensive list of resources for parents, including how to talk to preschool-aged girls about covert messages regarding body image in ads and entertainment aimed at children.

With older school-aged children, you can make up your own curriculum: follow two teams (one female, one male) playing the same sport on broadcast media. Keep a tally of how often sportscasters comment on the marital status and appearance of female athletes compared to males; note whether they refer to them by their first name, last name only, or both. The results will expose your daughter to compelling images of physically strong and accomplished women while raising her awareness of how female bodies are portrayed in the media.

CULTURE CURE: TALKING OUT LOUD ABOUT YOURSELF

When your six-year-old is mimicking the butt-bouncing moves of the latest pop sensation; when the shops are full of skimpy skirtlets and crop tops; when every trip through the checkout line urges your novice reader to get "5-Minute Flat Abs," "Shrink Your Inner Thighs," and "Look Leaner Naked," it may feel as if you are helpless against a tide that will make your daughter hate her body—maybe not today, maybe not tomorrow, but soon and for the rest of her life.

A mother can go a long way toward immunizing her daughter against the fantasy body image that is relentlessly peddled by the media. The trick is simple but may require a daunting change of habit: you must talk positively about your own appearance in your daughter's presence. Regularly. Refrain from self-loathing tugs, scowls into the mirror, and mutterings ("Oh, God, what the hell happened? This dress used to fit!"). You can think those thoughts all you want, just don't say them out loud or wince at your reflection when your daughter is in the room.

You might assume that giving yourself compliments is exactly what you *shouldn't* do in selfie culture, where teenage girls and certain adult women can't seem to stop pouting into their cell phone cameras. But there's a difference between vapid preening and demonstrating the many ways in which a woman can take pleasure in her physical being. As you're getting dressed or viewing your reflection, you might say:

> "Oh, nice! I didn't realize this new sweater matches my eyes."
> "I wasn't sure how I would look with bangs, but I like the change. It's fun."
> "Want to see my new boots? When I wear them with my trench coat, I feel like a secret agent."
> "This new lipstick color is a good one for spring."
> "Aunt Jane was wearing perfume that reminded me of being at the beach last summer, so I got some. Want me to put a little on you?"

Note that none of these remarks mentions body shape or weight. The joy of being female and feeling attractive (not in an overtly sexual way) is something any mother can pass on to her daughter. What matters is that your child sees you getting pleasure or satisfaction out of some aspect of your appearance. Think of how excited your children are when you and your partner get all dressed up for a party or date. You're glamorous to them! This is what makes growing up exotic and appealing, something to anticipate rather than dread. It's the same on an everyday basis: Do you like the way you present yourself to other people? At the very least, are you neutral? Or are you openly dismayed, always lamenting your flaws? What your daughter sees is the attitude she will absorb. And if you are the mother of boys, know that they don't like seeing you criticize yourself either. It's distressing to them.

Nearly every mother has had the experience of looking into a makeup mirror and having her young child slide in next to her, cheek to cheek. It's a poignant moment, seeing that plump cheek against the fading one. If only you could stop time and preserve her perfection! The next best thing is preserving her eager spirit by showing her how it looks when a grown-up woman respects and appreciates herself.

You may not feel it. You may be filled with doubts and feel betrayed by your deflated breasts and lumpy thighs. But act as if you do. And to get back to selfies for a moment: let your kids take your picture without moaning, "Stop, I look terrible." No, you don't. Not to them. They see you through rose-colored glasses, unless you insist on spoiling their view.

CLOTHES, HAIR, AND FOOD: THE CRUCIBLES OF POWER

One sentence sums up my philosophy about the thousands of hours spent arguing with a daughter over her choice of clothing, hair, and food: *Let her be.* If you allow your daughter to make her own decisions about most of these things, your account in the bank of goodwill will be overflowing and all other areas of family life will feel the glow.

Letting her be is not only the easy way out but also the best nourishment for a young girl's spirit and social development. The period psychologists call latency, between age four and puberty, is a time of exuberant exploration for all children. With boys, it's about adventure and collecting information and all the things we talked about in the last chapter. Girls need freedom and adventure, too, and they blossom during their forays into complex pretend worlds. But to a large degree they explore and express themselves through their choices of clothing, hairstyle, and food. Compared to little boys, who may be oblivious to their hair or shirt unless it itches, your daughter can seem like an insufferable diva. Again, try to reframe her pickiness as discernment. She's defining who she is by deciding who she is not.

Although it's counterintuitive, granting your daughter power within reason over her clothing, hair, and food gives you *more* leverage, not less, on the things that matter. These include being courteous to her grandparents, helpful to her family, responsible about the chores you assign her, and responsive to your requests without stalling.

By "let her be," I don't mean let her dictate, or that you must rush to supply whatever goods (the must-have tank top or shoes) or services (the must-get haircut) your daughter desires. You are not her fairy godmother. As you pick your battles, consider the following.

Clothing and Hair

Arguments with little girls over clothing and hair reflect both a mother's values and her pockets of nervousness. Some moms are affronted by the "shallow, sexist" plastic high heels the daughter wants to totter around on. Some are always running after their daughter with a sweater, trying to protect her from the cold. Others are appalled at the child's poor taste. One mother described her grade schooler as wanting to dress like "a dowdy old aunt! Prim little blouses buttoned all the way up and plaid skirts and *brooches.* She's eight and she's scouring thrift stores for this stuff! I cringe when I drop her off at school in the morning. How can I get her to stop this bizarre habit?"

"Don't give yourself an extra job," I advised. "The other girls will take care of this for you." As it turned out, the girls were entertained by her daughter's eclectic wardrobe, of which she herself tired in a few months. There's so much you don't need to worry about or protect against. Just compliment her sense of style and enjoy the spectacle of an eight-year-old dressing like a librarian from the 1960s.

Much of mothers' dismay over their daughters' attire has to do with the social hierarchy in the school, not only for the girl's sake (*Will she be excluded?*) but also their own (*What will the other moms think?*). As social institutions such as places of worship, civic organizations, and adult sports leagues become a smaller part of people's lives, the community of the child's school has ballooned to great importance. It's common for the parents' social life to revolve around the school's fund-raising efforts, seasonal events, plays, and field trips. This can make a mother feel exposed and vulnerable, but most other mothers are far too worried about their own parenting reputation to spend more than a nanosecond eyeballing your little librarian.

I've had the same mother who was "horrified" by her daughter's Princess Aurora costume come back six months later and say, "She only wants to wear olive green and black. She's wearing a Batman cape. She wants to cut her hair really short and I'm afraid this is permanent." It's just childhood—this is the fleeting world you don't want to miss out on by signaling your alarm or demanding explanations ("But why do you want to cut your beautiful hair?"). For both girls and boys, hair can be an expression of individual personality or of gender identity. In any case, hair grows back. And it's hers, not yours.

The mother who mourns a daughter's tomboy haircut might have spent hours brushing, braiding, and styling that hair. It might be a ritual they treasured, but just as often hair is a battlefield. Some children have sensitive scalps and the nightly hair-combing routine is a form of torture for them, even if you're being gentle. If hairstyling is a source of tension, provide your daughter with the tools and products to do her own hair, like a wide-tooth comb and spray detangler, and give her a few lessons. Then let her loose, no matter how imperfect or frizzy the results.

As I write this, dads doing their daughters' hair is becoming a popular trend. This is a fine way to get fathers and daughters together and give Mom a break. There are classes for dads and daughters, commercials featuring NFL players styling their daughters' hair, and hundreds of YouTube videos, including some featuring a trick only a dad would invent: using a vacuum cleaner hose to make the perfect ponytail.

Food, Frustrating Food

Food is more complicated than hair and clothes and arouses more anxiety in parents. Fortunately, the angst can be reduced by an attitude that takes the long view and by practicing some restraint in the grocery store. Your children can only eat what you buy, and if it's mostly good for them, you can eliminate 90 percent of the food fights.

A typical maddening dinner exchange goes something like this:

"What's for dinner?"
  "Salmon."
  "I hate salmon."
  "That's new. Last week you loved it. Remember, I grilled it with a panko crust and we had garlic sauce?"
  "No, gross, I hate it."

Entertain the possibility this isn't about salmon, or *your* salmon. Or even necessarily about power, unless you turn it into a power struggle. It's about development. Children's sense of taste is much more acute than that of adults (especially bitterness, and more so in girls than boys). They experience more pleasure and more revulsion. This explains reverence for Flamin' Hot Cheetos and, as with so many of your daughter's ever-shifting preferences, her heartfelt and honest refusal of a dish that was acceptable just last week.

How to handle the rejection? In a friendly but mostly disinterested tone, say, "Salmon, baked potatoes, broccoli, and apple slaw are on the menu tonight. You can eat whatever part of the dinner appeals to you. And over the weekend, if you want, you can give me some suggestions for meals you think everyone might like."

Today's parents are proud of children with sophisticated palates and are eager to please ("How about if I make you a salmon patty?"). But they're also seething (*Brat, you know you loved it last week*), worried (*She's got to get some protein in her!*), and despondent (*If I can't even get her to eat a piece of fish, how will I convince her not to take drugs?*). Beneath these objections may run a deeper woe: *I don't have control over one damn thing in my life, not even this frigging child's dinner.*

One reason parents are so overwrought about food is that in our culture it has assumed a bloated moral dimension, taking religion's place as the arbiter of good and evil. Healthy foods equal righteousness. Donuts equal failure. When women announce they've been "so good" this week or "so bad," everyone understands they're talking about food, not volunteer work. As we see ourselves reflected in our daughters, we apply the same culinary moral code to them.

A name has been coined for this obsession: *orthorexia nervosa*, literally "fixation on righteous eating." It's not yet in the diagnostic manual of mental disorders but accurately describes a condition so widespread that one school nurse told me the third grade teachers had switched from decorating gingerbread people at holiday time to using paper bags and glitter.

As for the actual impact of diet on a little girl, I ask concerned parents: Is the pediatrician worried? Is she growing? Does she have lots of energy for activities she enjoys? Has she missed a lot of school due to illness? If none of the answers raise red flags, remember that narrow preferences are just a brief snapshot in your daughter's life. So she only wants macaroni and cheese—that could change by next week as long as you don't make a big deal out of it and turn it into a crucible of power. Like the adorable speech impediments that disappear over the course of the year in preschool, her pickiness will fade as her palate matures.

What you preach about food has much less influence on your children than the items you keep in the house and your attitude about eating. The evening meal, whether shared at the dinner table or the kitchen counter, is a daily opportunity for rich family discourse if you can subtract the angst and power plays. Of course, there's a good chance the child who refuses dinner will try to sneak into the kitchen later and get a bowl of cereal. Or start complaining she's hungry. In a sincere and neutral tone (not wounded, pious, or sarcastic), you can tell her, "I respected your choice to skip dinner, and you have to respect the house rules and not snack on cereal. You can have a piece of fruit if you're hungry."

STOP TALKING ALREADY! WHEN GIRLS INTERRUPT OR GET BORING

Remember how the summer you were ten lasted forever, as did a trip in the family car? Compare that to now, when one Thanksgiving seems to follow the last in a matter of days. As we age, our perception of time speeds up. For your daughter it's a leisurely magic-carpet ride; for you it's NASCAR. The mismatch in perception goes something like this:

Daughter: What I have to say is brand new, important, and filled with details! Sit down while I tell you everything.
Mother: What I have to tell you is ordinary, low-novelty, and essential. Walk with me while I download it in sixty seconds.

Although time-deprived parents may give their daughters too little attention, it's also true that many loquacious girls don't realize when they're being repetitive, dull, or hogging the floor. Parents can do their daughters a great service by giving them some practical tips and feedback about when to speak and how to listen. A good time to instill some conversational etiquette is when you're alone with your child or among family.

Signaling That a Story Is Getting Too Long

Body language can be a first alert: stay still and gaze at her steadily without reacting much to her words. She may get the hint. If not, you can say (lightly):

"I get it."

"Yes, you said that already and I understand."

"OK, moving on: What happened next?"

"So you're saying . . ." (Summarize the story, then ask for different information or steer the chat in another direction.)

This gentle nudging of a conversation forward needs to occur on a regular basis for the child to develop a knack for storytelling and sense of verbal give-and-take. How much talking is too much? How can you tell when the other person is getting bored? Are you repeating yourself?

One woman told me that she was the youngest of six and had a problem with talking too much as a child. Her dad always made sure she was seated next to him at the dinner table, and when she started going on for too long, he would gently pinch her. If that didn't get through, he kicked her under the table. No one could see. This is an example of parenting that might seem unenlightened or mortifying but did no damage—she told me this story proudly, using it as an example of her father's love for his children.

Elementary school teachers have a creative technique for quieting students who blurt out answers or don't know when to stop talking. The teacher gives the student a secret signal, like touching her own ear or nose. Parents can do this, too.

Curbing Interruptions

This requires a two-pronged approach. The first part is to explain simple rules the child can remember: If someone else is talking, wait until there's a pause to start telling your story. If they're adults and they don't pause, after a little while you can raise your hand like in school and wave it around a bit (but with your elbow bent, not straight up in the air). Don't say, "Ooh! Ooh!" Do say, "Could I interrupt for a minute?"

The second part consists of your reaction when a child interrupts you. If you're on the phone or involved in a conversation, you can respond nonverbally by looking into the child's eyes with warmth, putting your forefinger to your lips in the "shh" gesture, and then raising it in the "just a minute" signal. This will acknowledge her wish to speak and your intention to wrap up your conversation. If possible, indicate with your fingers the minutes she'll need to wait (for example two, five, ten). Then turn your attention to her at the time you signaled. Following through on the message in this gesture is a healthy deposit in the bank of goodwill. You are a person who keeps her promises.

If you're not talking to someone but are focusing on a task, explain specifically what you're doing, why now is not a good time to stop doing it, and tell your child when you will be able to stop and listen to her. For example:

"I'm writing an e-mail to my boss and I don't want to forget anything or make a mistake, so I need to concentrate. I should be done in ten minutes and I want to hear your story then."

Not: "Give me a minute . . . I'm texting Susan . . . I said just a minute . . ."

When your task is complete, keep your word and seek your child out if she's left the room.

Teaching Her How to Listen

Children who interrupt or have trouble making or keeping friends because of their windy monologues can play a listening game with their parents. Devised by Peggy Post and Cindy Post Senning, authors of the wonderful book *The Gift of Good Manners*, it provides practice in a skill that for some children does not come naturally:

Say a sentence or ask a question in a variety of tones, emphasize different words in the sentence, and have the child guess what each version of the sentence really means. What is the difference between "We are going shopping *today*" (emphasis on time), "We

113

are going **shopping** today" (emphasis on the activity), and "**We** are going shopping today" (emphasis on the participants)? The same sentence can be made as a statement of fact, a question, or a command, depending on tone of voice.

Add physical gestures and facial expressions to the exercise. Saying "We are going shopping today" with a smile indicates a positive attitude; a frown indicates the reverse. Some children are very sensitive to tone and emphasis in speech, but most need explanations, examples, and plenty of practice to understand the myriad complexities of everyday conversations.

The generous and practical way to parent is to remember that your child is new to this world, this culture, our habits. With some patient guidance, she'll likely be able to learn everything she needs to communicate with sensitivity and grace.

FATHERS AND DAUGHTERS

Ten-year-old girl: Dad, did you know that ants never sleep?
Father: Really? Where did you hear that?
Girl: I don't remember! But I know it's true!
Father laughs, high-fives her.

Fathers teach a different set of communication skills than mothers do. Moms model listening for emotional nuance and offer solace and guidance; dads toughen girls up, teach them how to take a joke, and talk to them about things that are outside the personal, social realm in which women and girls are so absorbed.

As children grow, the value of Dad's contribution continues. Fathers use a less familiar vocabulary than do mothers, but because the words are used in context and children appreciate that Dad is spending time with them, the kids are motivated to figure out what he means and keep the conversation going. As fathers and daughters talk about business or sports or what's happening outside the car window, girls learn the meaning of terms like *gridlock* (where's the grid?) and *colleague* (sounds like *collie*!); the definition of *slam dunk*; the words needed to narrate a shared road trip (*pit stop, slipstream, thunderheads*). Obviously mothers also have vast and fascinating troves of knowledge; they have colleagues and watch sports, too. But because Dad-daughter conversations are less often hijacked by the "business" of the girl's schedule and activities, the topics of their conversations tend to cover different terrain.

The exposure to a wider vocabulary is only a small part of what a father contributes to his daughter's ability to engage with other people. Growing accustomed to his conversational rhythm and style and learning what to make of his nonverbal cues and playful teasing is her foundation. Talking to, playing with, and being quiet beside Dad gives a girl practice in what lies ahead: creating harmony with or standing up to men on teams, at work, in friendship, in love relationships, and with her own sons.

Where Mom protects her daughter's vulnerability, Dad sees her strengths and aims to endow her with more. Fathers bolster a girl's persistence and pride by challenging her and having high expectations. Dads teach girls how to manage bigger risks, including physical risks. They're often the ones pushing their daughters to take a few more chances on the playing field or to go ahead and jump into their arms in the cold lake. Daughters need that toughening up to be ready for a world of competition.

Dads also teach daughters the nuances of when it's worth it to break a rule and when it's not. Mothers typically prefer their children, especially daughters, to be more conservative. This goes back to neurochemistry and brain architecture. Girls are rule followers and pleasers; they're generally more hesitant than boys to step outside the lines. Fathers can give girls practice speaking up, challenging an idea, refusing to do something that goes against their nature or values. A girl can give her dad a hard time and he'll get mad, maybe shout at or punish her, and she'll survive. Moms get alarmed by the yelling and want to defend the daughter against this bogeyman. But the bogeyman she knows and loves is the one who can teach her how to stand up to overbearing or threatening characters she'll encounter later in life.

Fathers today are ambitious for their daughters. They might not be able to name the best third grade teacher, but they want to raise young women who can be independent and compete, and they know instinctively that developing nerve and resilience is crucial to their girls' survival.

PEARLS FOR FATHERS

When I was a little girl, my father always greeted a friend of mine, even if she had been over the day before, by saying, "Is that Shirley Capelli herself? Did I say you could come here?" Shirley always responded with a giggle: "I'm here to play with Wendy!" My dad is a natural with children, and when I parse the elements of his verbal welcome today, it's obvious why it put a guest at ease.

First, he knew Shirley's full name, as he did the names of all my friends. That was a sign of respect. Second, he was playfully reminding us that he was king of this castle and would be keeping an eye on the place. That made us feel safe. Finally, his faux tough-guy teasing demonstrated that he knew we could take some kidding around. To this day, when I phone my dad, he asks in a tone of incredulity and glee, "Is this Dr. Wendy Mogel herself?" I never tire of this game. Or of his playfulness and pride in me. (Once he thought my sister was calling, so I got to hear a different version: "Is this Sweet, Sweet Jane herself?" We'll leave that family dynamic for another book.)

From my work with parents and children, I've collected a few techniques like this that fathers can use to nourish their bond with their daughters.

Remember the first and last names of her close friends, along with some physical identifiers.

You'll get bonus points if you memorize the initials that go along with the popular names—"Is that Ella M. or Ella B.?"

116

Underpromise and overdeliver about attending events.

Unless you're certain you will be able to attend an event, do not say you'll be there. Also, don't say you'll "try to make it" if there's any chance you won't. Instead say that you will not be able to attend, tell her why, and then, if possible, show up. Your daughter will be thrilled.

Take her on father-daughter errands and trips.

Short trips to the grocery or hardware store are ideal "talking while doing" opportunities for dads and daughters, who may not have as many activities in common as fathers and sons. For the gold standard, take her on a road trip. Nothing—not the fanciest four-star resort—is as valuable as a road trip. Just a dad and his daughter cruising down the highway vying for control of the music, eating in dubious cafés, zoning out to the scenery, drifting into nonsensical or heartfelt conversations. Earbuds not welcome. It's a luxury to have so much time that a portion of it can be spent in companionable silence. Destinations can be landmarks, historic places, or the neighborhood and haunts of your boyhood. Another idea: the setting of a book she's read in school. After my daughter read *Huckleberry Finn*, my husband took her on a trip along the Mississippi River.

Praise her stamina, courage, enthusiasm, curiosity—characteristics that are not her physical appearance.

A father's uncritical gaze is a blessing to his daughter, especially because mothers are so attuned to the girls' personal grooming. The less a father comments on his daughter's looks, the more relaxed she'll be in his presence. He can then notice and cheer her other worthy attributes. Certainly if she's in a new party dress, or it's a special day, or she's in a costume or other creative attire, your exuberant appreciation will enhance the spirit of the occasion, "What rare beauty do we have here?" Otherwise, dads do best by keeping comments about their daughters' appearance to a minimum.

ONE WORD OF CAUTION FOR DADS

Be aware of the power of secondhand messages.

Let's say you've overcome your disappointment that she wasn't a son (or you're wildly relieved!). And you never criticize her appearance because you know that popular culture sends destructive messages leading women to believe that their worth lies in their looks. And it's easy not to let criticism slip out because your daughter is always beautiful in your eyes. And you're convinced that her potential is unlimited. Stay alert: what your daughter overhears is as powerful as what you say to her directly.

A father can undermine a thoughtful agenda of female empowerment by habitually speaking critically to or about his daughter's mother within her hearing or commenting on the appearance of female family members or women in the public eye. Even as I write this, I want to stop myself, speak for dads, and say, "Give me a break! An occasional snarky crack about a frumpy local politician is not going to doom my daughter's future relationships with men." But I'm not backing down because monitoring yourself for the "overheard" is simply another level of consciousness raising, an easily overlooked aspect of the power of a father's words.

GOODWILL IN GIRL WORLD

When you're not arguing with your daughter, the door to enchantment swings open and behold! Girlhood in all its chaotic glory. Goodwill for daughters has much to do with simple acceptance—just being along for the ride and making sure they know you're loving it and *you approve.*

Young girls are bursting with devotion to objects and people adults find ordinary or baffling. They start sentences with *Oh-My-God* at younger and younger ages. One mother recounted how her nine-year-old daughter Rose had been assigned a big science project:

I was pleased to come home after work and see lots of books open on the dining room table, maps taped to the wall, and long hand-written lists. I told Rose, "Wow, this looks great! I can see you've made a lot of progress on your volcano project."

She says, "This isn't my volcano project. This is my itinerary for our honeymoon." Rose is obsessed with the lead singer in a boy band. "See this map, Mom? First we're going to fly to Maui. Now see this list? It's our plan. When we get to the hotel we unpack, then we go straight to the bar to have champagne and watch the sunset."

Volcanoes . . . Hawaii . . . honeymoon! It makes perfect sense. Garner some goodwill by daydreaming about the vacation getaway with her for a few moments before directing her back to the science project.

With boys you're an anthropologist visiting a strange country, learning about its rituals and esoteric facts. With girls you're a sociologist. To fill the goodwill coffers, you need only listen to her describe her world. Little girls are experts at analyzing social structures. You're spellbound and patient, and you have lots of tolerance, even for gossip, silliness, and the granular details of her special third-grade universe.

Girls will espouse all kinds of stereotypes and assumptions that are wrong, but take care not to move in quickly to capture teachable moments. Appreciate the drama of her narratives. You're not looking for things to fix or improve, you're just observing and occasionally asking for clarification about concerns too subtle or confounding for your adult perspective.

Being your daughter's enthusiastic audience and letting her have control over her hair, clothes, and food will keep the goodwill account solidly funded. Here are a few other ways to cherish her.

Give her somewhere to roam free.

Girls need free play as much as boys do for all the same reasons and one that is specific to their gender: it's how they can learn the boundaries between risk and danger so difficult for parents to even consider in relation to daughters.

I'm a strong proponent of sending children away for a few weeks in the summer, either to a relative's house or to camp. You'll have to size up your daughter's readiness based on her eagerness to sleep at a friend's house, how well she does on school trips, and her overall enthusiasm for a parent-free adventure. Try to enroll her in a program where part of each day is unstructured. Scheduling "learning" camps next to school next to the structured family vacation will not provide her with the loose, lazy time she needs to find her own bearing.

The happy news is that some day camps are becoming more flexible, to the point where children are permitted to participate on random days without being enrolled for a specific program. They offer a place where kids can do creative, messy, unstructured activities. This type of freedom may cause you to feel that you're depriving your daughter of necessary skill-building opportunities or that you're being neglectful. If so, find one other parent who shares your values and it will put you at ease.

Let her teach you tech (especially dads).

Bonding over technology can be a good thing for parents and daughters. Yes, it's more screen time, and there should be limits set. But if girls and their fathers are having a hard time finding activities they both enjoy, watching a movie or TV show, playing video games, or tinkering with robotics may fit the bill. If your daughter isn't into building vehicles and actual robots, there are kits that let her build dollhouses, bunnies, Lego creations of all sorts, clocks, and much more, all with programmable pieces.

Go for a long walk or hike with her.

Leave your phone at home or in the car, and tell her you're leaving it. Walking outdoors, especially in parks or other wild or wooded areas, opens the floodgates of conversation and builds respect as only uninterrupted time together can. It says to a child, *You are worthy of my undivided attention.*

Being outdoors has other advantages as well. The greater the number of senses and the more physical movement involved, the more likely an experience will be etched in your child's memory—the smell of the wet earth, the texture of moss, tiny flowers, mushrooms, how the wind almost blew your jacket away. Hiking together will give her adventures to describe and will add to her storehouse of happy family memories. When you're on a path or nature trail, let your daughter choose which fork to follow. Even on a walk in the neighborhood you can ask, "Which way next? You lead."

Plant and tend a garden.

All you need is a few square feet for a vegetable garden or a patch of flowers. Flower bulbs look so plain, like a root vegetable, but plant them, water, wait, and a tulip or ranunculus emerges. Delight in that oddity of vocabulary: *ranunculus*, a word that combines the sounds of *ridiculous* and *uncle*. Tending a garden may well be your child's first experience with delayed gratification. And what a tremendous payoff! Watch your daughter's face as she introduces a friend to her flowers or offers her a taste of the first cherry tomatoes plucked from the vine.

Bake together.

This is valuable currency for both sons and daughters, but young girls are more likely to have fine motor and reading skills to follow recipes. (As mentioned in the last chapter, boys old enough to responsibly handle flames and knives love to cook.)

There's so much to learn from baking: The unique lexicon of the art—*sift, grease, brown, knead.* The visual acuity needed to gauge when a pancake is ready to flip or a cookie is just golden enough. Not to mention frosting and decorating the finished product!

HAND IN HAND, WHILE YOU CAN

It's a hot Sunday on a crowded street. A small girl catches my eye because of the confidence of her stride. She's wearing black boots, a lime-green skirt, and a black sweatshirt. I sense that her mother didn't argue with her about the outfit. ("It's going to be hot today. Black clothes are . . . Boots are . . ."). The child clearly loves these boots, wears them every day, and her mother chooses to let her choose. Instead of holding hands, they each hold the end of a pencil, no doubt at the daughter's suggestion.

The girl speaks: "I nevah, nevah, nevah want to go there. Nevah." She is not whining but stating a preference as strong as her stride. *I don't like it there.*

Mother (speaking in a calm, matter-of-fact, amiable way): "You don't like the farmer's market. We only need a few things. Then we'll leave."

I could easily imagine why she didn't like it. She'd have to maneuver between the forest of knees of a bunch of grown-ups, she's too close to the ground to see any of the vendors' displays, and she and her mom would probably have to switch from their playful pencil linkage to ordinary holding of hands. But mostly I was struck by the mother's reaction. She simply acknowledged her daughter's point of view and didn't try to change her mind by selling the current or future attributes of the errand ("We'll get to make a peach pie this afternoon!"). Or bribe her. Or say it's not so bad.

So many mothers I see are naturals at the art of conversation with daughters. Many more are just a few notches away, a few degrees of tamping down the anxiety and turning up the tolerance and curiosity. I think often of a little girl in a pink tutu I once passed on a dusty hiking trail. She was crouching by the side of the trail collecting rocks in the tutu's skirt while her mom stood next to her, not commenting, just listening and nodding while the girl exclaimed, "These all have stripes!" That was a mother who deserved a gold star.

It was an ordinary moment, one neither of them might remember. But I will, because I know how soon that girl will race ahead on the trail. Hold her hand now, slow your pace a bit, and learn how to talk with her while she's young, and you'll have her trust and friendship in all the years ahead.

CHAPTER 5

Hard Topics

Talking to Young Children about Sex, Death, and Money

Mom, what is this fish doing here? This fish has TWO black stripes and a circle around only one eye. Where is Goldie? Did Goldie die, Mom? She did! And you're lying! But you always say not to lie.

But WHY are they called privates? Like private school?

Are we rich? Is Zachary's family rich? Who's richer? We have two dogs, but they have a slide in their backyard.

In times that now seem as ancient as a rotary telephone, children's serious questions about sex, death, and money were ignored or met with bizarre formulaic responses. Babies were dropped off by storks. Providing nuanced or honest information about sexual feelings and activity was considered risky: knowing would lead to doing, which would lead to trouble. If a relative died, children might be told he or she had gone on a long trip or that God wanted another angel. Money fell into a special category. Discussing it was taboo for reasons never explained beyond, "It's not polite."

These forbidden zones deprived children of essential knowledge and parents of the opportunity to pass on their values and join in conversations about life's richest and most thrilling subjects. Nowadays parents are less squeamish but not necessarily more forthcoming. Where previous generations had an evasive, laissez-faire attitude toward sex, death, and money, today's parents are paralyzed. They recognize that a casual brush-off is both depriving and dangerous, but their fear of saying the wrong thing and having their child repeat it, setting off a cascade of outrage from the school or other parents, stymies them.

Parents are also afraid that if they allow their children to express the depths of their feelings or be exposed to ideas that are provocative, vivid, or sad, the kids will be frightened. Yet the opposite is true. Once children have talked about these mysteries with their parents, they are no longer as alone with the monsters under the bed.

Children have always taken joy in the sensual (*Ah, warm, squishy mud between my toes! Pulling on my penis, like a toy I never have to look for, so fun!*). They're fascinated with body systems (*When the baby grows in the mom's tummy, how does it eat? Does it poop in there?*). They're riveted by the cycle of life and death (*Goldie? Grandpa? MILO'S MOM?*). They're determined and curious, so if parents don't tackle these topics with readiness and aplomb, the children will be left to rely on less scrupulous sources.

They'll eventually see sex through the harsh lens of online pornography or clinical, scare-tactic sex-ed classes. Death will be revealed via superhero movies and video games, which teach that killing your adversaries is both cool and kind of fun. They'll learn to crave goods and services from our consumer culture while remaining ignorant about how money actually works. All this in addition to the normal misinformation that's been traded among peers from the beginning of time.

Every parent's conversational repertoire needs to include a way of speaking comfortably about the uncomfortable topics. There are excellent books that can do some of the heavy lifting for you, but ultimately your child will turn to you for answers both philosophical and practical. In all discussions about emotionally charged issues, a light touch will bring you to depths. Stay open, listen carefully, and let your child's questions be your guide.

HOW MUCH DO CHILDREN UNDERSTAND?

As soon as children can speak, they'll catch you off guard with questions that leave you groping for answers that are true yet not alarming. As they grow older, you'll get a sense of how they process information and the best approach for your particular son or daughter. Between the ages of four and eleven children experience tremendous cognitive development, and your answers will evolve along with them. But—and this is crucial—the answers do not have to be perfect.

Part of the parental anxiety that is so pervasive today has to do with what I call "AP Parenting," the notion that every decision has to be the right one, that we can't possibly come back to a child and say, "You know, I've been thinking about what I told you yesterday, and I have a better answer," or, "I gave it a little more thought, and that's not exactly how I feel." This flexible approach is a terrific model children can use with their own friends: you're allowed to change your mind. It's also the only approach that's realistic with a little person whose perceptions and comprehension changes almost weekly.

Even if a parent is aware of the general milestones of cognitive development, a child's ability to grasp information is never a sure thing. Consider the variables. There's the child's age and gender; the depth of his interest in the scientific side of things or the gory, artistic, spiritual, or commonsense side; the length of his attention span; what provoked a question in the first place; and whether the question he's asking is what he really wants to know. Children sometimes come up with convoluted queries that have little connection to what's actually on their mind. If you're relaxed about the questions, if you're curious and calm, your child will eventually get around to the heart of the matter, for example, whether he could be arrested for stealing a bag of chips from someone's lunch box.

STAGES OF COGNITIVE DEVELOPMENT IN CHILDREN

Many parents are aware of basic cognitive development in babies, for instance, the concept of object permanence. A newborn stares blankly at your game of Peekaboo. A few months later she's astonished and delighted by it. Between eight and twelve months the thrill is gone; she's figured out that objects continue to exist even if she can't see them.

Other milestones are not as obvious. Deborah Roffman is a health educator and author of uncommon wisdom.* She poetically describes a cognitive achievement that marks the emergence from infancy to very early childhood: "I am not one with the whole universe, not one with my parents. Humans are objects that begin and end; we exist in space as separate beings." This recognition naturally brings protest. *Whaaaa! I don't want you to leave me in this room all alone with the babysitter!* But it also liberates. *If I hide in the closet and don't move, or in the center of a round rack of clothing at the mall, no one can see me. Wow!*

By the age of five most children understand that time begins and ends. They understand the past best because they've had some experience with it. The future is still an abstraction: *very soon, soon, tomorrow, a long time*—these words are slower to provide reassurance to a child who is eager or worried about what lies ahead. By age six children grow in their ability to understand distance in a deeper way. Some are fascinated with the concept of movement over time, with locomotion and transportation.

These milestones concerning space, time, and distance are good to keep in mind when gauging your child's reactions, especially to

---

* See Recommended Readings for her titles and other books I regularly suggest to parents about subjects that typically cause nervousness or inhibition.

unusual or traumatic events. Whatever your particular child's understanding of these concepts, they are different from your own, and for that reason you can't assume that what a child hears is exactly what you meant. This is another reason it's helpful to be able to say, "I've been thinking this over, and I had some ideas about our conversation from the other day. Let's talk about it some more."

NOT ONE TALK BUT MANY

Once parents make up their minds to tackle a difficult topic, they sometimes try to explain the whole story, including all the precise mechanics, in one intense session. *Whew! Got that over with.* This doesn't work because children have short attention spans and limited capacity to take in new concepts and language. They can't absorb that much in a single gulp. **No matter what the age of the child, he or she won't remember the information if you download it all at once.** Even the brightest student will forget the details of a subject that is confusing, embarrassing, or "gross." This is a fundamental point to remember when dealing with any complex subject. There's no such thing as The Talk. There is the first talk and then many more talks.

A better approach is to patiently answer your child's questions as they arise, as often as necessary. Sometimes you'll be busy with another activity or unsettled because you're in foreign territory (you never would have asked such a question of your parents or any adult). You may be afraid of saying the wrong thing, unsure about the best response. It's always appropriate to say, "*That!* is a fine question. [Children respond well to emphatic declarations.] I need a little time to think about the best answer, and I'll get back to you." And then do it, lest your child conclude that certain topics are off-limits. Saying "Let me think about it" also saves you from impulsively responding in a jokey, mocking, or nervous manner and allows you to acknowledge and settle down with your own discomfort.

When discussing sensitive subjects, you'll travel together on the slow road. The conversations will be more effective if they aren't formal, lengthy, or preachy. Your child will come to see you as a trusty resource if you greet her queries in a welcoming manner and provide answers that are specific and brief. And you can always ask:

"What were you wondering?"
"Tell me what you already know so I'll know where to start."
(Here's where you get to correct misperceptions. "I'm not surprised to hear that, a lot of people think that way, but actually . . .")
"Interesting. Hmm . . . How did you hear about that?"
"Are you curious about anything else?"
"Does my answer make sense to you?"

IT'S YOUR CURRICULUM

Concerning sex education and the other provocative topics, don't assume the schools will give more than the most basic explanations. Most sex-ed programs focus on disease and pregnancy prevention. The curriculum tends to be either "Two forms of protection is the magic number—one for avoiding disease, one for avoiding pregnancy" or "Abstinence is the only sure path." Teachers are discouraged from exploring many subjects that might be controversial for fear that doing so will alarm a subset of parents and cause trouble for the administration. Intimacy and love; the precious and finite nature of all life; the relationship between money, class mobility, and success—these compelling issues get neglected in most classrooms.

In one regard this is good. It gives you the chance to educate your child on some fascinating subjects, to transmit your values, to keep up with changing times. But like all homeschooling parents, you'll have to prepare. This means taking a personal inventory.

What painful experiences from your own childhood might lead you to be overprotective or paranoid about your child's normal actions and questions? Or his naive but age-appropriate beliefs? What do you need to learn in order to raise a wise child in an ever-changing world?

While answering your child's questions gives you a sense of what he's capable of comprehending, you don't have to wait for a query to open a line of discussion. Food for thought is everywhere. Drive in the car or ride the bus, and billboards send messages to your child about body image, sexuality, drinking, illness, homelessness. If you catch your child staring at one of these, you can ask, "What's on your mind?"

Watch TV, movies, or videos, and the ads give you an opportunity to teach media literacy: recognition that many advertisers put profit over people's welfare. If information reaches your child through the Internet, you can explain that the motives of people who create web content are to attract viewers' attention, even if the message is not fair, kind, or true.

A stroll down the sidewalks of most cities will challenge you to discuss the range of people you see, including the elderly, people in wheelchairs, families who are fighting in public. You may not be able to answer your child's toughest questions about these people or displays, but you can be open to the dialogue.

Another skill you'll get to teach while out in the real world is public etiquette. Every child has loudly uttered some version of "Why is that lady fat?" or "Why is your skin brown and your mom's is white?" Without shaming your child, you can let her know there's a difference between things we talk about at home and what we say in public. When children are very young, you can help them understand when not to comment by making the boundaries simple: "It's not polite to say anything about how someone looks or acts unless you're saying what you like about it."

When your child gets older you can add some context. "We don't want to embarrass people or put them on the spot or hurt their feelings. For instance, Uncle Sal may always be saying he wants to lose weight, but it still isn't polite to remind him that he's already eaten two hot dogs."

Be prepared for your child's unintentional gaffes by agreeing on a code, such as pulling on an earlobe, that means, *Stop talking right now. I'll explain later.* You don't want to embarrass her, but you do want to raise her consciousness. Good manners are about protecting other people's dignity, and that's an abstract concept. Teaching it will take some time.

BUY THE BOOK: A FIRST STOP FOR HARD TOPICS

What kind of sticky issues will your child lay at your feet? Things like:

"Noah told me he got laid with Scarlett."

"How come Addie is allowed to sleep here but you always say no to sleepovers at her house? It's not fair. It's really fun at her house. Her parents are nice. And her brother's friends are really smart because they're in seventh grade."

"August said that Jackson's dad might have to go to jail. He said the dad tried to kill himself already."

"Lucy's mom has no hair on her head anymore. Or any eyebrows or eyelashes. She was wearing a scarf, but you could tell."

"Grandpa Mark will be home from the hospital before my school's open house, right? He has to see my painting. The boat looks like it's really far away in the ocean. Grandpa Mark showed me how to make a horizon line."

Simple answers such as "Sleepovers are best when all the kids are the same age" or "We're not sure when Grandpa Mark will be home" open the door a crack, but your curious child will keep pushing at it until you provide more information. While this chapter offers some guidance on common issues and a foundational technique for addressing complex questions, you can take advantage of the many excellent books for children on nearly any touchy or unusual topic. The books are geared to every age and cover a wide spectrum of political and cultural perspectives.

Acquire these books by going to a bookstore, not the library. You'll want to keep them around for a long time since you don't know when the conversational opportunity will strike and then strike again. Don't shop online because you won't be able to size up the physical attributes of the book: *Too long! Looks like a baby picture book. Print is teeny.* Or, *Oh, yes, interesting. I want to open this one and dive in!*

Examine the books for their design, illustrations, and general spirit as well as for the content. Does your daughter love quizzes? Choose a workbook. Does your son find that humor makes embarrassing topics more appealing and palatable? Find a book with clever cartoon illustrations or one that's written in a breezy style. You'll recognize which will intrigue and which will be rejected for being dull, preachy, or flat-footed.

WHAT'S SEX? WHAT'S SEXY? AND WHERE DO BABIES COME FROM?

Here's when children might start asking you about sex:

- At a younger age than you asked your parents, if you ever did, because kids are exposed to more sex-related media and advertising, billboards with alluring images, and billboards with stern but mysterious health warnings.
- When Mom is pregnant and they're curious about what caused it to happen; when it will be over and she'll be able to crawl around, jump, and play like before; or when and how their new little brother or sister will get out of her body.
- When they want to get the lowdown on the suspicious ("Or true, Mom?") information Zeke told them at school.
- Not until fourth or fifth grade, when they are studying plant and

animal reproduction and get to wondering about the human version.

One reason sex is so mystifying to children is that the word itself has several meanings, and unless they live in a cloistered environment, they'll hear it bandied about often and from an early age. In the book *Sex Is a Funny Word*, by Cory Silverberg and Fiona Smyth, the authors explain that "some words always mean the same thing (like *sunshine* or *crayons*). Other words have many different meanings (like *play*). . . . *Sex* is a word like *play*." The authors give three definitions of *sex*, which can be summed up as:

1. *Sex* is a word we use to describe our bodies, like *male* or *female*.
2. *Sex* is something people do together that feels good in their bodies. It also makes them feel close to the other person. Grown-ups call that "having sex."
3. "Having sex" is how grown-ups make babies. Another word for that is *reproduction*.

Children often ask, "What's sexy?" An impulse might be to launch into a tutorial on what it is not: "Well, it doesn't mean wearing tons of makeup!" Another option is to broaden the child's perspective. You might say, "It depends on each person. *Sexy* is one of those words like *wonderful* or *fun*—almost everybody has a different definition. *Sexy* can mean that a person thinks someone else is exciting or special, or they make them have good feelings in their body. They might find somebody sexy because of the way the person's hair looks, or their eyes, or they share a sense of humor."

The nuts-and-bolts reproduction questions are harder to finesse. Even if your own parents used baby names for body parts, you'll want to use the real words when talking with your child about sex. Then she'll be prepared if conversations about acceptable and unacceptable touching come up in school or with other children. If it's hard to say *vagina* or *penis* out loud, practice on your own the way you practice a few foreign phrases before a trip.

You're entering territory that previously has been somewhat forbidden, if only because parents and teachers do a lot of talking about keeping those specific body parts super clean and super private. "Close the door! Flush the toilet! Wash your hands! Don't talk about it in public." Elevating these very same body parts to starring roles in the magical, glorious Story of the Special Hug strikes children as a radical and surprising pivot. Adopt the following explanations as necessary to match your child's age and level of comprehension when the questions arise.

Where do babies come from?

Our bodies are amazing factories that make cells. When you cut your finger, your body first makes a scab out of cells and new skin forms out of cells underneath. All cells have specific important jobs. When boys start to become men, their bodies make thousands of sperm cells. These tiny cells have tails like tadpoles to help them swim fast. Girls are born with about a million cells called eggs. When girls start becoming women, these egg cells grow, just one at a time, in her body every month.

When a man and a woman cuddle and kiss and hug each other tightly, the man's penis fits into the woman's vagina and lots of sperm cells flow out of his penis and swim toward that egg. When a sperm cell reaches the egg they join together and start to make ALL the different kinds of cells that will become a baby.*

How does the baby get out of the mom? How does it fit?

At first the new bundle of cells is the size of a poppy seed. But it will grow as big as a watermelon in a part of the mom's body called her uterus, which people also call the womb. In the womb the baby

---

* Take a look at books listed in the Recommended Reading section for answering children's questions about other ways babies come to be.

floats in a special sac filled with warm water to protect it from being bumped around or hearing loud sounds.

When the baby gets bigger, the uterus stretches like a balloon. It takes nine months, about as long as a school year, for the baby to get big enough to breathe and drink milk on its own. When the baby is ready to be born, it travels out of the uterus, through a tube called the birth canal down to her cervix. Special muscles there can stretch and stretch like a balloon so the baby's big head can pop right out of the mom's vagina.

How does the baby eat? Does it poop in there?

The baby and the mother are attached to each other by a cord inside the sac. This is called the umbilical cord. To nourish the baby as it grows, the air the mom breathes and the food she eats travel through the cord. Mom eats pizza; baby does, too. The stuff the baby doesn't need after it has digested the food—its waste products, like your pee and poop—flows right out through this cord. When the baby is born, the umbilical cord comes out, too. The doctor, the midwife, or the dad cuts off the cord that attached the baby to the mom, and that cut heals. Your belly button is where your umbilical cord was cut!

FOLLOW-UP QUESTIONS AND PRESERVING YOUR PRIVACY

When you get to the penis-in-the-vagina part, most children will react with disbelief: "Oh, yuck! You and Dad did that?! Gross, gross, gross, gross, gross!" And after a week or two . . . "Did you and Dad do that more than *twice*?" Yet each child is different. While many are initially repelled, some are rapt, some bored, some excited to share the news. Typically months or years pass before you are invited into a conversation of more depth.

There are two responses that are especially helpful with questions about sex. One is, "I've thought about it and have some more ideas to add." For example, with an older child you might want to broaden an answer to include how same-sex couples, single parents, or people who are unable to conceive a baby can have one.

The other useful response is, "That's not something I share with other people," or, "I like to keep that private." It's a way to establish (and model) boundaries with children of any age, including precocious preteen girls who might ask about "the *first* time you had sex" followed by requests for details like your age, your relationship with your partner, the circumstances, or whether or not you were glad. When earnest parents ask me if they should be entirely transparent with these types of personal questions, I ask if they would feel obligated to answer their child's query about the *last* time they had sex. Your children are not entitled to any information about your personal sex life you do not wish to share.

PUBERTY AND BEYOND

By age ten or eleven most children are seeking more detailed facts about sex. It's now normal for children to enter puberty at earlier ages than in previous generations, so they need to be aware of the changes that will be happening with their bodies, emotions, and physical sensations. Some information is straightforward: when girls develop breast buds and a few pubic hairs, they need to start carrying a sanitary pad so they're prepared. This news may be stunning to a young girl, and it's ideal if a mother (or another older female) can explain it in person with a box of pads on hand so she can demonstrate how to use them.

As they move past puberty, teenagers will want to know practical information about sexuality in all its variety and splendor. Few teens want to hear these wonders explained by their mom or dad. Even if you manage to sit them down for five minutes while you describe how to put on a condom, their mortification may prevent them from really listening. Instead, hand your child an up-to-date and sensible book about sex and say, "This book explains about body changes, what sex is like, and what it's for. It should answer your questions, but if there's anything you're still curious about, you can ask me or, if you feel shy about it, write me a little note and I'll write back." Your child now has a trustworthy reference to study whenever he or she feels the need, and a willing parent to clarify or expand on ideas.

HOW LOVE CONQUERS PORN

Is there any way to completely shield your child from pornography? Nope. Not even if you move off the grid or to North Korea. I say this with deep regret, but it's true. Even young children who are only allowed on carefully vetted playdates can be exposed to these images because someone's got an older sibling with Wi-Fi and a screen, or a homework assignment reveals that whitehouse.com is not white-house.gov but links to a site where you can view graphic sex videos.

Accidental or intentional exposure doesn't mean your child is doomed to expect sex to be as depicted in pornography's alternate universe: *Women! They have no hair anywhere but on their heads, and you can do whatever you want with them, be you man, woman, or beast! Any time. And they like it. A lot!* It means that in addition to thoughtful books about sex and an open-door policy about technical questions, you'll want to provide some guidance about self-esteem, tenderness, and love, with an emphasis on the positive. Even books that are up-to-date about gender identity and embracing one's sexual orientation don't typically expound on pleasure, intimacy, and connection—about why adults would *want* to have sex more than the two times it took to create two children.

One way to transmit values such as respect and loyalty is by the way you treat your child and other family members, modeling love, commitment, warmth, compassion, patience, playfulness, and empathy. You're laying the foundation for physical contact and loving words in a nonsexual way: these are the emotions your child will recognize as normal and familiar in a love relationship when he or she is older.

Another way to share these values is through stories of your family history. Recount the tale of how you and your child's other parent got together (if you're still with that person and feeling kindly disposed). How did you know you were in love? Where did you go on your first date? How did you know that person liked you? If this feels too close to over-sharing, tell about how their grandparents met and fell in love, or about relatives long gone. Did they emigrate together? What was that journey like? Did they meet as newcomers to this country? Who introduced them? Maybe it was an arranged marriage and a very happy one, which opens another intriguing avenue of discussion.

You can also launch a conversation based on a song, poem, painting, movie, or book. Together you can listen to or read tales of love and heartbreak, smart and foolish choices, longing, delight, how romantic love can expand a person's life. In most contemporary animated fairy tales as well as some traditional ones, there are lots of opportunities to explore what makes a person lovable besides physical beauty. Bravery, loyalty, kindness, a playful spirit, sacrifice of some sort, and compassion for others nearly always make up part of the story line.

Obituaries are a surprising source of inspiring love stories, and these have the advantage of being true—something that will matter more as the child gets older. In tributes to people who have passed away, you'll often find moving recollections about the role their beloved played in their life. Teachers at your child's school may describe other true-life love stories from history. The biography section of the children's room at the library is another potential resource—ask the librarian for books or movies about couples who went on adventures, made significant discoveries, created a body of art, or worked for social justice. You're teaching your child the language of love in its various moods and phases: not just first blush of attraction but also the romance of companionship, shared passions, and mutual respect.

WHEN SOMEONE IN YOUR FAMILY IS ILL

There are awkward topics, and then there are wrenching conversations. Explaining to your child that a parent, sibling, or beloved relative is ill is one of the biggest challenges you may face. Like all the hard topics, it will require not one talk but many. The words you say to first deliver the news will be especially difficult.

There is no question that sooner rather than later you must tell your children what is going on. They sense the change in your mood; they hear the phone calls from doctors, the whispered conversations, the doors that are quietly shut. If you're not honest with them, their imagination will fill in the blanks with scenarios that may be more terrifying than the truth and may include self-blame: *Mom always said I was making her crazy, and now she really is sick!*

Children experience everything, including a loved one's illness, from the perspective of how it will affect them personally. *What will happen to me?* is the filter on all incoming data. So when explaining an illness for the first time (and in subsequent conversations), make sure to conclude by describing how the situation will impact the child's daily routine. What will change, and what will stay the same? Assure children that much in their life will be the same old, same old.

Betsy Brown Braun, an author and child development specialist, suggests that parents plan out in advance the story they will tell the child, keep it as simple as possible, and tailor the vocabulary to a level the child is sure to understand. Because circumstances can quickly shift, it doesn't make sense to give children too many details. To be specific in a way small children can understand, use simple words. For example:

Mom is having trouble with her breathing, and the doctors are going to take pictures of her lungs with a special camera to see what's causing the problem. She'll be in the hospital for a few days. When we find out what can be done to help, we'll tell you. Meanwhile, this week Carmen's mom will pick you up from school. You'll still be going to dance class on Tuesday, and I'll be home every night to have dinner with you and hear about your day.

Some illnesses require an operation and recovery period that is fairly straightforward; others will be an ongoing part of family life.

Cancer is a wild card. Patients often undergo rounds of treatment that must be explained to the child, with no guarantee about the outcome. In all cases, the parents' own worries will be apparent. One way to deal with the fear is to acknowledge it by saying, "It's scary and also we're hopeful. The two things are both true at the same time."

Try to maintain your child's usual routines as much as possible throughout the parent's illness. Small gestures can act as ballast in a household that's in the midst of a health crisis. One mom whose husband was recovering from heart surgery arranged her daughter's stuffed bear in a sitting position on the girl's pillow with a different toy in its paws each day. Regardless of how off-kilter the rest of the child's family life felt, the bed was always made and the bear was always waiting when the little girl got home. It was like a silent message from her mom: *You can count on me. You're in my thoughts when you're at school.*

Don't assume your child is insensitive if she's not reacting to the crisis the way an adult would: if she's not crying or looking sad, seems to forget about it, or wants to play outside with her friends. These responses are normal, as is misbehavior.

When someone is ill, a main cause of anxiety and depression for patients and their families is the loss of control, and that's true for children as well. Parents can lift a child's spirits by giving her ways to feel in control, for instance, by helping to care for the sick parent, assisting with household chores, or doing more of her own self-care. It's easy to think, *Oh, my poor child. I have to double up on providing for and indulging her.* But that drains your own resources and deprives the child of the chance to feel like she's an essential part of the family effort. Consider letting her help organize medical supplies, read to the parent who's ill, or take over some new chores. You could say:

I'm dealing with so many decisions these days. I have to be ready to talk to the doctor whenever she calls and to spend time at the hospital. You can help me out by taking charge of Bluebell—walking her, feeding her, and letting me know when we're running low on her food.

Ask for help from other adults, too. In our culture there's sometimes a cloud of shame around being sick and "weak." Seasoned caregivers know the folly of this viewpoint. You're modeling a healthy attitude for children when you show them that in a crisis it's natural to reach out to friends and family members for support.

A DEATH IN THE FAMILY

The loss of a beloved member of the extended family, such as an aunt or grandparent, has a deep and lasting impact on a child, and losing a parent or sibling is a tragedy that will surely affect the child's outlook and emotional development. It's also true that children are more resilient than parents may appreciate. They survive losses, and the ways in which they change may not be for the worse. Maturity, compassion, patience, and other worthy traits are often the by-products of these sorrowful events. It's not exactly a silver lining, and you wouldn't wish it on any child, but experiencing a death can lead to a more meaningful life.

In the past, euphemisms were used in an attempt to protect children, but today we're aware that kids become frightened and confused when they're told something like, "God took your sister to be with him because he loved her so much." (Child thinks, *What kind of mean God is that?*) Honest, specific, direct explanations work best. You can try using the word *very* to emphasize the extreme and unusual nature of what's occurred: "Something very sad happened. Aunt Laura died. She was very, very sick, and now we won't get to see her anymore. But we'll remember all the reasons we loved her so much. We're going to miss her a lot."

All the *very*s help to distinguish ordinary illnesses and accidents from this special case that has led to death. Making this distinction alleviates children's fear of another imminent death and loss. Reassure your child that he or she is healthy and so are other family members. Listing them will soothe your child: "I've recently gotten a checkup at the doctor's and I'm very healthy. So is Daddy and your brother. Grandma and Granddad are healthy, too."

Allowing children to attend the memorial service or funeral can help them comprehend and accept what has happened. Children age six and up are usually mature enough not to disrupt the proceedings, so encourage them if they want to go (they may change their mind several times, and if they decide against attending, honor their wishes). Imagination is often more frightening than reality, and many of their questions will be answered by what they see and hear. And as is true for all of us, they'll also have an opportunity to learn interesting or surprising or moving things they didn't know about their deceased relative by listening to the eulogies.

HOW CHILDREN PROCESS GRIEF

John Bowlby, who developed the psychological model of attachment theory, described three phases of a child's grief. First the child refuses to believe in the death and expects to see, find, or recover the lost person; next the child suffers from emotional pain, despair, and a sense of disorganization; and in the third phase the child is able to organize life without the person who has died. These stages are experienced differently depending on the age, cognitive level, and temperament of the child.

In general, from ages three to five, children do not understand that death is final but see it as a reversible state. They may search for the person who has died, from room to room in the house, in crowds, or in passing cars.

From ages five to nine, children know that death is "forever." In spite of this, they may cling to unrealistic hopes about the person returning and resist accepting that a death has actually occurred in their own family. Lots of questions and morbid fantasies are normal.

Children this age may experience sadness, fear, longing, confusion, and guilt. In order to protect themselves from being overwhelmed by these feelings, they may ignore, deny, or bury the feelings deep inside. Along with the awareness of the reality of death comes a concern that if someone close to them can die, they can die, too, and this can frighten them deeply.

It's normal for children to wonder if they're responsible for the death of a loved one and to worry about their own mortality. It's also normal for a grieving child to seem surprisingly unaffected by a death in the family. An unconcerned reaction, such as kicking around a soccer ball with a friend directly following the funeral service, doesn't necessarily mean that the child is denying the death. Children live in the moment, so with a ball, a sunny day, and a friend they may forget for a few happy minutes that Dad has died. It's disconcerting to adults but not at all unusual for children.

SHOULD YOU SHARE YOUR GRIEF WITH YOUR CHILD?

The conventional wisdom about grieving is not to hide your feelings from your children. By being open about your sorrow, you'll show your child he doesn't have to put up a false front. It's true that children shouldn't feel as if they have to conceal their emotions to protect their parents or for any other reason. Their experience of grief may include anger at being abandoned, guilt over the death, idealization of the person who died, and physical symptoms ("I can't breathe!" "My bones are hurting like Grandpa's did!"). They may also be embarrassed (*I don't want to be different than my friends who have dads that are alive*). The adults around them are likely to be on an emotional roller coaster, especially in the period immediately following the death. In those early days, the best that grieving parents may be able to provide is a loving atmosphere and tolerance for unusual displays of emotion from children and adults alike.

But as time goes on there's a risk that "Don't hide your feelings" can be misinterpreted as "Never hide a feeling." What if, as is common, a parent's sentiments about the deceased are more complicated than straightforward sorrow? What if he or she feels angry, guilty, disoriented, or abandoned? How much should a young child witness as the parent is working through the mourning process? It can be extremely distressing for children to see a parent who regularly weeps over small daily frustrations or disappointments, is lethargic, or is not keeping up with household tasks.

Having children regulates you as an adult. When a tragic event such as a death strikes your family, you can't stay in your pajamas all day or let the house fall into chaos. If you're unable to function well enough to run your home, you should see a counselor for your own sake and that of your child. This is when family grief groups can really help; the staff can point a distraught parent to additional psychiatric support if it's needed. Beyond that, time will be a slow but reliable healing agent as you find compassionate and thoughtful ways to share (not over share) your feelings with your child.

There are means by which you and your child can process grief together. One is by keeping the relative's memory alive through acts that reflect what the person brought into the world. You could say, "Let's go to the beach today in memory of Aunt Laura. We loved to have picnics in the sand with her, and this will be in her honor." Or, "We're going to keep Dad's garden going. Let's go to the nursery and get some new tomato plants, and we'll also buy some fertilizer so we can feed the flowers he loved so much."

Another way for your family to express how much you loved and miss the person is by encouraging your child to help you make a shrine, for instance, by arranging on a bookshelf or mantel a few photographs, a vase of flowers, and a trinket that reminds your child of the relative.

Let your child know that anytime she wants to talk about how she's feeling, you'll listen. You might say, "We can talk about it whenever you want, but I'm telling you in advance that on some days I'm sadder than others—I'll bet you can hear it in my voice—and I never know when that's going to be. You may feel that way, too. I can't predict when the sadness will hit me, but that doesn't mean we can't talk."

Parent Talk

As you and your child acclimate to the new contours of your life:

- Be available to listen. You don't have to have ready answers.
- Expect the child to repeat the same statements or questions over and over again.
- Offer reassurance about your child's safety and the health and strength of the rest of her family.
- Keep a watchful eye on the child to look for extreme reactions while bearing in mind that regression, apathy, and anger are normal.
- If other children are treating the bereaved child as the "death expert," remind him that he doesn't have to answer every question.

Finally and most important, give a grieving child permission to be happy again. Many adults and children fear they are being disloyal to the person who died when they find themselves starting to laugh and resume the rhythms of everyday life. It can feel as if you're forgetting the person, which feels like losing them all over again. This is a predictable phase of grief. Reassure your child (and yourself) that the person who's gone would want you to be happy. Set an example by enthusiastically participating in life the way you used to, before you hit this harrowing stretch of road in your family's journey.

WHEN A PET DIES

It's likely that your child's first experience with loss will involve not a person but a fish, dog, or cat. The grief children feel over the death of a pet is profound, and so is the anguish it triggers in parents.

Mother of five-year-old Lily: Goldie, Lily's pet fish, went belly up this morning. We only had her for five days! I knew Lily would be really, really upset, so I went to the pet store and got a replacement before she came home.

Me: To fool her? Lily's too smart for that, and think of the example you'll set if she uncovers your ruse. And you lose the opportunity to talk about death.

Mother: But I'm worried she'll feel responsible. Goldie lived on her dresser and Lily was the only one allowed to feed her.

Me: When Lily comes home today, you can explain that some animals have a short but happy life span. Tell her, "You were a good mom to your Goldie. I bought a new fish for you, and maybe you can give this one a happy home, too."

The decision to end the life of a pet who is ill has become more fraught as intensive medical interventions for animals have come on the market. Chemotherapy, bone marrow transplants, and other extreme measures can be very painful for pets, and many veterinarians have grave doubts about the ethics of such treatments. Each family has its own limits in terms of how much they are able or willing to pay for these interventions and how they define an animal's quality of life. Your child should not be invited to weigh in on these adult decisions, nor should she accompany you to the vet if there's a chance the doctor will advise you either to put the animal to sleep or embark on a treatment you can't afford or aren't convinced will improve the pet's quality of life.

Illustrated books are excellent conduits for mourning a pet and encouraging conversation with your child. It's nice but not necessary if the book features a child the same gender as yours. For girls, *Saying Goodbye to Lulu*, by Corinne Demas, is a fine choice. For boys, there's *A Dog Like Jack*, by DyAnne DiSalvo-Ryan, and Judith Viorst's classic *The Tenth Good Thing About Barney*, about a boy and his cat. *Jasper's Day*, by Marjorie Blain Parker, sensitively describes the decision to euthanize a pet.

After the pet has died, you can offer your child the opportunity to make a scrapbook or small memorial displaying one of the animal's favorite toys and a framed photo. If the pet was cremated, the urn with the ashes can be placed in the shrine as long as you and your child feel comfortable with it.

Parent Talk

When our daughter was four years old, a family friend took her to an insect exhibition. She came home with a female Mexican brown-haired tarantula. The first time "Tranchie" shed her carapace, climbing out and leaving the shell perfectly intact, we were confused and shocked. Had she cloned herself? When she died after sixteen years, we saved her body along with the collection of eight prior versions of Tranchie in a box that went on a prominent shelf in our den. It was part Guillermo del Toro, part loving memorial to a long life.

CHILDREN AND MONEY

As a species, humans have a hunting and gathering instinct. We are crows drawn to shiny objects we can take back to our nest. So it's only natural that children will beg, whine, or explode when their demands for goods are thwarted. Their urge to collect is exploited by advertisers, who are brilliant at appealing to pint-sized cravings and adult-sized weaknesses. "I want that!" is a running theme of childhood, and so is a parent's internal conflict about whether to say yes or no.

Not having enough money, especially compared to peers, is often a source of fear and shame for parents. They worry about their ability to protect their child not only in tangible ways, such as living in a safe neighborhood with good schools, but also in the slippery social realm of future options, acceptable appearance, and inclusion in desirable groups. All of these seem to depend on money, and they poke into the fabric of family life in the form of a child's demands for toys, clothing, shoes, outings, camps, sports equipment, video games, devices, and on and on.

Conversations with children about money are difficult on many levels and at every age. It's hard to say no to your children. When so much of their well-being appears to be riding on your ability to provide goods and services, it's hard to be honest with yourself about what you can afford. It's hard to be honest with the kids about that, too. It's hard if you're comparing yourself to your friends, neighbors, relatives, and the other parents at your child's school. And if you're wealthy, it's hard to know how to create a framework for spending that will keep your child grounded and appreciative. Given this thicket of emotions, most parents send mixed messages to their children about money.

Certainly safe neighborhoods, access to good medical care, schools with bountiful resources, tutors for special needs, and dedicated athletic coaches are beneficial to children. As a shield against an uncertain future they are the foundation. But to ensure your children a life of purpose, prudence, and joy, they'll need to develop social awareness and emotional maturity: the capacity for restraint, the development of a broad definition of treasure, and the recognition that helping others is both a responsibility and a reward. Where to start on the curriculum of cultivating these traits in your child? With conversations about money! The first step? Teaching kids about the difference between what they want and what they need, and reminding yourself what is owed your child and what is a privilege.

THE BUDGET: RAINY DAYS, SUNNY DAYS, AND GIVING TO OTHERS

The concept of a family budget provides a basis for all your discussions about money. (It works even if you don't actually have a family budget.) Here's the vocabulary for young children.

> **Budget.** When people work, they get paid in money. A budget is how we divide that money up for different things, like food, paying for the heat and water in our house, and paying for clothes and toys. Dollars are money. A credit card is also a kind of money.

> **Rainy Day.** We save some of the money we earn so we'll have it in case there is an emergency. We call that "saving for a rainy

day." A rainy day could be if the car breaks and we need to fix it, or you have a toothache and we need to go to the dentist.

Sunny Day. We also save some money for sunny days, fun things like family vacations, birthday parties, holiday celebrations, and surprise gifts—for instance, if we see something we know a favorite person would love.

Charity. We give some money we earn to places called food banks or shelters—they provide meals for people who don't have enough money to buy food or who don't live in a home with a kitchen to cook in. Sometimes that's because they lost their house in a flood; sometimes it's because they can't find a job. We also give money to organizations that support ideas we believe in, for instance, the idea that all people should be treated equally.

These terms demystify the world of material goods to which children are constantly exposed. Instead of saying "We can't afford that" (What's *afford?*), there is now a context. Your children may get tired of hearing you say "That's not in the budget," but at least they'll know you have a master plan, and you can remind them that it includes vacations and presents and celebrations.

The superpower that fuels children's crusade for stuff is their energy. Weary, weakened adults say no, no, no, then cave in and say "OK, fine." In behavioral psychology that is called intermittent reinforcement, and it's a powerful incentive for the child to try to wear you down again next time. This is the same psychological motivator that keeps gamblers glued to slot machines. So as much as you can, try to avoid giving in once you have refused a request. If you feel guilty, just remember that your child never has a problem saying no to you.

Most parents enjoy surprising their child with little gifts throughout the year, and this is a lovely gesture. My advice is to keep these surprises small and more heartfelt than expensive. Avoid saying no, no, no to a request and then surprising the child with it, lest the gifts become intermittent reinforcement, too.

A BROADER CONCEPT OF THE FAMILY BUDGET

As children get older, they'll lobby harder to convince you that they need specific items. They'll use slicker but often transparent and inane arguments like:

> "You don't understand how unhappy I am a lot of the time. This video game [or tattoo or piercing] will make me more popular."
>
> "I'm really shy when I'm at school, but if I'm wearing this backpack, I'll feel like I can hang out with anyone."
>
> "These sneakers are a great investment! They're a limited edition—collectibles! They're going to be worth a lot of money."
>
> "Everyone has them and I'll be the only one who doesn't."

The old chestnut "everyone has it" is still amazingly effective. Occasionally it's a legitimate argument—everyone does have the item and your child will feel like a pariah if he doesn't. So you have a choice: buy a $70 pair of sneakers he'll outgrow in three months, or pay ten times that for therapy sessions (yours and his!). Sometimes it makes sense to buy the shoes.

There's an upside to this scenario. A child who is old enough to say, "I need this because everyone else has it," is old enough to grasp a more complex definition of budgeting. You explain to him how running a household works and how he can contribute. This is not so he can "earn" the cost of a specific pair of shoes. These are everyday contributions as a citizen of the family.

A budget, in the broader sense, is made up of input and expenditures of effort, time, and money. Your kids can't pay the mortgage or drive, but they can make contributions by doing for themselves what you usually do for them. People think of chores in a retro sense that doesn't apply to most children these days. They don't have paper routes and few mow the neighbor's lawn. But there are dozens of chores parents do for their children and teenagers because it's easier, the parents are tired, they want to get back to their devices, or they value the child's completion of a school project—even if the child has procrastinated—more than having the table cleared. Yet simple tasks of self-care and household maintenance are crucial to teaching children about the connection between time, energy, and funds.

As they grow, your children will continue to request more goods and services. At that point they can be expected to perform more complex family chores (like taking the car in for a tune-up or driving the grandparents to appointments) and take more responsibility for themselves (like remembering and completing school assignments and showing up for volunteer activities). This way, they won't always be on the receiving end. Instead they'll be capable family members who contribute to the welfare of the organization and can also reap its benefits.

EXPERIENCES OVER THINGS

It's never too early to teach children the difference between money and value. One way is by saying, "In our family we often prefer to enjoy experiences instead of things." You can explain that many consumer items offer limited, predetermined satisfaction, unlike experiences, which deliver in different ways and over time. There is the pleasure of planning and anticipating the event, experiencing it, telling stories about it afterward, and savoring the memories.

> "We went to Yellowstone, saw a really big brown bear all by
> himself in the woods, but he didn't even see us at all!"
> "Mom let me choose two scary movies for a horror-movie

marathon. We slept until one in the afternoon the next
day."
"There were lots of kids at the beach with kites, and we had
a kite race to see whose went the highest. One kite got
mixed up with another and they both crashed!"

With an older elementary school child a parent can explain this
concept by reminding him of a family trip, then asking what he recalls
and if he's told a friend about it. The parent can share her memory,
too, and they can compare. A useful tip about timing: it's best not
to use this as a maneuver when saying no to buying something the
child is longing for. Instead, put it in the context of explaining how
the family makes decisions about money, for example, or why you've
decided to put a family trip in the budget for the summer rather than
buy a new but unnecessary car.

HARDER TRUTHS: INFORMING IS PROTECTING

I said earlier that there is no such thing as one talk; there is the first
talk and then many more. That's true. But no discussion of hard topics
would be complete without mentioning the talks that parents must
have in order to protect their children from societal forces that are
ugly, enduring, and real. They must explain how to stay alert around
grownups, even relatives, who may seem friendly but could do them
harm. Parents of children of color must educate them about how
to behave around authorities in order to minimize the likelihood of
conflict. Parents of gay or transgendered youth must prepare them
for the possibility of being taunted or victimized. Parents who are
undocumented must explain their precarious situation and what it
means for their children.

These talks are different from other discussions about safety,
such as warning children against strangers. Being kidnapped by a
stranger is extremely unlikely. Racism and sexism, and the brutality
that arises from them, are commonplace. The unfairness of these

conditions is confusing and outrageous to children, and observing it marks the beginning of the end of their innocence. Parents often shut down children's comments about, for example, skin color, thus shaming and confusing. Take their remarks as a cue that more, not less, conversation is needed. Problems develop when parents panic, unwittingly teaching young children that their observations or questions are taboo.

Even young children can grasp that human beings are curious about people whose appearances or mannerisms are unfamiliar. It is naive to believe that children are colorblind. One of the first things kids notice is contrast. They're fascinated by every sort of difference: skin color, accents, styles of hair. What do these external differences signify? When it comes to people, very little. Modeling multicultural interest and affiliations, plus having candid conversations, is the formula that works to inoculate children against prejudice.

THE CONCEPT OF CONSENT

In the face of unwanted touching or intrusion by a peer or adult, we want our children to take action right away even when doing so would usually be considered rude or unkind. Sexual harassment and assault is most often perpetrated not by strangers but by known adults or peers, would-be romantic partners, seemingly normal acquaintances, a parent or stepparent. To show children how to protect themselves against it, begin teaching the concept of consent when they are very young by demonstrating boundaries and giving them practice saying no.

This actually starts with parents themselves. How do you demonstrate respect for your child's boundaries? Do you keep tickling after he or she has begged you to stop? Interrupt carelessly when the child is talking or absorbed in work (play being children's work)? Wash her face, brush her teeth, or comb her hair without asking if she wishes to do the task herself or simply prefers to be forewarned?

The first building blocks of consent are in these parent-to-child behaviors.

When your child is a toddler, you can teach her about the two-way street of consent. It means that everyone has the right not to be touched or intruded upon if they don't wish to be. As children grow in understanding and experience, conversations about making distinctions between annoying behavior and harassment provide them with techniques for both protecting themselves and exercising control over their own impulses. You might say:

Sometimes people you trust or are supposed to be polite to—parents, teachers, your coach, a relative, a family friend, a new classmate, or a stranger in a public place—will want to touch you when you don't want them to. If you resist, they might tell you you're being silly. You might feel bad or confused. Sometimes in these situations your tummy or heart feels funny. It knows what's right when your mind is confused. That's called a "gut feeling." It's good to listen to your gut feelings and to practice saying, "No. Don't do that." And tell me or Dad right away.

Any grown-up who tells you to keep a secret from your parents is a tricky person. Don't trust them or do what they say. You can ALWAYS tell us.

Together with your child, come up with age-appropriate phrases that protect his or her boundaries while respecting the other person:

"Grandma, instead of kissing you on the cheek, today I'm going to blow you a kiss and give you a high five."
"No more tickling to wake me up in the morning, Daddy. I know you think it's funny, but it bothers me."
"I don't feel like talking right now."
"Please don't come into my room without knocking first."
"It's not OK for you to take my stuff without my permission. Stop saying, 'I didn't think you'd mind.'"

"Aunt Jess, please don't take my picture or make a video without asking me first."

PLAYING TELEPHONE

One day the school or a parent will call and tell you that your child showed or was shown, touched or was touched by, introduced or explained a body part or subject considered by the caller to be off-limits. The caller will use the word *inappropriate*. A spike of adrenaline will shoot through your veins as your mind races: *Did I mess up?*

It isn't fair to ask children to keep secrets, so you must assume your child will tell her friends about the conversations you have regarding sex or any of the hard topics, and that you'll have to deal with the fallout. Just keep in mind that what a teacher or mother has heard from a child is out of context and your message may have gotten lost in translation. When Ava's mom corners you with "Ava says you told Kristin about contraception," your reply might be "I did. We were watching a television show and one of the characters talked about birth control pills. I have a policy that when Kristin asks me something, I try to give her a basic, honest answer." Ava's mom may not approve, but her comfort is not your responsibility. Your priority is being open and "askable" with your child.

THE GREATEST STORIES EVER TOLD

Small children are natural journalists. They wonder about everything and have strong feelings about many subjects. Older children are interested in identity, justice, and community. Your assignment is to listen, clarify what your child is aiming to understand, figure out your own beliefs or dig up new information, and translate your answer into four-year-old speak, or seven-year-old, or eleven-year-old.

Hard Topics

Conversations about these subjects strengthen children's character and confidence. Whether the exchange lasts a few minutes or is an earnest if awkward sit-down, every hard conversation makes the next one easier. Sentence by sentence, you're getting to know your children on a deepening level, and as you do, you're building trust and rapport. You'll need both as they move into the teenage years.

CHAPTER 6

Spirit Guides in Disguise

An Introduction to Teenagers

*He capers, he dances, he has eyes of youth, he writes
verses, he speaks holiday, he smells April and May.*

—Shakespeare, *The Merry Wives of Windsor*

Sooner than most parents anticipate, and far sooner than they desire,
the grade schooler vanishes and the preteen appears. Often she is not
smiling. Especially at you. And just as you try to share a sensible plan
to solve her self-created drama, she flees to her room, slamming the
door behind her. How can you knock in a manner that won't elicit
a furious "*What?!*"

Then there's your teenage son. He's already in his room. Tech-
nically he's accessible, but here, too, you hesitate. What is going on
in there? Is it your duty to find out? You rarely see him unless food
or transportation is involved. When he shuffles into the kitchen
for sustenance, you may get a nod or a fond but pitying smile. Or
nothing at all.

Is this the most you can expect from now on?

In this chapter I'll offer comfort and advice on the vagaries of
conversing with teenagers, and in the two chapters that follow I'll
focus on teen boys and girls respectively. One theme applies to parents
of either sex. Your task for a few long years will be to resist making

summary judgments and to accept (and even feel compassion for) the teen's easily provoked anger, worry, hurt, and massive projections: "It's you! Everything is *your fault!*"

Your challenges will be many. First among them: wrestling with your sense of helplessness, panic, and nostalgia for the sweet elementary school days. You'll need to cheer your children on without trying to manage or exploit their successes. Acknowledge their victories without pushing them to do more. *Not* talk about it to all your friends. Tolerate being unliked and feeling unloved. Earn your own social capital, even in this busy time, so your child can look up to you. And all the while, keep the atmosphere temperate enough so that both of you can speak and be heard.

At no other phase of life is conversation between parents and children more difficult. Even infants are better at listening to what parents are trying to communicate and at getting their messages heard. Talking with teenagers rarely resembles what adults would define as conversation at all. Small successes are a triumph. Even if you were to scrupulously abide by every piece of advice I offer in these chapters, you'd still be in for a wild ride, and that's normal. If it's too right, something is wrong.

OH, THE PLACES YOU'LL GO

All parents of teenagers who come to see me are looking for a road map back to happier days and a detour that will bypass the mixture of grief and terror that is their natural lot. They suffer the heartbreaking loss of a beloved (*My baby! My buddy! My little beauty!*) and of control ("You want to sleep at Molly's? Who's Molly? Sorry, but we don't know her parents"). Their nights churn with visions of imagined risk-taking (*Sexting! Sex! Suicide by texting while driving!*). And all this uneasiness is followed by more loss: even if you can envision a bumper sticker on your car that broadcasts the family's achievement (*Chloe and Yale—it could happen!*), this child is still heading out where she belongs. She's awful now and then she's going to leave you.

The elf or pixie you've raised since babyhood is no longer cute and cuddly, but teenagers have other gifts to offer. Their wild devotion to certain bands, styles, foods, and causes; their sublime or cringe-worthy sense of humor; their creativity; their love of their besties and teammates—all this can engage and inspire the adults who are raising them.

I sometimes tell parents, "Your teenager is a spirit guide in disguise." If they look doubtful, I explain that in some cultures spirit guides assist humans in evolving from one level of consciousness to the next. They allow us to fulfill a potential we otherwise might not achieve. Your teenager is the only being with the power to nearly kill you yet also leave you humbled, more self-aware, and possessing of some authentic wisdom. You'll receive no formal recognition for the perilous rite of passage that is your child's adolescence, but if you're lucky, you will someday be rewarded with the company of a loving and reasonable young man or woman.

Conversing with teenagers relies on the principles and strategies you've cultivated up to this point, but the new pas de deux requires mastery of unfamiliar steps. Being enchanted by your child's enchantment evolves into an appreciation of your teenager's intense, kaleidoscopic world. Learning to respect your child's boundaries and individuality grows into an ability to separate from your teenager with less fear and more equanimity. As always, you'll be reminding yourself, *Today is a snapshot, not the epic movie of my child's life.* Nothing a teenager says is personal, permanent, or predictive, so relax and enjoy the show. It's got a short run, and the seats are limited.

MODERN PRESSURES ON A TIMELESS TRANSITION

The psychological process of separation has always been a bumpy one for teenagers and their parents, but today's moms and dads deal with extra layers of stress. Among the parents I see, these include alarm over technology and social media's impact on their children, and fear about the children's future, especially their ability to make a good living and build a loving and stable support network. These pressures cause some parents to cling more tightly to their teenagers. One mother described feeling like she had a phantom limb, the kind that causes measurable pain, when her daughter left for college.

Parental anxieties have found an outlet in the college-preparation process. The effort to pump up a child's academic résumé overwhelms parents' exchanges with their children from before ninth grade through high school, taking those years hostage. Less obviously, the race for college acceptance also provides cover for the parents' (often unconscious) resistance to letting go.

Let's briefly unpack each of these elements. If you're aware of the forces that have the potential to influence your conversations with your teenager, it's like installing an automatic pause button. You get a few extra seconds to make a choice before you speak.

Normal Teenage Separation

In all eras, a teenager's developmental job is to separate from his or her parents, try on different identities, and join a tribe. Nearly every culture has rituals surrounding this passage. They usually occur at the age of puberty, when the male child is pulled away from the females of the group and takes his place alongside the men, and the female is prepared for matrimony and motherhood. In the past, teenagers' physical, emotional, and cognitive maturity provided them with resources well matched to the demands of their lives. Boys gained the physical strength and courage needed to hunt and protect; girls developed the right balance of hormones and the emotional capacity to bond with a mate, procreate, and care for their young. The tribe or community benefited from the new attributes of the maturing youth.

Separation as a stage of normal development doesn't align with our modern drawn-out version of adolescence. In Western culture, rituals associated with the passage to adulthood—the bar and bat mitzvah, quinceañera, confirmation, sweet sixteen—are religious or social occasions that don't necessarily signal a change in the responsibilities or expectations of the child. True separation is marked by events such as getting a driver's license, getting a job, graduating high school, enrolling in college, joining the military. Even the age at which many teens get a driver's license has drifted upward from sixteen to eighteen, encouraged by parents who would just as soon chauffeur the kids or pay for a Lyft as see them take the wheel.

Regardless of their parents' wishes or the culture's demands, developmentally normal separation will begin when a child reaches puberty, which today is anywhere from age nine to eleven. It is first marked by the preteen's shift in allegiance from his parents to a peer group. A tight gang of friends is the bridge between dependence on Mom and Dad and more mature individual identity. Earlier puberty puts girls and boys in mating mode, adding more tension to the transition.

Another signal of separation is the teen's willingness to take risks. Teenagers aren't just oblivious to risk; they love it and actively seek opportunities to push the envelope. Researchers speculate that the attraction to risk helps teens separate. This actually works to the advantage of modern-day families: if the children take risks while they're still under the protective umbrella of parents and juvenile legal status, they'll possess a bit of worldly experience when they leave home with (hopefully) only minor dents to their reputation or well-being.

The stereotypical but legitimate complaints about teenagers as they separate are that the boys withdraw and the girls claw their way free by fighting with their mothers. All this is normal.

Digital Extras That Make Separation Harder for Parents

The blessings and curses of technology change dramatically as children become teenagers. By the later preteen years many are free to explore cyberspace on their own. This exposes them to social media, pornography, and dubious diversions, but it also opens infinite opportunities for creativity and learning. At a time when teenagers' schedules are packed with school and extracurriculars, the Internet may be the only place they're free to roam without parental oversight. Fearful parents like having the teens safe in their bedrooms, where they can take only virtual risks as opposed to those in the real world. But this robs teens of the chance to get street-smart, make mistakes, face consequences, and recalibrate their actions the next time. Self-control is what will protect your college freshman from the free-for-all of campus life.

Parents may insist that virtual mistakes are "educational" enough, but the vast majority of such blunders (*She texted a pic of her boobs to her boyfriend!*) have fewer long-term repercussions than parents fear. Online adventures are no substitute for the experience a teenager gets by interacting in person with human beings, city streets, parks, weather, public transportation, and other features of the 3-D world.

The cell phone is another obstacle to normal teen separation. The phones let parents track their teenagers' movements, spy on them, and stay enmeshed in their lives. And the stalking works both ways: a father of three complained that the "friend finder" app he made his daughters install backfired when they used it to monitor him. "They know if I'm at the store or work; they know if I'm on the way home. They hunt me down and text me and ask me for stuff. There's no escape."

The College Component

If parents have an all-access pass to their teenagers' lives via their cell phones, why aren't the kids rebelling, as is the time-honored tradition? They are, just not overtly. They're too frightened to openly revolt, having been raised on the myth that unless they get into a good college, they're doomed. A teen from North Carolina wasn't joking when he said, "My parents think it's either UNC-Chapel Hill or hobo." The road to college acceptance is too complex and fraught to handle on their own, the kids have been told, and in most cases it's true.

Spirit Guides in Disguise

The college-prep and application gauntlet soothes many of the parents' separation issues. Parent and teenager share a noble goal: to triumph over the teen's academic, social, and athletic challenges and gain entrance to a top-tier school. Parent and child pour over websites and applications, meet with tutors and experts, visit college campuses. The parent gets four to six years of close involvement, but the forced teamwork stalls or distorts the normal separation process for the teenager.

Since separation from parents is the primary goal of adolescence, these modern-day obstacles to it must always be kept in mind when you're asking yourself, *What's the best way to approach my teenager? What are we fighting about? What should we be talking about?*

TALKING WITH TEENS 101

Throughout the teenage years, your goal is not to be your child's friend. You're not going to be cool, because they can't think you're cool while they're separating from you. In your role as cheerfully unhip authority figure, you can nourish conversations by maintaining an air of open-minded, enthusiastic-but-not-gushing curiosity. Inviting your weary, wary teen into conversation lies not in being captivating but—I'm going to make up a word here—being *captivateable*. Pretend your son is an exchange student from Kazakhstan, or your daughter is a visiting niece from a distant state. Learn about the fascinating customs of their faraway cultures. Listen to understand before you assume, judge, or try to fix.

The crucial ingredient is restraint. Your calm tone, even cadence, and relaxed facial expression invite trust, which leads to candor and expressiveness. Learn to listen to your own voice—a raised pitch is much more common than shouting, and no matter how thoughtfully crafted your words, a tight-throated, tense, or irate delivery signals to the teen that you are lacking in conviction. This instantly opens the door to argument and defiance.

Teenagers don't perceive their environment the same way adults do. Their brain circuitry is evolving; studies using functional brain imaging show that adolescents respond more intensely than either children or adults to emotionally loaded situations and images. They're particularly sensitive to facial expressions of anger and disgust. Their hormonal systems are changing, and this has been shown to impact their response to stress. For these reasons, your teenager may perceive a slightly irritated tone as yelling, mocking, or demanding. An eye roll or shrug can feel like disdain or anger. This has everything to do with the teen's developing brain and body and may not at all reflect what you intended. But the kids aren't always wrong: teens are keen perceivers of emotional subtext. When your facial expression, posture, or tone doesn't match what you're saying, they trust the nonverbal expressions over the spoken words.

The best way to keep the peace is to control your delivery. Channel the masters of reassuring nonverbal communication: bartenders, hairdressers, the hotel concierge. This acting challenge may be hard to pull off when your baseline emotion is anxiety, but it's a necessary skill. If you want teenagers to talk with you candidly, you must play the safe and placid harbor in their raging life.

The shift in how you communicate will begin as soon as your child enters puberty. Preteens are a combo pack: unabashed narcissists who are also cruelly self-critical and embarrassed by their own existence. They keep up the facade of cool to cover their passion, shame, and humiliation. One sweet thirteen-year-old girl liked to hold hands with her mom when they walked down the street, but upon seeing any other teenager—even one she didn't know—she'd whisper, "Detach!" It was her mother's first lesson in that critical component of parent-teen communication: don't take it personally.

Keep in mind these basic principles:

- Acknowledge your teenager's anger, worry, or hurt without trying to fix it. Say "That sounds tough" or "You were disappointed" or "What are you thinking of doing about it?" Not "I'm calling that coach tonight!"

- Be temporarily deaf to the siren call of your own technology. When talking with your teen, let your phone ring, a text beep. Recognize that both you and your child long to be rescued from conversations that are confusing or embarrassing.
- Keep your list of rules lean but firm.
- Consider your teenagers' suggestions for alternatives.
- If they end the conversation in a snit or lash out and leave, do not follow.
- Allow them to have the last word even if your dad would have grounded you for the same behavior.
- When you explode, it teaches your teen that frustration is intolerable.

WHAT DO WE WANT? FREEDOM! WHEN DO WE WANT IT? NOW!

The engine driving most conversations with teenagers is their yen for freedom and your countervailing instinct to protect them. Humor and a light touch will improve the ride. Regarding rules and obligations, be good-natured and consistent: "Yep, these are the rules. I know your friends don't have any." If you're consistent, they don't have to test you. This means not only keeping your word but also being relentlessly predictable (even though they aren't) about things like dropping them off and picking them up on time.

Don't try to win arguments with teenagers using logic, evidence, or persuasion. Even if they see your point, it's not worth the loss of power, so they must resist: "That is totally unfair. You're ruining my life. NONE of my friends' parents [fill in the blank]!" And don't overexplain. Teenage males have limited attention spans, and the girls will become irritated or use your explanation as fodder for an argument. Instead, speak in a matter-of-fact and candid way about how increasing freedom is based on increased evidence of accountability:

"Show us that you reliably return home on time this semester and we'll consider a later curfew during spring break."

"Let's try this. We'll check your grades a month from now. If the teachers don't mention lack of preparation or overdue or missing work, I'll stop nagging you about due dates and assignments. I won't even bring up homework unless you do. But I'll still be here if you want to talk over strategy. Deal?"

Because a lot of teenage push back against rules is done to save face with peers, you can offer yourself as an excuse: "Mom and I are fine with being the bad guys. Tell your friends, 'My mother would kill me if she smelled smoke on me' or 'My dad would ground me for six months.'"

Feel free to suggest other justifications for responsible behavior as well. Even if teenagers don't appear to be listening, they are. If you made them wear a wire, you'd hear your words. For instance, they could tell their friends, "I'm playing basketball this season and that's why I'm not drinking." Sports practice is a handy reason to dodge any sketchy situation, as is rehearsal for group activities like theater, band, or debate team, or work commitments such as babysitting. With younger teens you can role-play these conversations. And you can always offer to respond to a coded text message—for example, the letter *q*—by texting, *Not emergency but need you at home right away. Will explain.*

A FEW TRAPS TO AVOID

Certain parental moves tend to either rankle teenagers or backfire and cause more conflict. Avoid these whenever possible.

Don't reprimand them in front of their friends.

When you must communicate your displeasure immediately (for instance, if they have been unacceptably rude to you in front of others), tell them, "You and I will talk about this later." If they continue to goad you, sternly say, "End of discussion."

Don't try to win back closeness by over-sharing about your life or gossiping about your friends or theirs.

Dealing with their own emotions and social life is hard enough.

Don't compare them to their sibling at that age or to their polite friend.

Resist saying things like, "Ramona finds me in the house before she leaves to thank me for having her over. You don't even look up when I come through the front door."

Don't criticize their friends or crushes.

What worked for dubious pals of your children when they were little is even more effective when they're teenagers: keep your enemies close. Instead of pointing out the blazing red flags about your daughter's boyfriend, invite him to dinner. The payoff is watching her gain new perspective on her own, leaving you free to say, "Oh, really? Yeah, I see your point. He brags a lot."

Don't provide goods or services and then grumble about it.

Whether it's doing their laundry, late-night chauffeuring, or ordering take-out pizza, do it graciously or don't do it. Avoid being a martyr. Learn how to say no without feeling guilty about it.

Don't promise to keep a secret from the other parent.

If the teen says, "Mom, I'm going to tell you something. It's really big. You have to promise not to tell Dad," you can reply, "I'll never make that promise, but I hope you'll trust my discretion." Allegiance between parents (whether or not they're still a couple) is critical to teenagers' peace of mind. The teen will probably end up confiding in you on your terms.

Don't say anything if they're ten minutes past curfew.

Teenagers have so few ways to assert their autonomy. If they're late by just a little bit, greet them with a friendly "Hi" sans irate undertone or raised eyebrows.

THE ART OF LISTENING TO TEENAGERS

Listening to anyone requires the excruciating practice of staying quiet and paying attention when you really, really want to be talking. The hectic schedule of most families adds an extra hurdle to listening to teens. Whether you're waiting out a torrent of gossip or trying to extract a few informative sentences, it all takes time, so factor that in to your approach. Then listen without defending yourself, correcting misperceptions, or apologizing. Listen to understand your child's perspective, not to decide whether it's accurate. Remember that listening does not imply agreement.

You and your children are not equals in ambition, experience, or street smarts. You want to stay close; they want to start moving on. As you listen, regard teenagers' phoniness and manipulative power plays as clumsy stepping-stones to separation. Curb any impulse to expose (and humiliate them for) their transparent excuses or shallow reflex apologies. It's easy to get defensive when they try to play you for a fool, but stay mum and let them have their say ("Mom, Dad, if I had known you guys would get upset, I *never* would have . . ."). As much as they may hope you're dumb, they know you're not. It's simply their job to try to get away with stuff, to lob and parry. Don't buy what they're selling, but don't retaliate with a character attack.

Reinforce your reputation as a serious listener by offering evidence. Recall their friends or rivals by name, and remark on specific situations they've told you about ("This reminds me of that time you and Sebastian walked the whole length of Golden Gate Park"). If the conversation offers you a chance, mention beliefs they've shared with you, for example, about injustice or karma. Don't use these convictions as evidence of a teen's double standards or your superior intellect, but as proof that you listened before and considered what he or she had to say important enough to remember—and that you are once again listening attentively.

You don't have to listen and respond in the same conversation. You can save your side for later. This is difficult because teens are insistent and their social lives are fluid. They want an answer NOW! By pausing the discussion you may displease not only your own child but possibly a horde of angry teenage zombies and their more lenient parents as well. No matter. If you need time to weigh the options, take it. You can bolster your confidence here by reminding yourself that you're being a great role model. When your child is being pressured by peers to "hurry up and take it . . . do it . . . grab it," she may recall your delayed response and say, "I need some time to think this over."

Finally, as critical as listening is, it's not always appropriate. Sometimes you can just say no. "Nobody's going to Lollapalooza. Not nobody. Not no how."

OLD YELLER (THAT'S YOU)

I find myself talking parents off the ledge of shame and guilt far more often than I do teenagers. The cause? They yelled at their kid. Mostly I say some version of "What else is new? You're the third parent to sit on that couch today with the same confession."

Why do parents get mad at their teenagers for making them mad? And then hold a grudge, stop giving them the benefit of the doubt, and get even madder next time? And feel terrible about it but aren't able to stop? Parents lose their tempers with teenagers more frequently than with younger kids because they are scared *for* them and scared *of* them.

When the thread of trust and connection feels so thin, it's hard to push yourself to stretch it further by confronting your teen about wrongdoing, cutting off his funds or freedom, or saying anything that will make him angry with you. Moms don't want to be *that* mom, the out-of-control screamer. Dads don't want to be *that* dad, the man who doesn't respect women or bullies a boy. But because you're a parent and not a child psychologist or crisis counselor, you will inevitably lose your cool.

And to your horror, it may feel great! Being mad is much more invigorating than feeling sad, hopeless, or impotent. All that grief (about your child growing up and you growing old) is less painful when eclipsed by righteous anger. When this happens, try to apologize before the end of the day. Without defending yourself you can say, "I'm sorry I spoke that way. I said things I don't actually feel because I care so much and want to [keep you safe, talk you out of your spiral of beating yourself up, or whatever is the specific issue]. I ended up saying things that, when I thought them over, are not accurate or fair."

Losing your temper occasionally is no reason to recuse yourself from the task of setting your teenager straight. I tell parents, "This is your job. Your kids are super smart and really dopey, and they do things that are devious and dangerous, and it's up to you to correct and guide them. No one in the family you grew up in was a master of diplomacy, so you're learning as you go." Maybe some people were raised with articulate, soft-spoken, fair, and forthright parents, but I've never met any. So calm or not, carry on.

TEXTING: TRAP OR TREASURE?

Texting gives teenagers a safe way to say howdy, share feelings, ask embarrassing questions, or admit to mistakes. The distance can allow for more sincerity and playfulness than do face-to-face conversations. It also allows for breaking happy news.

> *Mateo's family wants me to go to Utah with them again this summer!*
> *Who got picked to be County Fair and Rodeo Ambassadors? Who's*
> *getting a $1,000 college scholarship??? Me! Me and Katie! Yup!*
> *We did it, Mama!*

The best response to joyous texts? A short series of thumbs-up or confetti or shooting-star emojis unadulterated by flat-footed "where" and "when" questions. Those can wait until there's time for a more expansive in-person conversation that includes both hugs and hollers and the gathering of essential details.

But—and I see this increasingly in the once sanctified space of my consultation room—to parents, every text represents a possible red alert. It must be glanced at, just in case. Parents become like a cross between 911 operator and Task Rabbit. Only a fraction of teenagers' texts are genuine emergencies, but determining which fraction is a challenge because (even with emojis) you can't hear your children's tone. You can't see their facial expressions. You can't tell if they're choking back sobs or off-loading a concern so they can move on with their day. So unless they are Shakespearean in their texting content, it's out of context.

The surest way for a young person to become a confident and articulate communicator is to talk, especially to adults. Texting a parent makes it too easy to avoid such interactions. One client's son, who was new to driving, found himself at a gas station and didn't know how to pop the cover of the gas tank. Instead of asking someone nearby for help, he texted his mom, who was in session with me. Naturally she checked her phone and told the boy how to do it.

The most productive and confident teenagers and adults I know turn off or ignore alerts when driving, in a meeting, or working on an assignment that requires concentration. If you consider your teenager's increasing independence a long-term project, I encourage you to experiment with waiting a few minutes or a half hour before responding to a worried or wondering text, even if you're free. This pause will give your teen a chance to recover from a spike in anxiety or the motivation to find needed assistance or information. (And they have no problem waiting fifteen minutes or forever to answer *your* texts.)

A tougher behavioral modification for most parents is to cut down on their own texting. I counsel parents to pause before texting their child and ask themselves, *Can this wait? What will be the effect on my child—on her independence, privacy, social and academic life—to have Mommy or Daddy intrude on her?* Yes, it's efficient. You just need a little piece of information and you know this is when she has lunch. But you don't know what she's doing at this moment. Is she flirting? Is she comforting a friend whose parents are getting divorced? Is she talking to a teacher? Is she together with her own thoughts, figuring something out or enjoying a daydream into which you are about to insert yourself?

Rather than offering parents a set of ironclad rules about texting, I suggest they view it in terms of family citizenship. When children send you a text, they may be interrupting you. When you text, you may be interrupting them. The family can talk together about situations that are appropriate for texting during the day. The basic criterion is "Can this wait until we're together in person?" If it absolutely can't, keep the message as brief and fact-based as possible: *When do you need me to pick you up?* The less emotion, the better.

These guidelines don't apply to messages teens send to communicate things too heartfelt or difficult to say in person. In those cases, parents can respond quickly, with sensitivity, while still keeping their responses brief (in part because no digital communication is ever reliably private). The message can include appreciation that the child sent the message and a plan to continue the conversation in person: *Thanks for telling me. Talk tonight? XOXO.* This avoids the pattern I see so often, a frenzied back and forth, the teenager pleading or wheedling, the parent worn down and caving.

One final note on texting: don't get cornered. Texting is a great example of the principle of "just because you can doesn't mean you should." Frantic texts lend themselves to impulsive responses rather than reflection (about how the request, rebuke, or information download makes you feel) and investigation (for facts that confirm or refute your hunches).

LOST CONVERSATIONS: SIDE EFFECTS OF THE COLLEGE QUEST

A fifteen-year-old girl told me, "Every conversation with my mom feels like either a celebrity interview or a police interrogation." Teenagers need physical and emotional space. They need unstructured, adult-free time to learn to navigate their colorful inner world and the outer world as well. Today's teenagers also need to learn how to articulate what's on their mind. From formal research and casual feedback from employers, it's become clear that this generation communicates much better via text or online than in person. Learning to speak with ease and confidence is a skill that will absolutely give your child an advantage later in life. But if all you're talking about is school, the conversations will be tense and abbreviated. The teen will withhold what really matters to her, closing off an opportunity to delve into complex thoughts and feelings with a willing grown-up.

Among the families I see in session and meet during visits to public and private schools, certain patterns have emerged that are directly related to the parents' obsession with academic performance and college admissions. Test prep, test scores, which schools, how many— the relentless pursuit creates friction and highjacks opportunities for in-depth, heartfelt, mutually enjoyable dialogue. It dramatically degrades conversations between parents and their children.

My teenage patients have reacted to the pressure by becoming little psychoanalysts, able to dissect their parents' every frown and sigh. But ask them about themselves, and they shift into polite job-interview mode, formal and guarded. Like poker players avoiding the tell, they don't dare reveal their tentative passions or passing interests for fear their parents will smell résumé fodder and pounce ("You should do something with that!"). I recall a fifteen-year-old boy whose mother dropped him off for a session. She was no longer in the building, much less in the room with us. Still, he leaned close to me when he whispered, "Guess what? I'm writing a play."

Many teenagers get lost to themselves because their parents require so much emotional tending. Some (usually boys) go on strike, refusing to study or turn in assignments. It's what union organizers call "malicious compliance": they show up but don't work. Others, ever watchful and captive to their parents' need for status and security, joylessly overwork and even overplay (in competitive sports and/or frenzied rounds of socializing) until both their bodies and spirits are broken. I wish this were true only for the delicate outliers, but these are trends I see swiftly becoming the norm in my practice.

Parent Talk

Amid the rush to college acceptance, parents sacrifice the chance to observe their child evolving. They may think they know their son or daughter because they've brainstormed together about AP classes and community-service points, but they underestimate their spirit guide. Beneath their parents' radar, teenagers are hosting backyard concerts, doing photo shoots, creating webisodes, making beer from hops they planted by the side of the house. They can learn anything online, so they're following their interests and developing sophisticated skills and communities. Parents who are secure enough can watch this parade without getting judgmental or overinvolved, recognizing that self-expression is not a waste of time. Compassionate detachment is an excellent way to encourage teenagers' exploration of themselves.

"Parents try to fix too many mistakes before they happen. Let us enjoy failure so we can improve! Let me fail once," an articulate twelve-year-old boy lamented. Another said, "I'm just trying to warm up, to find out what I'm capable of." And a fourteen-year-old girl echoed the frustration of many others when she recounted this exchange: "I said to my mom, 'I hate it how my friends complain about getting B's. They think their life is over,' and Mom said, 'Why don't *you* feel that way?'"

TAMING THE TOPIC OF COLLEGE

Families caught up in the college race don't see how it creates shame and fear in their children (if they don't get into the "right" school) and resentment over all the time spent in test prep, which emphasizes tricks and memorization over intellectual depth. In the spirit of reducing unnecessary anguish and protecting students from having their high school years hijacked for the sake of their future, parents can take the lead in keeping the college campaign sane and realistic.

Since your community of peers is likely infected with the virus, gain perspective by reading about the financial, spiritual, and moral price of an overheated credentialing race. Try Yale professor William Deresiewicz's manifesto *Excellent Sheep: The Miseducation of the Amer-*

ican Elite and the Way to a Meaningful Life and Frank Bruni's *Where You Go Is Not Who You'll Be: An Antidote to the College Admissions Mania.*

To prepare for conversations about college selection, open your eyes to the child before you. Reflect on the questions below, which deviate from the usual "prep to meet your high school college counselor" worksheet.

- What did your child like to do when he was five or six or seven?
- In which kinds of environments does he seem both relaxed and invigorated?
- Is your child pushing for a particular type of school to compete with or distinguish himself from a sibling? To please you? To displease you?
- Is there a field of study he's expressed interest in but not yet been exposed to? A part of the country or world he's drawn to?

After you've had a few chats on these topics with yourself or your child, give him a book that will help him investigate his interests or appetites. It doesn't have to be about colleges; it could be a book about a particular state or city or field of study. There's so much college information online that a printed book can serve as a refreshing way to focus on just one enjoyable aspect of the search. It also signals your support of his individual passions over the pedigree of the schools. If he ends up with some eccentric choices on his wish list, let him pursue them (if the financials add up) but require him to pay the application fee.

When touring schools, always wait for your child's response before offering yours. Heed her gut reaction to the campus. My younger daughter had a Goldilocks experience: she described the students at one school we visited as "too happy," at another as "too sad." A half hour into our visit to her future alma mater she said, "Mom, this is home."

Remind your teenager that every acceptance involves an element of luck or an inside game (for example, status, influence, or wealth of the parents). Statistics about transfer rates can mollify a teen's disappointment or worry—one third of college students transfer to another school before graduating. Your child may or may not end up loving the college he attends, but if he doesn't like it, he can always switch to another school.

For students, the process of deciding where to apply to college, waiting to hear, and being accepted or rejected is like dating naked and getting your heart broken in public. It's especially hard because so much seems to be riding on their decision, yet they're too young to really know themselves. Your adult perspective and level-headedness are their anchor in this hurricane.

Last but crucially important: make the dinner table a college-free zone. You already have a family rule not to use phones during meals; make it include no talking about college, and see how the conversations expand into more varied and interesting territory. This also limits the collateral apprehension younger siblings will experience as they gird themselves for their own college marathons.

THE MISSING LINK MAY BE SLEEP

Next to college-admissions madness, lack of sleep has the most unrecognized detrimental effect on the relationship between parents and teenagers. It's not uncommon for parents to mistake their teenagers' sleep deprivation for a mood disorder, attention deficit disorder, or impaired memory. Panicky parents show up at my office when a teen's disposition or productivity tanks or when every conversation devolves into a fight. One of the first things I ask them about is sleep. Teens need an average of nine to ten hours a night. Current studies of children and teenagers connect poor sleep habits with increases in anxiety, depression, impulsive behavior, and decreased academic performance.

Getting by on just a few hours of shut-eye has become both a tactic for time management and a badge of honor among teenagers. Interviewing students about how much sleep they get, I was reminded of Navy SEALs or Army Rangers. One soberly stated, "I get ten hours," but the rest reported, "I get six," "I get four," "I don't get any, ever!"

For adults, sleep prevents excessive weight gain by allowing the body to process carbohydrates efficiently; strengthens the immune and cardiovascular systems; and protects against depression and irritability. All good. All worthy. But for teenagers, who are developing physically and laying down neural tracks that will last a lifetime, the benefits of sleep are more extreme. One example: during sleep, electrical signals in the hippocampus (the memory center of the brain) reverse their direction, going backward to "edit" unnecessary information from that day's input and reset the synapses so they can better absorb new information the following day. This is critical for teens, who are still growing and are tasked with a heavy load of learning. Sleep also increases response time in athletic performance. It literally refreshes teenagers' minds, bodies, and spirits.

Studies of adults show that when people who normally get seven or eight hours of sleep reduce it to five or six, they eventually become convinced they have adapted to the loss. But University of Pennsylvania sleep researcher Philip Gehrman reports, "If you look at how they actually do on tests of mental alertness and performance, they continue to go downhill. So there's a point in sleep deprivation when we lose touch with how impaired we are."

One way to determine if teenagers aren't getting enough rest is by how often they get sick, because sleep-deprived people are more susceptible to illness. If your teen is sleeping little and frequently falling ill, have a discussion about which activities can be scaled back. They may resist because they don't recognize how impaired they've become. Through trial and error, find a way to make adjustments. Like adults, some teenagers are larks and some are owls, so take that into account when devising a sleep schedule with your child.

CALMING A TROUBLED TEEN—AND KNOWING
WHEN THE TROUBLE IS SERIOUS

The average teenager is regularly flooded with dark emotions—shame, anger, hopelessness, helplessness. At these moments you may be tempted to minimize her sense of doom and remind her of the joy she's felt in the past and is sure to feel again. This isn't helpful because her capacity to think is frozen. She's stuck in an unbearable present, and imagining a vague future happiness is too abstract.

Jaime Lowe, in a piece for the *New York Times* called "How to Talk to a Stranger in Despair," interviewed crisis-negotiation specialist Sergeant Mary Dunnigan about her techniques for talking suicidal people off ledges. With some modifications these strategies are surprisingly apt for talking teenagers through their emotional turmoil. The key is to keep the conversation going even when your child is making scary threats, using distorted and illogical assumptions, or catastrophizing. Try these tactics:

- Listen attentively without interrupting.
- Don't criticize.
- Don't try to argue her out of her funk using common sense.
- Don't try to solve the problem right then and there.
- Repeat simple, comforting phrases such as "I'm listening," "Ouch," "That sounds rough."
- Say, "Let's take a minute because I want to make sure I understand. What I think you're saying is that your art history teacher plays favorites. Is there more to it?"
- Gently and tentatively offer a longer view. "His class will end at spring break and you'll never have to take anything else with him, is that right?"
- Try to turn the teen's attention to a small problem or discomfort that can be attended to right away. Is she hungry? Feeling grimy? Would a hot shower help? ("You have to get them to feel the cold and get hungry, so they're not only thinking about their internal despair," says Dunnigan.)

Occasionally (but not as often as the more hysterical corners of the Internet would suggest), a teenager falls into serious despair or depression. It's trickier to know when to worry about teenagers than it is about younger children because teens are so secretive. Still, there are signs that will let you know it's time to seek the help of a professional.

Are they hiding in their room more than usual?

All teenagers escape to their rooms, but if you notice a drastic increase, you may want to pay closer attention to what's happening in the rest of their life.

If they consume a lot of social media or games, are they mostly just observing?

Research has shown that this behavior signals a higher risk for depression and anxiety because the teens are making social comparisons but not using the sites to connect. In order to figure out if this is the case, you'll need to discreetly ask about their online habits, since any sites or apps that matter to them will probably be blocked to you. Listen for what they say they've discovered online, who they've met, what they're doing. Does it sound like an active portal into a community that's exciting and matches their interests, or like passive consumption? This may not be obvious. For instance, one thing boys do that puzzles parents is watch videos of other people playing video games. That's passive, but it's also fun and he's learning new gaming strategies. You can always ask in a genuinely curious tone, "What is it you like about watching the other people play?"

Are they participating in class?

Some students are always more outspoken and engaged than others. To find out if your child's behavior has changed or if she seems to have mentally checked out, confer with one or more of her teachers.

Have their grades dropped?

Grades that are significantly lower than what is normal for your child may be a sign of emotional distress, but it may also mean that the student's workload is too heavy. Because parents are so focused on children taking the most advanced curriculum they can, it's common for the kids to be placed in classes for which they're not developmentally ready. They're overwhelmed but ashamed and afraid because they've swallowed the Kool-Aid, too. The stress, shame, and fear can result in depression.

Have they withdrawn from friends?

It's normal for middle and high schoolers to shift alliances, but pay attention to excessive isolation.

How do they act around younger siblings or cousins and extended family members?

Does your child's sweetness still come out, or has he or she gotten distant and hard?

Are there signs they could be injuring themselves?

This is more a problem among girls than boys. If they're cutting themselves, they'll wear long sleeves, pants, or long skirts when the weather calls for lighter attire.

Are they losing weight or going on extreme diets?

You'll see evidence of the weight loss, but the teen will deny the reason for it. It's common for teens with eating disorders to tell their parents, "I already ate."

What do the grandparents say?

If your child is close to his grandparents, ask them about this list. Maybe they've noticed (or your child has confided to them) something you've missed.

To ascertain whether your teenager could benefit from some sessions with a psychologist, look at his behavior in as many environments and get feedback from as many observers as you can without being overly intrusive in the child's world. If the different pieces of information form a troubling pattern, you'll want to make an appointment with a specialist who works with teenagers. You don't have to bring your son or daughter to the initial meeting. Just tell the therapist, "This is what we're seeing. Should we be worried? Do you want to meet with my child?"

WHAT TEENAGERS WISH THEIR PARENTS KNEW

When I give a lecture, I frequently spend part of the afternoon interviewing small groups of local middle and high school students about what they want their parents to know. At first their good sense, generosity, humor, and insight startled me. Now I just expect and enjoy it. Before we dive into specific tactics for talking with teenage boys and girls, take a look at what students from around the country would say to their parents if they had the chance.

What do your parents worry about that they don't need to?

> "They think bad grades wipe out good. They don't understand that when you judge us it just adds to judgment by class-mates, teachers, college-admissions people, and ourselves."
> "They worry, but I'm already worried. Or they ask if I'm wor-ried when I've decided, 'I'm just going to see how it goes.'"
> "They expect me to be as smart as my brother."
> "They ask too many questions. 'Who did you sit with at lunch? What did you eat? Tell me everything that hap-pened between eight and three.'"
> "They ask, 'Who are you texting? What are you texting about?'"
> "They think you have to save the entire country of Darfur to get into Yale."

What's one piece of advice you would like to give your parents?

> "If I ask you to check my spelling and maybe grammar, it doesn't mean I want you to rewrite the paper."

"There's a difference between pressure and motivation."

"My room is my temple."

"Don't act like there are only two positions at any moment: ahead or behind."

"Just because you were wild doesn't mean I'm going to murder someone or get someone pregnant."

"Please listen instead of thinking up the next thing you're going to say."

"Ask about my life, not just my grades. Say, 'How are you?'"

"Keep doing what you're doing, but calm down."

(A version at EVERY school) "Chill!"

What are the sweetest things your parents do that they may not realize you appreciate?

"When my favorite kind of ice cream just appears in the freezer."

"My dad watches *The Walking Dead* AND *Family Guy* with me."

Fiercely blushing sixth grade girl: "This will sound lame, but I love it when Dad tucks me in an extra little bit if he comes home late. Even though I'm already tucked in."

"When Mom talks to me about the world and not about college."

"She texts before a test, *Good luck, I love you,* instead of texting after. *How did you do?*"

"Mom gives me tiny surprises, like a ring shaped like a pancake that was pancake-scented."

"Dad says to Mom, 'Let him.'"

CHAPTER 7

The Exchange Student from Kazakhstan

Teenage Boys

Nobody loves me but my mother,
And she could be jivin' too.

—B. B. King, "Nobody Loves
Me but My Mother"

His clumsy footprints trail through sitcoms, movies, blogs, and comic strips. He avoids speaking directly to adults, especially his parents, from the age of thirteen until college orientation. The subject matter of any voluntary utterance is limited: skateboard heel flips, his totally original *Clash of Clans* strategy, the catharsis and truth of hip-hop lyrics. Getting him to answer questions directly is nearly impossible. Decoding the messages hidden in his mumbled private jokes and slang is taxing. And the yield? Likely just another excuse or refusal, the usual dissembling or transparent lie shouted from behind his closed door.

The stereotype may make for great satire, but it's based on science: the neurobiology of normal child development. As a boy grows taller, his regard for his parents shrinks. How did the world's bestest dad morph into an irrational tyrant? The sweetest mom into a pesky nag? He doesn't know. But he does know where to find sanctuary from their badgering. After a stop at the fridge, he's safe behind the closed door of his bedroom. Freedom from the public humiliation of a surprise erection . . . his beloved bed with the old, worn *Star Wars* comforter. Headphones! Video game heaven! His guitar! Privacy, decompression. *Ahhh* . . .

Teenage boys' silence and secretive ways invite parents to fill in the blanks with their imagination. The news media prods their fears, implying that every teenage male is one frustration away from shooting his classmate, facing sexual assault charges, or online gaming himself into partial brain damage and debt. This noisy message from the outside joins up with a quiet despair hidden in the parents' hearts. They're grieving the loss of the precious little guy who begged a parent to lie down with him until he fell asleep, to read one more story, to listen to the funniest joke ever! That boy is gone, replaced by a guarded and gruff fellow who averts his eyes and stiffens if you lean in for a hug.

As he travels the road from boy to composed and generous young man, your son's reticence is to be expected. He's keeping a wider berth, one that can accommodate a posse of favorite friends at school, teammates, new inspirational adults, perhaps a girlfriend. If you don't take his brusqueness personally, chats with your teenage son can be funnier and more enlightening than those you'll have with anyone else. But certain rules and conditions apply. When it comes to talking to teenage boys, there are distinct dynamics between a mother or father and a son. Let's look at those first.

MY NERVOUS, NOSY MOTHER

For a teenage boy, self-control is a limited resource and his cache is used up before dinner. All day long he deftly follows a series of complex code-switching rules: he addresses teachers with respect; determines the precise blend of boasting, camaraderie, and playfulness that allows him membership in his friend group; and listens with care to the subtle but crucial directives of the orchestra leader, swim coach, or tutor. He arrives home depleted from the mental and physical exertions of his day. But wait. Who lurks just outside his bedroom door? The woman formerly known as Mommy, eager to hear EVERYTHING: "So! How do you think you did on the social studies test? Did you decide if you want to try out for the musical? Feeling ready for the meet on Saturday?"

The boy knows it's wise to avoid this conversation because his honest responses ("I don't know. Not yet. Not really.") will both disappoint and arouse suspicion. Which Mom will pass along to Dad. Which Dad will interpret as a call to arms. So the boy just mumbles or pretends he's sleeping or tries a stall using as few words as possible: "Later, Mom, lots of homework."

Adolescent boys back far away from Mom in part because she's female. She has breasts, which he will feel when she hugs him or see when she leans in to look at his homework. Since he can't predict how his body will react, it's best to keep a safe distance.

But it's also more complicated than hormones. Mom's default protectiveness—a natural and understandable impulse—will lead her to look for the dangerous potential in what the boy is telling her rather than to respond with neutral curiosity. Boys know that if they sound excited about an upcoming overnight trip to a nature reserve with their biology class, distracted Dad will probably respond, "Cool!" while Mom will say, "Cool," and then veer into a litany of questions about the weather, mosquitoes, adequate clothing, food, and the type of vehicle that will be transporting the students. As a mother, you might find it hard not to convey wariness in your tone even if you manage to monitor your words. You'll need to wean yourself away from those habits if you want to convince your son that it's safe to talk to you.

Throughout a teenage boy's development he longs to be confident of his mother's devotion and affection. This may come easily, or it may require the mother to take an accounting of personal injuries perpetrated by the males in her life: brothers who were permitted to torment her or whose cruelty was ignored; the emotional gap created by the absence of her own father; the lack of strong, kind men overall in her childhood or in her current work environment. This self-inventory allows a mom to protect her son from her own prejudices and projections. It also lessens the chance that she will unintentionally treat him as a scapegoat, an easy target for revenge.

When talking to your son, resist beginning every encounter with a flood of queries or words of any kind. Allow for some warm-up time. A relaxed facial expression and friendly gaze send a simple nonverbal message: *I'm happy to see you.* Proffering food, rather than inquiring whether some is desired, knocks his defenses right down. For conversation to flow, it's essential to pick up cues, to sleuth out and demonstrate fascination about his current enthusiasms and convictions. Consider this shopping list a sixteen-year-old handed his mom when she asked what he wanted at the supermarket:

- Broccoli and cauliflower, organic, locally sourced
- Organic almond milk, unsweetened only
- Cashew butter, raw, organic
- Beef—grass-fed

Telling me about it later, the mom said, "Can you believe this? Since when is he so pure? Two nights ago he was wolfing down tacos from a street cart. 'Beef—grass-fed' costs twice as much as regular beef!"

Though it might strike the mother as outlandish, this list is the type of item that invites sincere probing if you can control the urge to roll your eyes. Why grass-fed beef? Is it about sustainability? Taste? The likelihood that grass-fed cattle are treated more humanely than those housed in an agri-corporate feed lot? The boy's replies will tell you about his current sensibility, and your questions will assure him that you value his perspective.

Around the house you can take advantage of two avenues into conversation. One is accidental: he wanders into the kitchen, you're fixing dinner, and you say, "I need help chopping these veggies. Thanks!" If he forgets that you prefer the carrots to be of uniform size and sliced on the diagonal, maybe don't mention it. Or, "We've got two rakes and lots of leaves in the yard. Let's give it a go." Or, "These towels need folding," "Help me decide which magazines to toss and which to keep." As you're working side by side, he'll start to talk. You'll listen, offering occasional murmurs of interest or asking a question that pertains directly to what he's discussing (and does not detour into an area of his life you're worried about).

The more intentional version of this is an offshoot of the family citizenship from which no child, no matter how scholarly or talented, should be exempt. Your son needs to be responsible for some household chores, and while he's doing them, you can be there, too, working on tasks of your own—not grilling him but making a general comment about something that does not involve him, like the news or a piece of local gossip. Even if he's wearing headphones, your presence in the room may disturb the airwaves enough for him to unplug and add his two cents to your remarks.

One thing I caution moms against is demanding too much tech support from their teenage sons. Just as I ask parents of small children, "What percentage of your conversations consist of nagging, chastising, and reminding?" I ask parents of teen boys what percentage consists of pleas for help with devices. If it's too often, the boys may feel exploited.

For mothers of sons, then, the main tasks are to actively look for ways to engage on topics of the boys' choice and to tamp down a natural tendency to worry and overthink. A reliable antidote for the anxiety: confer with a trusted friend or relative (not your partner) who knows your son well. Seeing him through the eyes of a loving observer will supply a new perspective and possibly allow you to get a good night's sleep.

MY WEIRD, JUDGMENTAL DAD

Teenage boys withdraw from their fathers because, from their point of view, *Wow, Dad has really changed.* At five, boys see Dad as heroic—up so high, especially when they're riding on his strong shoulders. It's a privilege just to be near Dad! The majesty of playing Monopoly *alone* with Dad, going to the dog park together and stopping on the way home for donuts, of strapping bikes onto the car and driving to the lake for a ride and a swim—all this makes a young boy feel powerful and protected.

Then, sometime between nine and fourteen, the admiration fades. The natural rhythms of boy and man diverge. Now a father-son fishing trip can seem like an innocent but oppressive abduction—slow-paced, even lonely. Dad's taste in music and movies, his pride in scoring box seats at the playoffs . . . *meh*, compared to the son's love of, as psychologist Carl Pickhardt describes it, "the renegade, the urban, the percussive." Now he's enthralled by YouTube DJs, the way his coach curses *all the time*, and, of course, every single thing about his nineteen-year-old cousin Kai, so cool and perfect and, unlike Dad, "really fun and understanding."

It's not just that father and teenage son may now have fewer interests in common. Spending time with Dad means he may be judged in a negative way because of his father's outdated grasp of . . . everything! Yet even though the teenager views his dad in a less exalted way, he still wants his approval and fears his criticism.

Fathers do tend to be more critical of their sons as the boys grow older. They mean well; they want to make sure the boys will be able to fend for themselves out in the world. But dads sometimes aren't aware how much the ground has shifted for young people (and will surely keep shifting). If the American Way decrees that every generation must surpass the previous one, how are these boys going to surpass their fathers? The dads assume their own road to success is the most reliable path for their sons, but that path may not even exist anymore, at least not in a way the fathers would recognize. Parents don't understand the new economy, and dads don't necessarily understand what makes an appealing college candidate. The sons know this, but at the same time they're comparing themselves to their fathers and thinking, *How will I make him proud of me?* The whole predicament is overwhelming, and the easiest response for the boy is to withdraw.

How can fathers connect with this vulnerable yet prickly creature? By doing what they've always done best: hanging out and having fun together. A great many dads who adored goofing off with their boys when they were little don't realize that shared leisure time with a teenager is vital for maintaining that bond. Start with up-to-date versions of old pastimes: maybe a fixed-gear bike for his birthday so you can go riding together and he'll look cool while mastering a new skill. If you ski and your son snowboards, go to a mountain that permits both on the same slopes.

On the home front, you can binge-watch his favorite show with him and stretch to see the wit, thrill, and emotion in it. Order two pizzas. Calm down. You're not going to do this every day, but the shared experience gives you a new set of references and in-jokes— something to talk about that's actually interesting to your son. All these activities require faith and commitment because they're outside fathers' accustomed problem-solving mode.

Dads who fear they'll never regain their teenage son's respect and admiration can take comfort from Mark Twain's famous observation: "When I was a boy of fourteen, my father was so ignorant I could hardly stand to have the old man around. But when I got to be twenty-one, I was astonished at how much he had learned in seven years."

CONVERSATIONAL PLAYBOOK FOR TEEN BOYS

To set the stage for conversing with a teenage boy, it helps to recite a brief internal pep talk: *I'm going to pretend this young male is a student from a foreign land. He acts confident but is unsure of the territory. Behold his energy and enthusiasm! But don't confuse his size and IQ with maturity.*

Effective communication with adolescent boys is brief and direct. They won't tolerate lectures or long-winded explanations. Be brief but not blunt: you can be direct while also being tactful. Humor eases the way, but not if it's at your son's expense. Even if you both enjoyed joshing around when he was little and his main mode of communi-cation with friends is throwing shade, at this stage he's too sensitive for emotional roughhousing with parents. Sarcastic comments from Mom or Dad can cause shame and bitterness.

Testosterone is steering your son's moods and desires. The changes in his body unnerve him—sudden growth spurts and a cracking voice, or months when *nothing* happens and he doesn't grow an inch. Strong feelings are stirred but must be hidden, tears suppressed. On the bright side, unlike when he was a little boy and you had to speak to him loudly and face-to-face, in this new phase of life he possesses excellent hearing and full command of language. His lack of response to "a simple question, damn it!" doesn't mean he hasn't heard or understood you. It means he's thinking about it or doesn't want to respond. Therefore, as teenagers themselves so often say, you don't have to yell.

Expect to feel envy. You used to be his hero, but now your son is looking elsewhere for inspiration. His ability to attract mentors is a sturdy predictor of his future success in the outside world, so default to encouragement rather than suspicion when he lists the mind-blowing attributes of a favorite teacher, coach, older student, or new girlfriend.

Speak openly but not too often about your own missteps or foibles. Share these anecdotes lightly, with the acceptance that no one ever outgrows doing dumb stuff, making mistakes, or feeling embarrassed.

Be on the lookout for free information. If he starts to talk, put down your device or swivel your chair away from the screen. Allow him to continue speaking until he draws the conversation to a close. If he's negative—complaining about the assholes at school, unfair grading policies, or favoritism—consider it a compliment. Letting off steam is welcome here. If his tale is dull, overlong, or lacks a compelling narrative arc, listen, listen, listen, and then ask questions both to show your enthusiasm and to subtly demonstrate how to summarize the story.

The Exchange Student from Kazakhstan

Parent: You're saying you want to be a DJ?
Son: I have everything I need! Jasper's getting paid to be the DJ at Sophie's birthday and he only has five hours of music.
Parent: And you have four days!

Don't use reason or evidence to disprove his ignorant views, exaggerations, or distorted perception. Don't insert your own agenda or pivot to a related topic. Keep in mind that today's goofy or outrageous talk is a foundation. It will mature into serious sharing of feelings and opinions if you prove yourself a trusted traveler. This will take time and patience.

In all conversations with your teenage son, keep in mind the following.

Tone and Pitch

A soft tone has power to calm, reassure, and convey respect even if your message carries a needed rebuke. Instead of shouting, try repeating what you said more gently. Or evaluate the importance of your question or comment. Consider letting it go.

If your son's tone is contemptuous, resist responding in kind. Despite his braggadocio, his pride is exceedingly delicate. A caustic tone feeds the self-mockery he battles as he wakes up to find the worst acne eruption yet, recognition that he's the second shortest boy in eighth grade, disappointment that he didn't make the baseball team. A polite tone conveys respect, which feeds his self-respect.

If he hasn't followed through on a responsibility or agreement, try not to sound indignant or disgusted. Simply say:

"We agreed that I wouldn't get involved in your homework if your grades were solid. They've slipped, so now I'll be monitoring how you spend your time."
"I'm sorry you're not feeling well, but you need to take out the trash cans."

When he talks about his feelings, use an accepting, questioning, almost tentative tone: "Sounds like you're disappointed in Carter?" Be aware that your interpretation could be wrong, but if you're right it could be even more painful for him. If he denies it, acquiesce: "I wasn't there, so I don't know the details. I'm sure you have a better take on this than I do."

Tempo

Slow it down, lest your quick-thinking son feels he's in a debate. Insert a pause between his query, attack, or petition and your reaction. This gives you time to reflect, even if only for a millisecond. When your impatient son demands, "I've got to know *now*!" remind yourself of your right to ponder.

Facial Expression

While little boys are often too busy dashing about or hyperfocusing on a game to study a parent's countenance, teenage boys have an uncanny ability to read your nonverbal messages through walls. If your son is near enough to see you wince or smirk, even if it's just a flash in his peripheral vision, he'll register it. Sometimes you'll want to communicate with just a look. At other times, exercise the same mindful discretion with your expressions as you do with your words.

Body Language

Mothers: A brief affectionate pat on his back, arm, or head (calibrated by how comfortable he seems with the contact) is probably acceptable while you're talking to him. Other than that, maintain a respectful physical distance. Don't crowd him or attempt to snuggle close on the couch.

Dads, sometimes you get to hold him tight. Think about the spontaneous body language of football players celebrating a big win:

bear hugs, butt slapping, and yelps so exuberant that these graceful men lose their balance and end up in a pile of joy and fellowship on the ground. If you and your son share in a personal best—"Dad! We actually hiked this sucker in under three hours!"—you can let loose, holler, and hug. If even in jubilation he shies away from unabashed physical intimacy, stick with the hoot and holler and some hearty high fives.

Timing

If the conversation is important and could potentially take tricky turns, pick a time when your son is not hungry or fatigued. Most people aren't at their best first thing in the morning, and this is especially true of teenage boys on school mornings. The optimal time for discussions he'll need to remember depends on your son's sleep schedule and internal clock. Pay attention to when he seems to be most calm and alert, and time your chats accordingly.

Setting

Most males prefer to talk while you're sitting next to them or doing a physical activity together rather than engaging in prolonged eye contact. Listen or float ideas while driving, walking, in the bleachers at the stadium, waiting for the movie to begin, cooking together, playing fetch with the dog, or in his bedroom with the lights down low. Dim light or darkness can provide teenage boys a welcome shield from parents who want to read every nuance of their facial expression: *Did I see a tear? A look of contempt?* It also offers cover to the boy who is self-conscious about his still uneven proportions, hair, or acne.

WHAT *NOT* TO SAY TO A TEENAGE BOY

"What are you doing in there for so long? With the door closed?"

"Why didn't you say something?"

"How did Simon and Jack do on the test?"

"What's wrong with you?"

"What were you thinking?"

"So what's Tyler's mom like?" Prodding for intel about their friends or friends' families will arouse suspicion: Why do you need to know? Don't you trust him to choose good affiliations?

"See what you can do when you apply yourself?"

"You're amazing! You are *so* gifted!" The paradoxical alchemy of boys' motivation is that telling him he's talented is likely to discourage him and, because of his natural self-doubt, invite rebellion.

"I can't believe you like this band! They have zero talent." Don't denigrate his taste. It's similar to criticizing his friends, which is like criticizing him. But you can say in a good-natured tone, "I must admit, I'm not getting this music yet." This puts the onus on you and makes your son happy because you're acknowledging how unknowable and separate from you he has become.

"We need to talk." These words will cause your son to shrivel up or quake. When delivering new rules or negative feedback, just come out and say it in the simplest way possible.

WHAT *TO* SAY TO A TEENAGE BOY

Be businesslike.

A frank, professional approach works best when communicating responsibilities, questioning him about his schoolwork, or discussing any of life's chores. Avoid pleading, grilling, or tense reminders of what he promised to do. Detach! Bargain and give him choices when appropriate. Ask, "What's your plan?" in an earnest manner.

Be straightforward.

When your son's body can't be trusted not to betray him (see acne, erections, cracking voice), it's natural for him to be a bit paranoid. Teenage boys typically expect their parents to have a hidden agenda. By communicating in simple, direct, and honest terms, you're taking into account his islands of thickheadedness and suspicion.

Be relaxed and specific with your compliments.

To minimize his embarrassment, give positive feedback in an offhand way: "Nice moves on the field today." Express your thanks sincerely and specifically: "You and your friends did a fantastic job cleaning up after the party."

Be agreeable.

Find opportunities to say:

> "Sure."
> "Yep."
> "Certainly."
> "You bet, name the day!"
> "Thank you, sir."
> "Good idea. I hadn't thought of that."

Help him expand his emotional vocabulary.

Just as you did when he was younger, when he talks about feelings, mirror back what you sense he's experiencing beyond the basics of sad, mad, and glad: "Sounds like you were relieved . . . proud . . . grateful . . . confused . . . feeling left out . . . frustrated." Although teenage boys obviously know the definitions of these words, they still may need some subtle guidance attaching them to specific emotions.

Let him know you cherish him and enjoy his tribe.

As a counterforce to our male-bashing culture, and because you do, say, "I love you." And also:

> "I sure lucked out in the son department."
> "Hungry? What can I fix for you?"
> "Your friends are welcome to stay for dinner."

Start every day with a welcoming "Good morning" and a smile.

Even if he's scowling or glum. Give a warm salute. Or pat his shoulder or tousle his hair (if he hasn't already styled it just so).

Let him know he's on your mind during the day.

Say, "I thought of you today when . . ." followed by something you know he'd appreciate. This is a love letter to children of all sexes and ages.

GOODWILL FOR TEENAGE BOYS

The teenage boy's most valued currency is respect—for his privacy, agency, opinions, and growing pains. Look for ways to convey your respect and the bank account will steadily accrue.

Knock on his door and do not enter until he has given you permission.

This is a Triple-A Bond of Goodwill for all teenagers. It also increases the likelihood that he'll respect *your* closed bedroom door.

Trust him.

"I ran into Louise, and she asked if you could walk and feed her dog while she's away this weekend. She'll pay you. She left directions on her kitchen counter and the key is under the back door mat. Here's her number. Just give her a call and let her know if you're available."

Let him speechify without cutting him off.

You are not a fact-checking journalist or the PC police. Delete the belittling word *mansplain* from your vocabulary. Try to discriminate between innocuous fibs and statements intended to cover up serious wrongdoing. Only call him out for the latter.

Don't take his public standoffishness personally.

Resist feeling rejected if he pretends not to know you when you're walking down the street. He's practicing independence. Extra points if you don't mention it at all, even when you're both back home.

Get a dog. Don't ask him to help take care of it.

For boys, dogs are the opposite of parents. They don't talk. They're not nosy. You can scratch their belly and it makes them happy. Their ears are velvety. You can touch them as much as you want (you can't touch Mom's hair the way you did when you were little). You can tell a dog all your troubles, and it'll lick you and not offer advice. You can go on a walk with a dog and not feel self-conscious, like you're going alone and have no friends. You can go to the park and other places where there are humans who will mostly be looking at your dog and not ask what grade you're in or where you're applying to college.

Why shouldn't caring for the dog be one of your son's household responsibilities, as it might have been when he was younger? Because for teenagers, dogs and cats can act purely as antistress drugs and the cheapest, funniest form of therapy that's available. Nothing else can serve quite the same purpose.

Be flexible.

A demand for rigid compliance invites rebellion. Accept approximations of politeness and cooperation. Keep in mind that even when he's a head taller than you, he's a beginner at most of the everyday details of adult life. So if he didn't notice the gas tank was empty, let the first oversight be for free.

CHAPTER 8

The Visiting Niece
from a Distant State

Teenage Girls

Success is not a straight line, but an unpredictable scribble.

—Madeline Levine, author of
The Price of Privilege

If trying to converse with your teenage son feels like the world's most frustrating game show, at least he doesn't corner you. Most teenage girls produce a tsunami of parent-directed (mostly mother-directed) verbiage. Your daughter may rail against you, insult you, and treat your rules like human rights violations, but at least she talks. This gives you something to work with.

Parents suffer feelings of loneliness and grief when their adorable baby girl reaches puberty, just as they do with sons. But with daughters it's compounded by fear about the potential dangers that await her, especially sexual coercion or assault. Arguments and power struggles often leave parents of teenage girls outraged, hurt, or bewildered. But farsighted parents can encourage the separation process, making for less friction as the daughter pulls herself free. With practice you can detach from the drama but be there for her with good sense, good humor, and great-but-not-perfect expectations.

Parent Talk

MY MOTHER? MY SISTER? MY FRENEMY?

When a daughter gets home from school, she doesn't necessarily make a beeline for her room. Often she'll stop to download her day to Mom. Locked eye-to-eye across the kitchen table or bent together over a cell phone, mother and daughter get stuck in a feedback loop of concern over the girl's appearance, grades, and popularity. Teenage girls are much more easily rattled than boys. The boys may be painfully self-conscious about their looks or height, but they also figure, *I'm a pretty good ball player* or *My band is going to be BIG. I know it!* A boy is less likely than his sister to agonize over the difference between a B plus and an A minus, or to feel devastated about not getting invited to Ellie's party. And a son isn't about to relinquish any of that info to his parent anyway. A daughter is much more likely to share (and share and share). And just as she did when her daughter was younger, Mom feels and mirrors the girl's emotions.

Suniya Luthar, a developmental psychologist and preeminent researcher on adolescent vulnerability and resilience, found that mothers of middle school girls are the least happy of all parents. "Mothers are essentially the 'first responders' to children's distress," she writes, "and now they must figure out how best to offer comfort and reassurance, as the old ways—hugs, loving words, and bedtime stories—no longer work." Comforting a teenage girl may require a level of sensitivity and patience you've never before had to muster. There's no reliable formula because the girls are so mercurial. You just have to experiment. Contentment comes to those who endure, Luthar promises: "Our data clearly show that the happiest mothers are those whose children have grown into adulthood." Talk about delayed gratification.

Over the years I've seen a troubling trend: mothers who have been devoted and insightful parents get unmoored when their daughters enter their teen years. It's commonplace now for a sibling dynamic to creep into the mother-daughter relationship, and the girls are put in the position of being both Mom's adversary and her pal. Some mothers angle to be popular with their daughter's friends, hoping to catch some of the sparkle and beauty of youth, to hear the jokes and the gossip. Few daughters welcome this version of Mom as big sister.

Today's increased academic pressure further complicates the teenage girl's passage into independence. Because girls lack the boys' ability to shut the door and withdraw, the forced collaboration with Mom is more troublesome. As mother and daughter toil together like yoked oxen, the daughter's criticism, exasperation, and hostile comments—all natural expressions of her need to separate—may be experienced by the mom as a deep betrayal. Against such a torrid backdrop, the traditional thorny relationship between mother and teenage daughter has become especially volatile.

DADS AND DAUGHTERS

The challenge for fathers of teenage girls is twofold: resist backing away from the daughter once she enters puberty, and find ways to stay connected even though her mother seems so much more plugged into her life. Dads often feel pushed aside by the tight bond between mother and daughter, even if theirs is a love-hate relationship. Mom knows every detail of the girl's academic progress because she visits the school's web portal daily; Dad barely knows it exists. Mom spends hours shopping with the daughter and parsing the details of her social life; Dad loses track of the shifting friend groups. (These are generalizations based on thousands of families I've talked with over the years. I'm not referring to gender here but to domestic and child-rearing roles and responsibilities.)

Fathers who cede all territory to Mom feel the loss deeply. Prior to puberty, his daughter was a little pal, almost like a girl-boy even if she was wearing a tutu and tiara. They could hang out together, go to ball games or ice skating or Home Depot. They could wander the aisles of Costco tasting all the samples. She could sit on his lap, hold his hand, hang over his shoulder to read his magazine. As she looks and sounds more like a woman, adopts a saucy style and speedy slang-laden patter, or gets a boyfriend, it's easy for Dad to feel left out or awkward. But although she may not acknowledge it, a teenage daughter needs her dad.

To stay close, choose from a wide-ranging menu of activities, especially those that Mom doesn't object to but is unwilling to participate in: horror movies, music festivals, food trucks or ice cream shops, political demonstrations, going to a skate park. You can both take banjo or tennis lessons. Dad's customary role as Fun Czar doesn't have to come to a halt when his daughter turns twelve; he just has to investigate a bit to figure out where her new interests lie.

A father's ignorance about the minutiae of his teenage daughter's academic and social life isn't necessarily a handicap. In fact, it's usually a blessing. His presence can be a refuge where the girl feels unwatched and free. Here, she learns what it feels like to enjoy the company of a man who cherishes and respects her. This is the foundation of any woman's self-esteem. That's why it's vital for single moms to find a trusted man (brother, uncle, granddad, family friend) who can fill this role in the life of a teenage girl.

As mothers do with sons, a father should light up when his daughter comes home or climbs into the car after school. Eyes that beam love and approval, a smile, and a warm "Hi, sweetheart" should be the touchstones she can rely on every day. I've found with the families I counsel that fathers sometimes withdraw and stop talking to their daughters because they become afraid of them. Lacking the mother's willingness to plunge into personal topics ("Are you and Connor having sex?"), they go silent. Paradoxically, Dad shutting down (or being physically or emotionally absent) is what leads many young girls into earlier sexual activity, latching on to what I call the "teddy bear boyfriend"—a warm body to fill the space Dad left.

Mom's role in the healthy father-daughter relationship is to step back, not micromanage, and not criticize if events (especially meals) don't unfold exactly as they would have on her watch. A perceptive mother will hand over the reins and take advantage of the time off. A big-hearted and confident mom will encourage Dad to take the daughter on a college tour and trust his observations when they return.

THE STICKY WEB OF SOCIAL MEDIA

During the teen years girls are influenced by their phones nearly as much as by their parents. The social dance of their day never ends, measured in likes and followers and numbers. The rational part of a girl's brain knows she should put these digital quantifiers in perspective, but the emotional part takes them literally. Social media creates a trigger of envy and insecurity that perfectly fits the teenage girl's neurological development. On a minute-by-minute basis, she's gauging her worth and predicting her future. All the things mother and daughter fret about together are amplified by her digital footprint.

A study by psychiatrist Ramin Mojtabai and researchers at Johns Hopkins Bloomberg School of Public Health found that depression among teenagers increased significantly between 2005 and 2014, with a big jump in 2011. Girls were more affected than boys. The factors normally associated with depression—sociodemographics, household dynamics, and substance abuse—did not account for the increase. Worth noting: Snapchat and Instagram both launched in 2011 on the iOS (iPhone) platform. The study's authors don't remark on that correlation, but citing previous research they observe, "Adolescent girls may have been exposed to a greater degree to depression risk factors in recent years . . . mobile phone use among young people has been linked to depressed mood."

Parents' loving attention can counterbalance some of social media's pull. Your example makes the biggest difference, so silence your phone when you're talking in person with teenagers. You don't need to answer every text instantly or consult Google whenever someone forgets a celebrity's name. You grew up having conversations without peering at a phone—show the kids how it's done! Impress them with your ability to chat, confabulate, and crack jokes using only your mind and memory.

Teaching teens about the effect of technology on the brain may help them understand why their mood shifts so dramatically depending on the "likes" they do or don't receive. There's a growing body of research on this topic, the gist of which is that "likes" stimulate the same part of the brain as winning money or eating chocolate. No need to lecture them about tech addiction; just briefly and conversationally mention the research so they have a new context in which to view their reactions to social media.

CONVERSATIONAL PLAYBOOK FOR TEENAGE GIRLS

Conversing with teenage girls begins with a quiet moment of talking to yourself: *I'm going to pretend this lively young girl is not my daughter but my niece from a distant state. Behold her passion! See how her friends admire her. Marvel at her style. Note how quickly it changes. Wait at least one day before weighing in on anything she says.* Now proceed, keeping in mind the following guidelines.

Tone and Pitch

Avoid talking in a baby voice or whining, which is irritating to teenage girls. Don't yell even if she's yelling at you. Aside from that, the usual rules apply, with one caveat: you can't win. If your voice is calm and steady, she'll say, "Mom, why are you talking in that fake zombie voice?" She'll pick at the way you phrase things, how you pronounce words, how you ask questions. Refuse to take her bait and keep your tone modulated, but know that you'll be walking on eggshells anyway. Ignore her needling as much as you can. And don't worry, she doesn't talk to her teachers or friends this way, only you.

Facial Expression

Try to cultivate a pleasantly neutral "resting face," but recognize that it may not matter. Everything that applies to boys in terms of teenagers' hypersensitivity to facial expressions is also true for girls, but girls will challenge you rather than retreat ("Why did you get that look on your face? Mom, I can see you. What's wrong?").

Tempo

Like young girls, teenagers speak very quickly and are passionate advocates for their cause. Consciously remind yourself not to speed up when she does. Speak at your normal rate. You may find it helpful to practice some subtle deep breathing while she's talking as a counterbalance to the tension that's a natural response to listening to another person's anxious monologue.

Timing

You don't want to have a significant conversation with her when she's rushing out of the house, preoccupied, fighting with a friend, or has just gotten her heart broken. But when *isn't* she involved in some urgent matter? There may be no pause in the action since girls are so often texting or FaceTiming or otherwise communing digitally. Aim for a moment when she's well-rested and not running late. Then ask her to silence her phone while you talk.

Setting

Keep her company in her room while she's packing for a trip without offering a single suggestion unless she asks your opinion. Watch her apply individual fake lashes or change the laces (why, oh why?) on her brand-new Dr. Martens. Acquire a taste for chopped-up micro-conversations as you walk one block from store A to store B (she's still got a good memory and can pick up the thread). Recite the mantra, *Visiting niece from a distant state, visiting niece from a distant state,* and find out why she's a passionate fan of (anything).

Avoid trigger settings, for example, in her room if she's "casual" and you're a naturally neat type. Seeing the expensive dry-clean-only dress she begged for lying on the floor under a muddy boot, or two open bags of chips on her night table, can set an ugly conversational agenda. Instead find neutral territory.

SHE'S A COMPLEX PACKAGE

Mutually respectful, enlightening, loving conversations with teenage daughters are rare. They absolutely happen, and when they do you can put them in your affirmation pot. But more often you'll be contending with "Lisa Bright and Dark," as a client referred to her daughter. One minute she's furious with you, insulting you, barraging you with a combination of sensible arguments and absurdity:

> "UNFAIR! Alexander got to stay up past midnight when he was my age. I don't care if he was babysitting. It's time on a clock."
>
> "You make all these strict, bizarre rules because you have a lot of personal problems. And everyone knows this about you. And they talk about it all the time."
>
> "You're tired? Why are you so tired? What did you do today? You got to go to work and do interesting things. I was in PE with my sadistic volleyball coach!"
>
> "You think I should buy these boots? Are you insane? Yes, you are. You're an insane person. Do you see how shiny the zipper is?"

Five minutes later she'll want to sit on your lap or brush your hair. She'll ask you how an outfit looks. She'll beg you to make popcorn and watch the new sci-fi series with her. Savor these moments of camaraderie and consider them a preview of the relationship you'll enjoy when she returns home on college vacations. But be prepared for the pendulum to swing at any moment.

The Visiting Niece from a Distant State

Teen girls are agile and inventive litigators. I've heard hundreds of eye-popping stories, but here's a favorite. One morning a father who lives in Chicago had to go into his fifteen-year-old daughter's wallet to retrieve a credit card he had loaned her. There he spied a Texas driver's license with his daughter's photo and a stranger's name. Age: 21. He got his wife, and together they woke the girl, showed her the license, and demanded to know what was going on. Without missing a beat she said, "Yes, that's a fake ID. I have it so I can go to bars with Hayley and Karlie and Reed. I never drink! I go to bars because if I didn't I'd be going to house parties where there's drugs and it's unsupervised. So you should be glad! Bars are supervised. Mom, Dad, I *swear* I never drink."

They gave her back the license.

Years later, when the father was telling me this story, he still couldn't believe both he and his wife had fallen for it. "But she was so convincing," he said, and the admiration in his voice was clear. With daughters it's complicated.

ESTABLISH RULES OF CIVILITY

"She follows me from room to room yelling at me."
"The vicious things she says about the way I look make me feel like crap. How did I raise such a monster?"
"I feel like her punching bag. And I feel like punching HER!"

Teenage girls are mean to their mothers because they're under so much social and academic pressure and Mom is safe. It's no different from the dynamic that was going on when the children were small, but it's more painful. Lisa Damour, the author of *Untangled: Guiding Teenage Girls through the Seven Transitions into Adulthood*, offers an excellent approach to this problem. She makes a distinction between respect and politeness. Daughters don't need to respect their mothers, she says, and mothers don't need to demand that feeling from their daughters. The daughter can feel any way she likes. But in order to have the privilege of your attention she is required to speak politely.

Each family will define this term slightly differently, but here are some general rules of engagement that can be applied in both directions:

- No yelling.
- No global insults. (How to recognize? Sentences that begin with "You always" or "You never.")
- No interrupting the other person as soon as she begins to speak.
- Listen to points you don't agree with.

You can tell your daughter these rules and explain, "In this house, people speak to each other politely." But it has to be true. When I work with families where the parents are frequently unkind or critical of each other in front of the children, I remind them that while they've grown accustomed to eruptions and skirmishes, the children are learning about what to expect in relationships.

Snarky comments often come from Mom, who's criticizing Dad for things he's saying to the daughter that will supposedly damage her irreparably. It's unfair, but just as when the children were younger, fathers can get away with a looser approach than moms. I tell the mothers, "I'm sorry, but he can say things that are teasing and it can feel affectionate and connected. You say the same thing, and it hurts your daughter's feelings." When Mom develops more tolerance for Dad's verbal joshing, it's often the turning point to a higher level of civility among the entire family.

If you and your partner are being polite to each other and the kids, you're on firm footing for demanding the same of your daughter. She doesn't have to approve of your taste, your clothes, the questions you ask, or the food you serve for dinner. Remember, none of her behavior is permanent or predictive. Use the strategies below to establish rules of civility and end a conversation when *you* want to end it.

The Visiting Niece from a Distant State

WHAT TO SAY WHEN YOUR DAUGHTER IS . . .

Being Rude or Mean

Daughter screams, uses profanity, insults you. "I know you're very upset, but this is not a conversation. It feels like an attack and it's not going to get us anywhere because I won't listen to it. When you can tell me what you want me to hear in a calmer way, I'm ready to listen." Then stop responding to her. Do not get seduced into a counterattack.

Advocating a Cause That's Not Reasonable in Your View

Your ninth grade daughter says, "There's nothing to worry about. Willa's brother Miles is driving us all to Coachella. He's really nice. Don't you trust me?" Your reply can be one or more of the following:

"I do have a lot of confidence in you, and your judgment tends to be excellent. It's the situation I don't trust."
"It may be perfectly fine, but the temptation [or risk, or lack of supervision] is not something I'm comfortable with."
"Not yet. With your good track record I'm sure you can do this at some point, but I'm not ready for it yet." This is positive reinforcement instead of "Are you kidding? Maybe in two years!"

Refusing to Let a Topic Drop

This often turns into a daughter stalking you around the house, demanding that you engage. You can say, "This conversation needs to stop. I'm not thinking straight. Soon I'm going to say something I regret." You can tell you're running out of fuel when your thinking starts to get global and your fantasy punishments primitive: *She always flakes on the French homework just to piss me off. I'm going to ground her for a month. I'll take her phone and she won't get it back until Christmas.*

DON'T CRITICIZE HER STYLE, DO RAISE HER AWARENESS

Regarding your daughter's terrible taste in makeup, nail polish, hair, or clothing, my advice is to hold your tongue. She's trying on identities, like she did when she was a little girl playing with costumes. If her style gets too extreme, the school will rein her in. She may no longer ask for your honest opinion, but if she does and it's negative, use the same techniques you employed for younger girls. Either play the biased-Mom card ("You always look beautiful to me") or globalize it ("That's not a look I like on anyone").

Dressing in unflattering styles is painful to see but not risky for the teenager. But what about seductive clothing? It's possible that what you perceive as clearly provocative (teensy shorts, cleavage thrusting out of a demi-cup bra squeezed under a super-tight tee) does not appear to your daughter as risqué; it's just fashion. If you try to instigate rules, she can change into her preferred attire as soon as she's down the block. I'm not suggesting you let her wear anything she likes; I'm just acknowledging the limits of a parent's power. As you're sending her back to her room to change into something less skimpy, it might make some impact to say in a concerned tone, "A skirt that short is going to attract the attention of men of all ages, including creepy adult guys." Don't expect her to thank you for this insight. Your goal is to place the idea in her head where, ideally, it will grow from a tiny seed of hesitation into a healthy flower of self-awareness.

Teenage girls want to wear trendy outfits and feel the power of their sexuality, but they can't truly comprehend the effect tight, revealing clothing has on boys and men. Social media undermines their confidence about their physical appearance while all media pushes highly sexualized fashions. At the same time, there's a rapidly growing awareness of the pervasiveness of sexual assault and of violations of women's rights and dignity. It's confusing for a young woman (and adult women, too). How do you encourage your daughter to embrace her sexuality and develop a personal style that doesn't cheapen and objectify her body?

One approach is to talk about your own aesthetic sensibilities. Whose style do you admire? There are dozens of movies with female characters that can broaden your daughter's view of women and fashion. You're not expecting her to agree with your taste today, although she might. You're giving her ideas for tomorrow.

Commonsensemedia.org has a list of classic and new releases under a wonderful category called "Movies with Strong Female Characters." Watch these movies together, taking care not to let an agenda of consciousness raising crowd out your shared pleasure.

WHAT *NOT* TO SAY TO TEENAGE GIRLS

"Olivia's mom told me she's doing a college-interview boot camp this summer. Doesn't that sound like it would be so helpful?" Don't use comparisons with other teenagers as inspirational hints.

"Enough with the upspeak!" Upspeak is ending a sentence in a questioning tone. ("We were going to meet at the movies and then she canceled? And we had to reschedule?") Most girls outgrow this habit.

"You sound like a bored character on a reality show." The creaking, low-register, monotone delivery called glottal fry is irritating to many adults. Young people perceive it differently and may consider it authoritative and empowered.

"Do you know how often you say *like, you know*, and *um*? And end sentences with the word *so*?" Leave her alone about verbal tics and slang. Again, it's just a phase.

"Stop biting your nails, twirling your hair, playing with your split ends . . ." Psychologists understand these behaviors as products of teenagers' naturally high energy with too

211

little opportunity for release. Forced to sit through biology instead of hunting, gathering, or chasing after small children? Tapping your feet, talking nonstop during breaks between classes, leaning precariously back in your chair vents some of the pressure. Teenagers have to move. All these habits will likely disappear on their own.

WHAT *TO* SAY TO TEENAGE GIRLS

Compliment her choices, not her looks.

If you approve of something, she'll probably reject it. Opposing you gives her power. So if you want to pay her a compliment, make it about specific observable facts, not your personal judgment. Don't say, "You look adorable in that jacket" or "I love those earrings." Instead say, "That leather jacket looks so soft" or "Those earrings really stand out against your dark hair."

Remember issues she brought up and ask her about them without offering judgment or advice.

"I know you were frustrated in calculus last week. How's the new unit?" "Did you decide what kind of glaze you want to use on your bowl?"

Take the indirect route.

Broach awkward subjects or tender feelings by talking about characters in a movie or TV show. Don't be the one to point out the similarities between those fictional people and your daughter or a situation she's in. If she mentions the connections or shares some insights, tread lightly. These are precious and intimate moments when your best contribution is to listen closely and murmur an occasional "Wow. Interesting."

Stay open-minded.

"I hadn't thought of it that way" is a powerful and liberating sentence. You can model listening and changing your mind by saying, "Good point" or "I didn't realize there would be adult staff supervising the event. Now that you told me, you can definitely go."

GOODWILL FOR TEENAGE GIRLS

There are reliable ways to build credit in a teenage girl's bank of goodwill, and they are surprisingly simple.

Be discreet.

Daughters will feel safe about sharing experiences of shame, pride, heartbreak, loneliness, love, and appreciation for their friends—and may even ask for and follow your advice—if they trust that what happens with Mom or Dad stays with Mom or Dad.

Get a family pet. Don't ask her to help take care of it.

As with teenage boys, pets are therapeutic for adolescent girls. The dog or cat never criticizes her weight or gossips behind her back. Its love is unconditional and always accessible. She can hug it and stroke it and sleep with it. But while some girls thrive on caring for animals, others are not so eager. Some may even see dodging the pet care as a way to assert their autonomy. So just as with boys, don't insist on your daughter caring for the animal . . . just be thankful for the emotional support it provides.

Let her decorate her room and don't butt in.

You're not obligated to buy her a fantasy bedroom, but within the budget you set, let her go wild. Give her dominion over as much as possible, because she feels completely powerless.

Surprise her with little gifts.

This is risky because her tastes change from moment to moment, but it's worth it, especially if she's having a hard week. Say, "I remember you admired this when we were at the mall. If you don't like it, it's easy to return."

Be effusive when she does something thoughtful for you.

When you see generous or kind behavior, be very appreciative: "Sweetie, I'm so grateful to you for doing this. It really gave me a lift today. Thanks—you're the best daughter ever."

CHAPTER 9

The Opinionators

Teaming Up with Your Partner, Your Ex, the Grandparents, and "Olivia's Mom"

We live in an era of bountiful resources, available at the touch of a screen. When we no longer require the services of the online experts or real-life specialists we have summoned, they politely recede until the next time we need them. Not so your child's other parent or grandparents. They always have an opinion, and you *will* hear it. Not to mention the imagined rebukes of the other moms you see each day at the playground or at pickup.

To be fair, your child's other parent deserves an equal say in the rearing of your son or daughter. Grandparents are often able to cherish and encourage a child without worrying about developmental milestones or test results. And among the other moms you'll find not only insecure show-offs but also intelligent, generous, loyal women who will become lifelong friends. These Opinionators are your inner circle. Observing how you interact with them shapes your child's understanding of human relationships—*human* meaning imperfect, hopeful, extraordinary, fallible. A work in progress.

TALKING TO YOUR PARTNER ABOUT YOUR CHILD

The push and pull between mother and father is an ancient dance that's revised every decade. Roles mutate as the nuclear family strains to accommodate modern pressures and the definition of *average household* expands to include two moms or dads, college graduates returning to live at home, moms as primary breadwinners. Yet despite the changes, most families are still founded on a set of two parents, and that means two perspectives on child-rearing multiplied by a thousand ways to disagree.

From infant to high school senior, your child is listening. When you were growing up, you were alert to how your parents greeted each other at the end of the workday; you sensed the warmth or tension between them, and it reassured or rattled you. You know your children do the same, so you try to be a model of maturity and forbearance no matter the mounting store of grudges or frustration you've tucked away. Then you curse yourself for failing. What is reasonable to expect of yourself? Of your partner?

Let's begin with what is *not* necessary to be a successful parent. It's not necessary to be right about your child-rearing decisions. And I don't mean right compared to your spouse; I mean right, period. There is no "right." The perfect solutions to this week's crisis might not work. Or they'll work for some families and not others. They'll work on Monday but not Tuesday. Families are evolving organisms.

It's not necessary to present a unified front to your children. There's a myth that if they see a crack in the wall of Mom and Dad, they'll either exploit it or get scared, but it all depends on how you disagree. Civilized debate and compromise is a skill you can model for your children.

It's not necessary to always use your inside voice. Some families are hot, some are cool. Some homes are full of noisy verbal jousting, and others are mellow. Some families enjoy merry self-mockery; others delight in gallows humor. There's room for every flavor as long as the foundation is respect.

When it comes to raising children, no two parents will have identical sensibilities about appropriate levels of risk, fun, manners, or enrichment. But when one of them harbors a deep commitment to unearthing the very best choice and deep ambivalence about what it might be, the less anguished parent is often seen not as sensible but as neglectful and disloyal. In a great many of my sessions with parents I find myself repeating, "It doesn't matter." Yet we're living in an era where parents behave as if it *all* matters—as if every decision is life-and-death.

We parents have a huge investment in the quality of our children's lives. But it's not an entirely noble impulse: their well-being has become a proxy for our fears about the future and our dissatisfaction with ourselves, our partner, work, sex, aging, in-laws, and money. It all gets displaced onto the children, and arguing about them stands in for the other conversations we should be having. It's made worse by the culture's frantic pace. Urgent feels normal. When a disagreement with our partner arises, we rush to settle it instantly. No room for reflection, no time for compromise. No bandwidth for asking ourselves, *Could my spouse be right? Why am I reacting this way?*

PROXY BATTLES AND HOW TO RECOGNIZE THEM

In the average family (where no one is mentally ill, addicted, or abusive), most arguments about the children are proxy battles. The proxy battle is usually triggered by emotional wounds (mostly unconscious) from your own childhood. You're reliving and trying to correct the mistakes your parents made, and your partner is doing the same thing. Women (and some men) get into a habit of feeling victimized, carried over from a childhood where they had too little power or respect. Men (and some women) feel pushed around and confined, their confidence diminished, their playfulness stifled, carried over from a childhood where they worked hard to please a critical parent. These are only two of countless examples.

It's not possible to cleanse your memory and nervous system of all prior experience and solve each of your child's dilemmas through pure reason. Besides, those memories don't only result in neuroses and bitterness; they're also what made you the insightful, patient, and soulful parent you are on your better days. At the same time, you can learn to recognize when legitimate concern over a child is overlapping with hurts from your past or other unrelated issues. It's best if you can catch yourself doing this before you start discussing it with your partner, but it's easier to see the connection when you're trying to explain yourself out loud.

As always, tone is the first warning. Is your pitch rising? Do you sound dismissive, contemptuous, offended? How does your body feel? Is your heart pounding, is your throat tight? Are you clenching your hands, shaking your head, or jiggling your leg impatiently? Is your breathing shallow? Listen to your words. Are you saying, "You always . . . You never . . . I can't believe you . . . ?"

When you notice these signals, pause. Put the conversation on hold. This may be extraordinarily difficult because the problem is going to feel like a calamity and you're late for something and why hesitate when you know you're right? All the more reason to wait for a window of time when both you and your partner are rested, fed, and have fifteen minutes or more to devote to the conversation. Aside from a medical emergency, just about everything can wait.

BASIC MANNERS AND VOICE LESSONS FOR PARENTS

My mantra for both mothers and fathers is: *Stop worrying about the influence of the other parent and concentrate on your own behavior.* For example, understanding that children tolerate gruffer behavior from fathers than from mothers can help you mentally shift from alarmed to reflective: *Hmm. He just yelled at her to stop climbing the refrigerator like a monkey and get the hell out of the kitchen. Not what I would say, but his tone was light. Let's see how she reacts.* A sense of humor and trust in the good intentions of the other person build a more relaxed and loving home.

The surest way for parents to sustain this healthy perspective is by observing some old-fashioned manners. For instance, just as Mom holds her tongue regarding the monkey comment, Dad resists treating Mom like a servant, mocking her, or correcting her. The parents are consistently decent toward each other. They don't insult, curse, or bully each other. This models appropriate behavior for the kids, and it also signals that the parents are on the same team, even if they sometimes disagree, which makes the children feel safe.

Good manners for parents are the same whether you're a couple or are parenting separately (assuming that an objective third party would find both parents decent and well-meaning). You don't have to fake feeling affectionate or kiss your ex hello, but you can still be respectful and polite. Manners are behaviors, not feelings.

Traditionally, manners consisted of a lot of artificial-seeming rules about forms of address, who stands first, who pulls out a chair for whom. Though they may appear arbitrary, those rules meant that everyone knew what to do. They kept the social gears lubricated. In the same way, there are fundamental rules of conduct and vocal delivery that will make for a smoother, more gratifying relationship with your partner.

- Speak audibly and clearly, but don't yell.
- Limit shouting from other rooms.
- Keep your shoulders relaxed. No finger-pointing, frustrated shrugs, or "WTF?" gesticulation.
- Say please and thank you automatically and often.
- Use the person's name or an affectionate nickname at the beginning or end of a comment or question.
- When your partner is leaving the house, bid him or her farewell.
- When arriving home, wait in the car or on the street for a few moments. Take some deep breaths. Oxygenate your brain and body. Make your entrance without trailing in friction from the office.
- When your partner returns home, stop looking at the screen and swivel your chair or get up to greet him or her. Give a hug, a kiss, or a pat. If you're on the phone, end the call. Do this even if you're talking to your mother about your child.
- Don't greet the returning partner with a list of chores or reports of a child's misbehavior or crisis.

- Resist interrupting the other person when he or she is telling a story. Even one you've heard before. Listen without vetting it for child-safe content. Don't debate the facts or steal the punch line.
- At the dinner table, assign each family member a permanent seat. Children should not sit in the parents' chairs. Let them look forward to this honor when they become parents themselves.

Tone and body language carry more meaning than content. Groans, sighs, and smirks telegraph resentment, suspicion, or condescension. Other behaviors to avoid:

- Mumbling or speaking so softly that the other person must walk over to you to hear you.
- Vague or noncommittal responses: "Stop worrying! It'll get done."
- Delays in decision-making.
- Forgetting what has been agreed upon.
- Uttering the guaranteed-to-irritate "Fine!" or the teenaged "Whatever."

CIVIL DISAGREEMENTS

In a marriage your partner is always in close-up. As the image becomes sharper, it's easy to see the flaws. You assumed your spouse would forever retain all the qualities you fell in love with; instead, the two of you keep changing as you grow older. Friction is unavoidable.

You're going to disagree, but you don't have to fight. And you don't need to put on an act for the children; it's good for them to see how you deal with conflict. The unity you present to them isn't a facade of clench-jawed cheeriness and rigid rules, it's a habit of unwavering respectful communication.

It starts with awareness of nonverbal signals. When you disagree with your spouse, do so directly and verbally, not with covert grimaces or eye rolls to the kids. No head in hands indicating disbelief over how dumb men are, no raised eyebrows or openmouthed astonishment mimed to the children as the other parent leaves the room. You don't want to conspire with your child against your partner. If you can't help but express your surprise and dismay over something your partner has said or done, do it to his or her face and if possible with a touch of humor: "Yikes—you're taking the kids swimming now? Your parents are coming over for lunch. What, you don't want to see them?" Be generous in your assumptions. Maybe the other person forgot your plans.

When criticizing the other parent, first acknowledge what he or she did right. Aim for candor without rancor. If you're too angry or if the proxy-battle alarms start ringing, say, "I can tell that if we talk about this any longer, I'm going to say things I regret." Or, "We're not going to be able to solve this now. I'm too tired. I had a hard day. I definitely want to get back to it. We can talk it over after the kids are in bed [or tomorrow, or over the weekend]."

If you don't agree but don't want to argue or delay a decision, say, "I'm going to defer to you on this one. I'm not sure it's the best course of action, but let's try it."

If the kids are there: "Mom and I disagree about this and it's an important topic. We're going to think about it, discuss it some more, and then we'll let you know what we decide." Don't treat your spouse as a foolish clown who's refusing to bow to your superior wisdom or as a fun-hater who's always out to spoil a good time.

Certain recurring situations warrant your taking a child aside and having a conversation about the other parent's temperament, all the while keeping it respectful. "You know how traffic frustrates Dad. It's best not to talk to him while he's driving." Or, "You know how Mom is before she has to teach a new class. She's concentrating and can't give you her full attention. Come to me if you need help or have a question." Children may not recognize these predictable traits or patterns on their own, so this kind of familiar, even affectionate talk teaches them that being sensitive to another's temperament is a good way to avoid emotional land mines.

When a disagreement with your partner starts to heat up, the best way to avoid escalating it into an argument is by practicing active listening. That means paying full attention to the other person, not just waiting for a chance to jump in with your own comment or selectively listening for things that prove how "wrong" your partner is. Psychologist Harriet Lerner, author of the classic *The Dance of Anger*, says we automatically listen for negatives: "You can tell you're defensive if you're listening for inaccuracies, distortions, or exaggerations instead of what you would agree with." You don't have to correct everything you disagree with. You don't have to cross-examine or nitpick. You're going to give the other person the benefit of the doubt. All this is more likely to happen if you make a practice of not diving into the argument the moment it erupts but waiting until you've both cooled down. And if you end up saying things you regret, you can always ask, "Can I have a do-over?"

SCENES FROM A MODERN FAMILY

What do we fight about when we fight about kids? Oh, everything: grades, food, their friends, athletic potential, screen time, devices, bedtime, the importance of religious school, the money we're spending on them. When they're teenagers, tension revolves around all of the above plus the teen's spending, curfews, clothes, cars, and accountability. Often one parent makes excuses for the child or shrugs off bad behavior while the other is astonished that parent number one doesn't see the pattern and the swift downhill trajectory of the child.

There is no set of commandments that will resolve the top ten parenting arguments, but parents can clear the debris so conversations about these topics become more comfortable. Most of the couples I see have common blind spots and assumptions about each other's feelings and motivations. Their stories are almost like set pieces from a repertory company—same plot and script, different actors. Some of the scenes relate directly to issues such as sleep and bedtime. Others are habits so ingrained that the parents don't realize they're blocking the way to more fruitful discussions. Here are the situations I most often encounter.

Musical Beds and Bedtime Rituals

At night the child gets into the parents' bed and the dad moves to the couch. Or the child gets scared and the dad climbs into the child's bed. A related pitfall is the bedtime ritual that ate the marriage:

> **Father:** Our five-year-old, Isla, won't go to sleep unless my wife does an elaborate bedtime ritual. She has to sing certain songs in a certain order, help Isla arrange her stuffed animals at the foot of the bed, read to her for half an hour, and finish up by checking under the bed and in the closet for monsters. The whole routine takes longer and longer every night.
>
> **Me:** How long?
>
> **Father:** Up to an hour and a half. And then Isla gets up a couple of times in the night and comes into our room. She insists that her mom walk her back to her room.
>
> **Mother:** She screams if I don't comfort her before bed. She's afraid. I don't know why Jeff can't understand that.
>
> **Father:** I'm afraid, too. I'm afraid for this marriage. I don't know why you can't understand that.

At issue here are habits of dignity and mutual respect. Everyone is so frightened of strong emotions—as if no child should ever be scared of the dark and no parent should ever have to experience their child being scared—that they take the easy way out, which is to be a human blankie. Then it becomes a habit, and the parents' sleep and privacy are sacrificed. In some marriages everyone agrees on a "family bed," but among the couples I've counseled there is much resentment from fathers about the children encroaching on the parents' bedroom. The child's nighttime jitters can also be a handy camouflage for the parents' eroding intimacy.

Playing Blame Badminton

Parents often think a child's problem traits are a direct result of their partner's bad behavior, which they see as an intentional choice. But is your spouse's behavior really so careless, dangerous, or cruel? Or is he or she simply doing things differently than you would? Our culture leads us to believe one false move can ruin a child forever, so parents turn on each other—often sarcastically and in front of the children:

> "Nice move! Your 'honest' answer to his question about what happened to the prisoner's head after it was chopped off by the guillotine is something he can't unhear."
> "I see you caved in to her demand for waffles. When she gets a mouthful of cavities, it's on you."
> "You're still putting on his socks and shoes? Really?"

Blaming the other person can be tempting because you feel like you're taking action in a situation over which you actually have little power. Parents are helpless about children going through developmental phases. They can't change their children's temperament or influence the outside forces (good and ill) that affect them. One of the paradoxes of parenting is that you have only limited control yet feel all the responsibility. That's why the blame starts pinging back and forth.

Mom's in Love with Her Little Buddy, and Dad's Out in the Cold

Fathers become especially resentful and inhibited when Mom clearly prefers spending time with her son. Part of the reason mothers are so smitten is that the child is a younger, cuter, more malleable version of the husband. In today's style of parenting, no amount of together time is too much, and that provides new cover for the ancient rivalry between father and son for the mother's love. Mom is very close to her daughter, too, but they do bicker, and Dad usually shares her deep affection for the little girl. The rivalry, if it exists, is subdued.

In my sessions with couples who are struggling over Mom's devotion to her little boy, I'll sometimes say to the wives, "You know, Aiden's going to grow up and fall in love with another girl. Tom's really cute, too, and he's the one who'll still be hanging out with you." If the spotlight you're shining on your child is so bright that your husband is left in the shadows, consider expanding your view.

Do Something! But What?

A mother complains to a father about the child or an event involving the child, and the father thinks she wants him to do something about it. He doesn't know what to do and he's not fully committed to the idea that something needs to be done, so an argument erupts. Often, though, the mom just wants him to listen. The stereotype is that men take action and women are more circumspect, but among modern parents the roles are frequently reversed. It's the mothers who want to jump in and solve the problem right away. In these cases an option for the father (or the more tranquil partner) is to be quietly supportive or noncommittal: "I'm not entirely sure why you're so upset, but I respect your opinion."

Texting a News Scroll of Irritations

Parents sometimes fall into a habit of texting each other a stream of child-oriented complaints: *She left her racket at the court . . . Stella says Mona posted an ugly pic of her . . . Fever 100.5 now . . .* This is outsourcing your distress when you haven't metabolized it or tried to solve it on your own. The news feed stokes the coals of parental anxiety and doesn't give a couple time to miss each other. When they reunite at the end of the workday, what do they talk about? All those minor problems.

Technology in the Bedroom

Diving into your online world is a solitary journey. You may occasionally share a funny video with your partner, but then you get sucked back into your social networks, news sites, or communiqués from work. Although neither person may intend it, a custom of tuning each other out while unwinding can lead to one or both partners feeling isolated and ignored.

All committed couples must decide how to balance the allure of the Internet against that of the person with whom they share a life. Unplugging when you get into bed may feel awkward at first, but those few moments each night when you get to be alone together are too valuable to lose.

ELEVATING THE ATMOSPHERE

We cherish our children and put much effort into cultivating their social, academic, and creative skills. Then we look over at our spouse and give a weary shrug. There's no energy left for the grown-ups to nurture each other.

Elevating the atmosphere in your home requires devoting a percentage of your effort to your partner instead of your child. A teaching I found in Christian pastoral counseling literature is a brilliant example: it suggests that every morning before a couple parts ways, they ask each other, "What can I pray for you today?" This allows them to connect deeply for a moment as they either leave the safety of the home and go out into the world or prepare to manage the children and household. At the end of the day, the parents get back together and ask if their prayers worked.

This little ritual nourishes what spouses need most in each other:

a loving partner who cares deeply about them but doesn't feel responsible for their challenges. Bringing God into it can be a metaphor, a way of saying, "What's on your mind?" And when the person comes home, "How did that go?" With or without the prayer, parents can ask these questions.

Deciding to change some of your self-talk is another way to subtly lift the atmosphere. Just as you train yourself to view your children with the slightly detached interest of an anthropologist, you can do the same with your partner. What are the ways of this tribe? Among my clients, differences in perspective trigger knee-jerk assumptions. Fathers tell me, "My wife has far too much information about the kids. She can't be objective. She's exaggerating" or simply "She's crazy." Moms say, "It's so clear the damage his parents did to him" or "He's absolutely on the spectrum" or "He's never around the children and doesn't know what he's talking about." Instead, when your partner says or does something that plucks at your parental anxiety, you can say to yourself, *That's interesting.* And to your spouse, "Tell me more" or "I hadn't thought of it that way. Help me understand."

A few condescending looks or words can do considerable damage to your relationship, but tiny packets of gratitude are equally powerful. Another elevated habit for parents—including those who are divorced—is staying alert to traits or events for which you or your child truly appreciate the other parent. Then tell that parent:

"I'm so glad he inherited your singing voice."
"When she got home she was so excited about going roller skating again!"
"He loved the movie—thanks for taking him."
"You taught her how to use a power drill! I wish my dad had taught me."

If you're divorced, you may think you'll sound phony or that these comments won't have much impact. But they'll disarm your ex, lower tension levels, build trust, and increase the chance that he or she will consider your point of view or be accommodating when your plans suddenly need to change.

My final suggestion for elevating the atmosphere is to resist the unhealthy lure of detailed conversations about your child's progress and promise. Lively discussions about topics that have nothing to do with your child are more important than dissecting the talent of his third grade teacher. Your child's teachers, friends, and obsessions will soon dissolve into history, to be replaced by next year's edition. You probably need to be talking less about your child, not more.

TALKING TO YOUR EX

Parenting separately has become commonplace, which is not to say it's any easier than it was decades ago when divorce carried a heavy stigma. Some exes grow into amicable blended families after time has passed, others remain at war, but in the early days before rules and routines have been established, most parents struggle. You're still Mom and Dad but no longer husband and wife because unendurable conflict, disappointment, betrayal, or failure to communicate drove you apart. Now you're free from some of the old frustrations but forced to encounter new ones. What's fair? How is *on time* defined? What about *clean? Rested? Protected from unwholesome influences?*

Effective communication with an ex requires diplomacy, and diplomacy requires strategy. Even when you're heartbroken, dizzy, and still nursing fresh wounds. A helpful mind-set for displaying a nonthreatening and supportive attitude when talking with your ex about the kids: pretend your child is a dog. If you were placing your Labradoodle in the care of a friend for the weekend, your instructions might be, "Muzzy has been having some trouble with her tummy. It might have been her food. She seems to be better now. I took her for a walk this morning. See you Sunday night, and thanks!"

Some parents have a tendency to be less than candid with their ex about little crises or bouts of illness. Neither parent wants the other to think something's gone badly on their watch. Others tend to over-direct. The Labradoodle trick helps you deliver the basic information and then relinquish control: "I wanted to let you know she's been crying every night about the breakup with Luke. This may continue, or she may feel better when she's in a different environment." Or, "She's incredibly worried about the history final and that's why she looks stressed." But not, "Therefore you've got to make sure she studies at least two hours a night. I'm sending her with the flashcards. Put them in two different piles. Make her go through the whole set at least once each day."

DON'T MAKE YOUR CHILD PLAY MESSENGER OR SPY

Divorced parents sometimes try to avoid direct contact with each other by communicating via the children. Every marriage and family counselor warns against this, but it can take superhuman self-discipline. It's so easy to say, "Remind your mom that I'll be out of town next weekend." What could possibly go wrong? Item number one on a long list: your child could forget.

Texting is an efficient way around the problem, but remember only to text information that falls within previously agreed-upon parameters: pickup times, playdate addresses, or—and this is the outer limit of text-appropriate communication—a respectfully phrased request for schedule changes. Never text emotionally. I see text wars between ex-spouses all the time—Team Husband and his new opinionated girlfriend against Team Wife along with her friends and maybe her mother. They're all parsing the meaning of the texts. Texting is an impulsive medium and e-mail is a cold one, so if you can't control yourself when texting, stick to a brief but friendly e-mail or the phone. Just don't use your child as the messenger.

When a child gets home after staying with the other parent, it's tempting to launch a cross-examination in the guise of a happy-go-lucky interview: "So where was the dinner? What did you order? Did Mom's new boyfriend sleep over?" Children aren't fooled no matter how offhand the delivery. They know they're being asked to spy, and it makes them feel disloyal and trapped. And criticizing the ex can drive children to be protective of their mom or dad, pushing them prematurely into a adult role.

Confiding to your child about the separation, divorce, or ongoing tensions is similarly unhealthy. Even though children will never protest, may give great advice, and may even feel special and grown-up, placing them in this role burdens them, stealing more from the carefree quality of childhood than they've already lost through the breakup of their family.

DON'T INTRUDE, DO ENGAGE

You'll earn a nod of appreciation if you refrain from calling or texting your child or ex when they're together. It's easy to rationalize it as a reassuring dose of love—*Night, sweetheart!*—but it can be an intrusion. You don't know the rhythm of the moment or the activity you're interrupting. Contacting your child conveys lack of trust and is sometimes spurred by unconscious envy or your pang of loneliness. And it's unnecessary because bad news travels instantly—you'll know if they need you.

One last habit that will foster goodwill in both your ex and your child: take a moment when picking up or dropping off to initiate a brief chat about something that has nothing to do with the kids or logistics. It can last as long as the two of you are able to sustain a friendly tone. Thirty seconds or thirty minutes are both fine. And when you leave, you can drop one of those genuine compliments that relate to your child: "Can you believe the amazing model she made of a city street? Looks like she inherited your talent for engineering."

FORGING BONDS WITH THE GRANDPARENTS

Chef Massimo Bottura attributes his love of cooking to his deep ties to a cherished grandmother. When his older brothers would torment and tease him, he recalls, "My safety place was in the kitchen, under the table, where my grandmother was rolling pasta." She'd shoo the brothers away with her *matterello*, a three-foot-long rolling pin, shouting, "Leave him alone—he's the young one!" From under the table Massimo would watch flour drifting down, and when his grandmother turned her back to gather ingredients, he'd reach up and steal fresh tortellini.

Hearing Bottura talk about this table as a source of shelter and nourishment, I thought about the division of emotional labor in families. His nonna didn't feel an obligation to build the character of her grandsons ("Boys, sit down right now and listen. It's not nice to scare your little brother. How would you feel if someone did that to you? Massimo, you mustn't steal food"). Instead she went about her work while standing up for love and freedom and the vulnerability of the young.

In the best-case scenario, where your parents are living, engaged with your family, and sane, they will provide that kind of uncompli- cated devotion to your child. But often it's not so simple. Changing values and attitudes about health and safety leave both sides frustrated: the grandparents find the parents' worries and restrictions bizarre, and the parents find the grandparents' ignorance and relaxed attitude dangerous. Your parents may be hurt and puzzled when you ignore their advice or insist they abide by your rules. "Why is our daughter so cranky, rigid, and paranoid? Only organic food? Organic cotton, too?" And as the child gets older: "What's wrong with drinking from the garden hose? Building a fort with real wood and nails? Getting some street smarts on an actual street?"

Certain issues—like food allergies, tutors, and specialty summer camps—are especially controversial. Grandparents are perplexed by how "delicate" the child is and how "neurotic" the parents are. The price of the tutors and camps strikes some grandparents as outra- geous; the need, doubtful. Another point of contention is therapy or medication for the child. Grandparents tend to be of two schools, neither very compassionate toward the parent. It's either "Why didn't you do it sooner?" or "Are you crazy? That's what children are like. It's the way you handle it that's making it worse." Meanwhile, parents think the grandparents are so out of touch with current child-rearing challenges that their opinions are nearly worthless.

It's true that the world you grew up in was very different from the one in which you're raising your child, and that grandparents are easily confounded by the shifting challenges. They think you're exaggerating problems, and in some cases they may be right, but often they're wrong. Still, there's a silver lining to this conflict: grandparents and grandchildren have the best human relationship that exists because they have a common adversary (you) and neither one wastes too much time worrying about sugar or paraben-free shampoo. Plus, they're in love. You can reap a lot of benefits from encouraging this love affair, and so can your child.

If you don't count against them the fact that they're not exactly like you, most grandparents are perfectly serviceable in the role. They have the patience to listen to a preschooler's rambling and illogical story. Their expectations of the child are refreshingly low: "Sit here on the couch with me, sweetheart, and tell me all about your new hamster." Grandparents can reveal secrets about what you were like as a child—pranks, passions, and near-disasters that happened "when your dad was seven years old, just like you are now!" And they can spin remarkable tales about life in the olden days when they were growing up: "We didn't have computers—there was no Internet. We were allowed to run around the neighborhood by ourselves all day! There were no cell phones, and the moms would stand in the street and yell their kid's name when it was time to come home for dinner."

There's an extra hidden advantage of children spending time with grandparents. Even kids who adore Nonna and Poppy will have a renewed appreciation of their own parents after being away for an afternoon or weekend. You can see it in their happy faces as they ride off on Dad's shoulders, eager though they may be for their next visit to the grandparents.

DOES IT MATTER IF GRANDMA IGNORES YOUR RULES?

While waiting in an airport terminal, I overheard a man talking to a couple who were on their way to babysit their five-year-old grandchild. It was the first time they'd be caring for the boy over a period of several days. The man said, "It's easy. Here's what you do. The parents are going to hand you a list. Study that list carefully, like it's the Constitution. Nod your head a lot and listen while they go over all the details. Then the minute they walk out the door, throw the list away and do whatever you want."

That's excellent advice. Why? Because children are bilingual. They easily adapt to different rules in different households, just as at school they know how to speak to teachers and interact with other students. Children with divorced parents learn a different set of rules for each home. So if the grandparents don't enforce all the items on your list, it needn't have any effect on the way your children behave with you. Children are usually too smart to say "Grandma lets me!" but if they come home with new demands you can simply reply, "I know, that sounds like fun, but our rules are different."

Of course, there are exceptions. If the grandparents are alcoholics (or now married to one) living with an unfenced pool and an unpredictable dog, if Grandpa habitually shouts insults at Grandma, if they casually disregard your child's legitimate health issues, they can't be permitted to spend unsupervised time with your children. If they're reasonable people who also have a weakness for M&M's consumed while watching silly television, let it go. Remember, too, that they are a generation older than you and get tired looking after small children for long stretches. That's why they watch so much TV.

DEALING WITH A GRANDPARENT'S ANNOYING COMMENTS

Grandparents' suggestions, corrections, or outright disapproval can be grating, and daughters are particularly sensitive to perceived criticism from their mothers. Instead of allowing yourself to become inflamed by a grandparent's comments, you can learn to manage them. Aim for a vocal style that signals respect, cheerful self-reliance, and noncommittal openness to their input. Here's a typical exchange between grandmother and adult daughter, with some diplomatic responses.

"Jess, I'm worried that by raising Maya as a vegetarian you're making her too finicky. She's going to be rude or wilt from hunger the first time someone offers her a hamburger. Are you sure you want to do that?" (Note the irksome rhetorical question structure.)

"Mom, I can see why you're concerned, but we do expose her to all sorts of different foods. We're not worried about this. Is there anything you've read or heard about kids who are vegetarian becoming lifelong picky eaters?" It's unlikely Grandma will have scientific evidence to back up most of her opinions. Instead her response may be something along the lines of "Anyone can see . . ." or "Everybody knows . . ." Or she may simply shake her head. It's kind to acknowledge her worries without getting into heated debate. She's not going to be raising or ruining any more children of her own.

Another approach is to seek her guidance: "Do you remember any foods I wanted to eat too much of when I was little, or refused to eat at all? How did you handle it?" If you were a finicky eater, this might open up a discussion about things your mother did that were ineffective (like forcing you to choke down green vegetables). Or your mom might have some enlightening advice about what did work. If she can't recall having to deal with this while raising you, it may put a pause on the conversation while she silently admits to herself that she has no firsthand advice to offer.

You and your mom might even detour into some recollections about your childhood dinner-table antics or the food she ate when she was a girl. Her fear about your child's diet could be residual anxiety from her own childhood, since issues around eating go back generations in some families.

With practice, it's possible to listen to a grandparent's comments without either arguing or caving in. Don't expect to change or educate them, but stay open to the possibility that you might learn from their experience.

LET GO OF OLD GRUDGES

When you talk to your parent, two conversations are happening at the same time. One is inside your head and arises from childhood memories of your family. On an unconscious level you may get drawn back to when you were hurt, angry, or felt you were being treated unfairly. Without realizing it, you're still trying to right those wrongs, some of which you may have exaggerated and some that are legitimate.

This internal narration affects your external exchanges with your parents: the words you use, the tone, how often you speak, what you refrain from saying. Old grudges become ingrained assumptions. Until you have children, the dysfunction mainly affects you, your parents, and your siblings. But when you become a parent, you have fresh motivation to raise the standard of discourse. Let go of long-held grievances, and you'll be setting a good example for your kids. You also have fresh motivation to set boundaries, insist on being treated respectfully, and remove yourself from your parents' company if they refuse to accept their role in past injustices or aren't kind to you, your partner, or your children. Whatever your relationship with your parents, conversing with them in a civilized manner is a deposit on your future, because the way you speak to your parents is very likely the way your adult kids are going to speak to you.

Ongoing friction with your parents affects your ability to be an energetic and nurturing mom or dad. You have a finite amount of emotional fuel. It's depleted or refreshed depending on your habits of sleep, diet, and exercise; how much you enjoy your daily activities; and the quality of your relationships. Your children are entitled to a generous portion of your energy. If you expend it feeling resentful, stressed, or exploited by a parent's demands, you have little left over for telling bedtime stories or listening to your child describe his best friend's new dog.

If you're confused about your feelings toward your mother or father, take this test. When you look at your phone and see that it's your parent calling or texting, what's your first thought? How does your body react? After the call, do you feel lighter and grateful for the companionship? Or do you feel angry, humiliated, weak, or ashamed? If it's the latter, consider making some changes. Talk to a therapist. Or reduce the tension by setting clear boundaries: "Mom, please don't call or text when I'm at work unless it's an emergency. I'm happy to catch up with you over the weekend." In some families no amount of careful phrasing or modulated vocal tone can improve the tenor of the relationship, and your contact with your parents will have to be more limited.

STRINGS ATTACHED

Accepting gifts of money or time from grandparents is not necessarily a problem. Some grandparents pay the children's college tuition because they can afford it and college has become terribly expensive. Others gladly offer to babysit the grandchildren because they enjoy spending time with them. But in many families it's more psychologically complex. I have clients who accept money from their parents because they're convinced that education at an elite private school or attendance at costly summer programs are essential preparation for social and academic achievement. I ask these parents, "Are you selling a part of your soul for this money? Are you giving up your dignity and authority?"

The grandparents in these families sometimes view the parents as weak or helpless because of their dependency. They have more respect for their grandkids than they do for their own children. This doesn't only take place among wealthy families; the same power plays can develop if the grandparents provide regular child care or allow the kids to stay at their house while the parents go on a vacation, however modest. If you take the phone test and are having negative physical or emotional responses to your parents, the strings are too tight.

The Opinionators

For most of human history, marriages were arranged. Now that adults in Western countries marry whomever they want, it's frightening for both sets of parents. In what may be a protective instinct for the species, in-laws initially tend to be skeptical of the person their child marries. This can flare up again when a grandchild arrives.

To improve and maintain their relationship with the in-laws, I advise parents to think of them as foreign dignitaries. Observe the proper rules of decorum. When you're on their turf, put aside your idiosyncrasies ("Room fresheners give me a headache," "We don't drink soda") and even your valid complaints ("Can't you PLEASE turn down the television?"). When they're at your house, a few gestures in the same vein (such as keeping Diet Coke on hand) will take you far.

I learned some splendid in-law tactics from the members of a group of Chinese businesswomen who attended a weeklong parenting seminar I taught in Beijing. Many of them lived with a mother-in-law who was helping raise the grandchildren. I asked them to role-play the part of their mother-in-law, and they jumped right in:

> How can you make my son this breakfast? You know he likes eggs for breakfast! You know how he likes them prepared. He has to work very hard all day and you're not even trying to pay attention to what he loves. Clearly the only one who will ever understand him is me!

These women were highly accomplished and self-disciplined. They sat in the hotel ballroom for eight hours a day, never checking their cell phones and rarely taking bathroom breaks out of respect for my time and role as a teacher. They feel the same way about their in-laws. In response to a mother-in-law's criticism about breakfast, they would say something like, "I am so honored to learn from you and find out how to be the best wife to your son." On the page it sounds subservient, but in person it was lovely.

The Chinese women explained that this is how they disarm their husband's mother and dissipate the tension, which they understand to be caused by the mother-in-law's envy of their youth and opportunities. Many of the mothers-in-law were from farming families and had grown up in rural poverty. In China the difference between the generations was so stark that it was easy for the younger women to feel generous and compassionate.

In Western countries this type of respectful response to criticism can take the form of a question. Just as when your own mother criticizes your choices, you can deflect your in-laws' judgments by saying in a nonchallenging tone, "Tell me what it was like when you were raising Jon. Did he have chores? Did he ever get punished? If you had it to do over again, would you do anything differently?"

Asking these questions gives the elders a chance not only to share their experiences but also to reflect on their opinions. If you say, "What was it like when my husband was seven and had to do his homework? How did you encourage him?" They might respond, "Well, they didn't give homework to seven-year-olds back then!" Point made. Now they have a little insight into what you're up against.

GOODWILL FOR GRANDPARENTS

With so much attention focused on the children, grandparents sometimes feel taken for granted or as if they're hired help. Acknowledging grandparents and showing your appreciation fosters goodwill.

Send paper birthday cards (not e-cards) and include a warm childhood memory.

Now that you're a parent, these memories will more readily spring to mind. The grandparents can reread the card, show it to their friends, and keep it on their nightstand.

Ask the grandparent to demonstrate or teach your child a skill.

The most obvious example is making a favorite recipe, but your parents possess a lifetime's worth of tricks and talents: Grandpa's technique for knotting his tie or tuning a guitar; Grandma's method of dispensing with spiders or shuffling a deck of cards.

When my daughter Emma was in high school, she and her friends drove for two hours to have my parents teach them some dance moves. The kids were preparing for a swing dance party and knew where to find the experts. My parents met on a blind date—a mutual friend thought they might be a good match because they were both good dancers. I know Emma appreciates this fun part of her family heritage.

Ask the grandchild to record an interview with the grandparent.

If Grandma and Grandpa prefer not to appear on camera, suggest they speak into a microphone. Most everyone loves reminiscing about his or her life. And unless a grandparent is hobbled by illness, long-term memory stays strong until the end. Grandchildren provide a new audience and no recriminations, so the grandparents may be more willing to open up. Even relatively young children can do these interviews; look online for lists of questions to get them started.

Think of opportunities for the grandparents to be involved (and don't forget Grandpa).

Aside from babysitting, what skills do your parents possess that could contribute to the family? Grandfathers cherish the children, too, but they often get neglected amid the lovefest or ongoing battle between Mom and Grandma. I've noticed that many grandfathers are far more willing to be involved with their grandkids than they were with their own children (perhaps a side benefit of waning testosterone levels and competitive drive!). And these older men often have good instincts about what will delight a small child. When my daughters were very young, they enjoyed standing on my father's feet as he walked with them, gently singing, "Bah-dum, bah-dum." When he stopped they would say, "More bah-dum! More bah-dum!"

Parent Talk

TALKING TO "OLIVIA'S MOM"

Having children is a gateway to new friendships forged at Mommy and Me, on the preschool playground, or during the endurance trials of chaperoning field trips. A few of these will turn into lifelong alliances that outlast the bond between your respective children. Some of the parents will become trusted advisers and reliable fonts of support. Others will generate the kind of self-doubt you haven't felt since middle school. (I've listened to moms in session agonize over what to wear and where to sit at the school play, fearing that the popular crowd would not welcome them if they didn't make the right choice.)

When my daughters were in school, it seemed that every other girl was named Olivia. An "Olivia's mom" might be overheard saying, "I don't know how Olivia does it! Always up studying when we go to bed, and when we get up in the morning, she's already made breakfast for the whole family and walked the dog! She started a microfund NGO for indigenous women in Colombia [pronounced by Olivia's mom with full Spanish accent], and we think Dartmouth will be recruiting her for diving." Olivia's mom was not exactly lying. Maybe her daughter made breakfast once and walked the dog for a few days, then dropped it. Her family *hopes* she'll be recruited by a college for diving. If I weren't in the business of hearing the inside stories of so many families, I might have felt disheartened comparing my own daughters to Olivia.

Today, far more than in the past, school communities are often the center of parents' social lives. The closeness leads to a heightened sense of both insecurity and competition. Other parents can start to seem like an in-your-face barometer of your parenting skills and social standing; their children's moment-to-moment successes become the standard by which you judge your own child. My conclusion after many years practicing therapy: people's depictions of their family life are about as authentic as their Facebook page.

Until a child enters middle school, it's possible that you'll be interacting with the other parents every day. You may feel the same jitters your child does when you wait at the gate the first day of the year or venture on campus for Back to School Night. Eager to be liked and accepted by the other moms, you may lose perspective about what to say. A good rule of thumb: when getting to know another parent, use the kind of discernment you would with any new acquaintance. If you're eager for instant closeness or popularity, you'll be tempted to reveal too much too soon. Don't sell your child's secrets as the currency of friendship. The test: How would you feel if your child overheard you? We all need friends to help us gauge our child's behavior, but wait and see if this person shows herself worthy of your trust. Do you believe she won't tell her child? Because as soon as she does, *your* child is likely to find out, too.

Finally, resist the temptation to bond with other parents by scapegoating or joining in vigilante-style uprisings over the decisions of school administrators, the actions of less-than-perfect teachers, or the influence of a troubled child in the classroom. For a passing thrill, you'll degrade the atmosphere of the school or make another child's life harder. It's not worth it.

We need the community of other parents. I tell my patients, "Find a parent with a child a little bit older than yours who is turning out pretty well: down-to-earth and fairly enthusiastic. When in doubt about a decision regarding your child, ask that parent instead of polling the moms on the playground." Parents who don't become your best friends can still be a valuable source of news and feedback about teachers, coaches, tutors, and other adults who care for your child—the trustees we'll meet in the next chapter.

CHAPTER 10

The Trustees

Getting the Best Out of Nannies, Teachers, Coaches, and Other Adults in Your Child's Life

It takes a village to raise a child . . . and the other villagers may be thoughtless, delightful, irritating, or inspirational. Some may seem to hold exorbitant power over your child's future. Others are loving allies and mentors. These are the trustees, temporary stewards of your child's developing mind, emotions, and talents. As your children watch how you interact with these adults or hear you discussing them at home, you are teaching lessons about how to treat authority figures and cope with challenges and honors. In conversations with the trustees, your default assumption should be: *This person wants the best for my child.* Your internal mantra: *My child is not a special case.*

Your approach, attitude, and comments can either put the trustees at ease or cause them to label you *difficult.* You don't want that label. It's very hard to shed.

THE NANNY: A LOVING PROFESSIONAL

If you have a nanny, your relationship with her or him is a unique one. Just look at the hiring process. No license, degree, or objectively measurable skill set is required of candidates. An agency will conduct a background check, you might get a name from a friend's nanny, you'll call references, but mainly you grant a stranger full responsibility of your family's most valuable and vulnerable asset based on intuition. And usually it turns out well. It's obvious that hiring a nanny enables both parents to hold jobs or eliminates the need to commute to and from day care. But it's the other profound benefits of this role for both child and parents that led me to include nannies among the esteemed trustees.

When a nanny enters a child's world, it begins to expand. The unfamiliar becomes accepted and appreciated: new people (other nannies and children at the playground); new foods and flavors; the accent of her speech; her passionate expressions of affection (*mi corazon, mi vida, mi amor*); new games, songs, and knowledge. It's practice for the separation the child will experience and the flexibility he'll need when he enters preschool or kindergarten.

Your interaction with the nanny will be your child's first exposure to an employer-employee relationship. It may also be your first experience as a boss. Under your child's curious eye, you'll be negotiating, handling conflict, and issuing instructions, corrections, and praise. Yet this is no ordinary employee because the nanny is in your home every day, seeing your family in excruciating close-up. And the power balance is a strange one: in many households both the parents and the nanny feel a little paranoid. The nanny is afraid of angering the parents and getting fired, while the parents are fearful the nanny will lie, steal, or suddenly quit, leaving the child grief-stricken and the parents forced to hastily hire a replacement. (Although it's wrenching for children to lose a beloved nanny, if you've fired her with cause, you are actually protecting your child. If she's quit because of changes in her life circumstances, you can invite her to remain connected with your child through visits or holiday and birthday cards.)

Because this professional relationship is also personal, lines get blurred, usually to the detriment of the nanny. Mothers strain to be nice in an effort to keep the nanny happy, but overly cautious phrasing results in directions the nanny may not understand. Getting too sisterly with the nanny—sharing details about your marriage, health, friends, or work—erodes your authority and intrudes on the nanny's privacy, even if it feels like bonding. And telling yourself the nanny is "just like a member of the family" opens the door to subtle exploitation of her time and love for the child.

SET EXPECTATIONS BEFORE YOU HIRE THE NANNY

Much of the drama can be avoided if you have the presence of mind to set expectations while you're interviewing the nanny. This isn't as easy as it sounds, because parents can be blinded by relief at ending the search process, a quick emotional connection with the person, or a friend's glowing recommendation. Sitting before you is a warm, intelligent, experienced individual available to work right away, and you don't want to put her off by talking about a lot of rules. But contrary to your worries, nannies are reassured by parents who can clearly explain the job. Along with the hours and housing arrangements (if she'll be living with you), you can outline what you expect from her and how you see your own responsibilities. As an employer, fair treatment of a nanny typically includes:

- Not asking her to stay late at the last minute (or doing so only in a genuine emergency).
- Paying her overtime.
- Paying her if you'll be away on vacation.
- Telling her in advance when vacations will occur.
- Instead of reimbursing her, provide a credit card and cash for child-related expenses.
- Arriving on time to relieve her from duty.

If you're explicit about rules during the interview, it will be much easier to enforce them when the nanny is working for you. Regarding phone use, you might say, "When we're playing with Mila, bathing her, or putting her to bed, we put our phones away and we'll want you to do the same. When you're at the park, we'll expect you to be watching her and not using your phone to play games or check in with friends or family, because an accident can happen in a moment. We'll only text or call you if there's a change of plans or an emergency, and we'll expect the same from you—we don't need you to check with us about minor decisions."

MUY CONFUNDIDO

Several years ago I led a workshop for nannies in Santa Monica. Most of the women who attended were native Spanish speakers, but all had some English-language fluency. My plan was to talk about effective discipline strategies and how to communicate with the children's parents. While the women appreciated the advice about discipline, what they really responded to was the session about talking to moms. Their most frequent complaint: "If she had just told me how she wanted it done or what she wanted me to do, I would have been glad to comply." I heard lots of *"confundido"* and *"frustrado"*—"confused" and "frustrated."

In her book *Secrets of the Nanny Whisperer*, Tammy Gold addresses the mix-ups that most often provoke nannies. In adapted form, here are her six rules for better communication:

1. *Never pose a direction as a question.*

Not "Do you think you could change the sheets today?" but "Please change the sheets today."

2. *Never use the word* if.

"If you get a chance, could you . . ." makes the request seem optional and low-priority.

3. *When you want the nanny to do something, tell her directly.*

Women have a communication habit of couching their wishes in suggestions—think of all the times your mother said, "Doesn't it seem cold to be leaving the house without a jacket?" Don't ask or hint, just say it: "Please make three sandwiches to bring to the park so Sammy will have some to share with his friends."

4. Don't attribute your needs or requests to someone (or something) else.

Parents sometimes do this in an attempt to add weight to their directives, but it can backfire. Telling the nanny that a new study says babies should stop using pacifiers by twelve months can be perceived as information, not an instruction. The nanny may think, *I've been taking care of kids for twenty years and it hasn't hurt any of them.* Own your decision: "We're weaning Cora from the pacifier. Please don't let her use it. Thanks!"

5. Don't give frequent feedback or directions in e-mail or texts.

Resist interrupting your nanny's time with your child or her time off. Short messages about schedule changes are essential, but, despite the efficiency of instant communication, don't deliver negative feedback or complicated instructions over a device. It's too easily ignored or misunderstood, especially by nannies for whom English is a second language.

6. Your nanny is not a mind reader.

Even if you think the nanny knows your values and routines, tell her out loud exactly what you want her to do or not do. This is true for all nannies but particularly those raised in environments where the cultural norms may be different from yours. Don't assume the nanny knows what you mean, what you intend, or what you would prefer.

THE WEEKLY CHECK-IN

I advise all parents with nannies to schedule a brief weekly check-in. It doesn't have to be on Friday afternoon, but it should be a meeting you observe religiously. As much as any other strategy, this will keep the parent-nanny relationship low-stress and also alert you to problems—both by listening to what the nanny tells you and noticing what she doesn't say. Nannies are prone to downplaying concerns or not mentioning them at all. You'll have to earn her trust over time by reacting calmly and not switching into prosecution mode when she gives you less-than-rosy feedback (as you'll also learn to do with an older child's teacher).

The weekly meeting is how you'll get a sense of the relationship between the nanny and your child. It's not reflected in the number of concerns she reports but in the details she shares about the child. The meeting can begin with you asking, "How did the week go? Is there anything I should know, anything unusual you've seen in Derek's behavior?" Maybe she'll grin and say, "He's starting to be very careful about how he parts his hair, and he's looking at himself in the mirror a lot. He says he has a crush on Kylie." A loving, astute, fresh observation is a sign she's attuned to your little one and not on Facebook or texting her friends. Vague phoning-it-in answers signal the opposite.

If you're not getting any stories like that from the nanny and she appears preoccupied with personal problems, you can say, "You've seemed a little worried lately. Is it something you'd feel comfortable telling me about?" If she insists everything is fine and you're still uneasy, investigate. Come home unexpectedly, have a friend drop by unannounced, or show up at the park ("I got off work early"). Don't ignore your gut feelings.

Your children will probably behave better with the nanny than with you. That can be confusing, leading you to fret that they love the nanny more than their own mom or dad. But this is the same principle you'll see when they come home from school in a gloomy, babyish, or hostile mood: their day is long and demanding, and they act the worst with the people they love the most. If your child loves the nanny, too, you've succeeded! Mastering the triad of nanny, parent, and child is excellent preparation for the bonds you'll soon be forging with your child's teachers.

TEACHERS ON TRIAL

When most of us were growing up, our parents didn't fret much about whether our teachers were fair-minded and inspiring. They also didn't fetishize grades. Mom and Dad's loyalties were clear: obey the adults. If we were sent to the principal's office, our parents' ire would be aimed directly at us. We could insist that it wasn't fair, that we had a side of the story, too, but even if they listened to us, most parents didn't take it upon themselves to plead our case. Their response was usually, "That may be, but I've got news for you. *Life's not fair.* Get your act together."

Not anymore. The venerable alliance between teachers and parents has ruptured, and today many parents reflexively side with their children in classroom disputes. They play puppet master, calling or e-mailing teachers to badger them, often in the politest of tones, into providing a second chance, a more flexible interpretation of the rules, a "but he was provoked" or "he'll never do it again" pass for their child. It's the dark side of devotion, and it can backfire in ways parents don't intend.

We know that when children are protected from the consequences of not turning in work on time, playing video games instead of studying, or breaking rules, they acquire a Photoshopped view of life that makes the adult world harder to master. Why, then, are parents so intent on running interference for their children? The same forces we've been discussing throughout the book are in stark relief at school. Parents see a pristine report card or transcript as a passport—vital fortification against an uncertain future. Their child's social transgressions? Innocent missteps unlikely to be repeated. Accolades and triumphs? Validation of the parents' worth. With so much at stake, parents' emotions overtake their common sense.

In this charged atmosphere teachers are no longer viewed as colorful supporting players in the saga of a child's life, but as agents of good or evil. They're scrutinized, kissed up to, gossiped about, lobbied against. Rarely is today's teacher left to do her job with a sensible measure of hands-off parental trust and support. Educators in private schools and in high-tax-bracket public districts contend with parents who believe that their dollars buy them round-the-clock access to the faculty. Teachers in underprivileged neighborhoods have a different challenge. Parents may be hesitant to engage due to lack of English-language fluency or their own negative experiences in a classroom. They may be weary from juggling multiple jobs or unaware of the benefits of showing up for parent-teacher conferences. In these cases the parents don't interfere, but their lack of involvement leaves teachers without the kind of connection that can support student learning. Teachers find themselves at either extreme: fending off helicopter parents or fending for themselves.

Helicopter (or "snowplow" or "kamikaze") parenting has been on the rise for about twenty years, long enough to have had a permanent impact on teachers' classroom approach. Some of this is positive: administrators and teachers have become more alert to signs of learning disabilities; more aware of the long-term effects of bullying; more respectful of gender orientation, ethnic and social class diversity, and the strain of prejudice. There were drawbacks to the days when parents automatically sided with the school without thoughtful regard for a child's heartfelt complaints or legitimate learning struggles.

But in the course of this sea change, teachers and parents have become warier of each other. As parents have stepped in, some teachers have stepped back. They've reconsidered what they're willing to say to a parent or recommend for a student. Paradoxically, the more a parent pressures a teacher, the less likely the child is to benefit from the best that teacher has to offer.

The most glaring and widespread example of this is grade inflation and its by-product, candor deflation. I titled my last book *The Blessing of a B Minus* because so many parents react to a B minus by panicking, hiring tutors, and pestering or petitioning the teacher. With parents in such a tizzy, the grading scale has become distorted. A capable but uncommitted student who doesn't reliably participate in class, hand in homework on time, or prepare for tests won't get a D or usually even a C. It's not worth it to the teacher to ruffle the parents, who may complain to the administration that their child isn't thriving because of the quality of the instruction.

Not only are teachers using a vanity grading scale, they've also become hesitant to offer frank assessments when they see children squandering their gifts or casually giving up on tasks that don't come easily. The teachers don't lie, but many have learned to be less than forthcoming because they've experienced the consequences. The result is that parents are deprived of useful information about their child.

STEALTH TUTORING, PARENTAL REWRITES, AND OTHER SIGNPOSTS ON THE ROAD TO PERDITION

> You cannot airlift kids to the summit, plant the flag in their hands and call it their accomplishment.
>
> —Julie Lythcott-Haims, author of *How to Raise an Adult*

At its most damaging, parental interference crosses the line into dishonesty. In many of the families I counsel, the children have tutors in one or more subjects as a kind of grade insurance. Some are "stealth tutors," meaning the children are cued not to let the teacher know they're getting the extra instruction. Asking children to keep secrets from their teachers sends a confusing message: it's OK to lie to an adult when it buys you an advantage over your peers. It's also an example of how the rules don't apply equally to everyone. This secret is an unfair and demoralizing burden to place on any child.

Another area where the ethical lines get fuzzy is homework. When I meet with teacher groups, I always advise them to inform parents at the beginning of the year about how involved they want them to be in everyday assignments or special projects. If your child's teacher doesn't give you guidelines at Back to School Night or in a "Welcome to Fourth Grade!" blog post or newsletter, ask her directly. When the expectations are unclear, it's easy for well-meaning parents to give too much help, especially since the amount of homework, sports practice, and other extracurriculars has gotten out of hand at so many schools.

The problem only increases as the child gets older and community service obligations, rehearsals, and sports team travels fill their calendars. Now Mom or Dad rewrites a paper out of sympathy mixed with ambition and again hints that what happens at home should stay at home—the child shouldn't tell the teacher. Then there's a test on the material and the child bombs it. The teacher's got the paper and the test in front of her and calls the parents. The parents can be candid, or they can improvise an excuse: "Oh, right, she was coming down with the flu the day of the test, that's why she wasn't able to concentrate. Why not let her retake it next week?" If there's a pattern of deception, no one is fooled, and the teacher is going to write off that family. Not the student, the family.

Faculty and administrators are aware of the stresses some of their most privileged (on the surface) students face. The parents are always traveling or working. Mom or Dad is depressed, an addict, or ready to separate. There are money problems. The child is feeling lost or neglected in a blended family. The teachers know they can offer the student precious attention and care they may not be getting anywhere else, and of course they want to be a nurturing presence in the child's life.

Teachers don't blame children for their parents' behavior. However, if they sense that their recommendations are being met with superficial compliance but deep resistance and lack of follow-through, or that the parent is continuing to lie or cover up for the student, many teachers will pull back on their efforts with the family. That usually amounts to being less scrupulous about transmitting information and less creative about finding solutions to the child's academic struggles.

At public schools the same problems exist, but the teachers often have a greater number of pupils per classroom and little patience for tiptoeing around parental shenanigans. They may shrug and let it go (bad for the child, who concludes that cheating works because teachers are dumb, don't care, or both). But it's just as likely that the teacher will pull the student aside and demand to know what's going on, forcing the child into a humiliating confession or a lie. She may even call the family in for a meeting with the principal, where the parents will be questioned and the student further embarrassed or disciplined.

For too many families, the bad habits continue when the student is in college. The parental "edits" where the paper is essentially rewritten, the excuses, the cover-ups have by then become absorbed into the child's ethical framework. *It's OK to cheat, just don't get caught. Everyone does it.*

Unintended consequences of stealth tutoring and parental deception include:

- Loss of intrinsic motivation. (*I'm doing this work for my parents and teachers, not for myself.*)
- Loss of gratification and pride. The kind that comes from figuring out how to meet learning and creative challenges on your own.
- Lowered self-confidence. (*I must be pretty defective if my parents have to hire a high-priced specialist to come to our house or lie to my teachers to make excuses for me.*)
- Unwittingly teaching children that problems can be solved quickly and neatly by spending money.

Good parents make bad choices because they want reality to be different from what it is. I tell them, "Please don't deprive your child of reality. It's a wonderful teacher and it's free. You don't have to pay any tuition for reality. You have to pay a lot of money to protect your child from reality."

HOW TO TALK TO THE TEACHER AT THE
PARENT CONFERENCE (OR ANYWHERE ELSE)

Your goal in talking to your child's teacher is to create a spirit of partnership. You want her to be candid. You want to reinforce what she's trying to accomplish in the classroom through your actions at home. In order to give her the confidence to be honest, you need to communicate that you can take it. If you really want to gain her trust, you may need to confide that your reflex response to unfavorable feedback is panic or denial. Any mother can say this because it's true enough. Then tell her how much you value her opinions and want her to feel free to share them.

Your words and demeanor should express humility and emphasize your amateur status. This isn't kissing up to the teacher; it's acknowledging her expertise in an arena about which you have little knowledge, even if you've read a lot of books. If you're a child development professional, it's still true that you don't teach at your child's school, and even if you do, you aren't privy to the dynamics of your child's particular classroom.

There are two reasons it's important to explicitly communicate respect and openness right at the start. The first is most parents' tendency to side with their child. The teacher is battle weary and will assume that's your stance, too, unless you assure her that it's not. The second reason is that the teacher might be intimidated by you. If your child goes to a private school, it's likely that your family income and social status are more elevated than hers.* You can level the playing field by talking about what you *don't* have: her knowledge of children. It only takes one thoughtful remark, such as, "It's so good to be here. Second grade is new territory for us, and I want to learn how we can help Gabe meet your goals for him and for the class in general."

At Back to School Night most teachers will describe the normal developmental milestones and typical behavior of boys and girls at this grade level; social issues that typically arise; and subjects with which students commonly struggle. Unless you have a terrific memory, take notes so you can refer to what she's said when you meet one-

---

* In private schools and public schools in high-tax-bracket districts, you can distinguish the teacher parking lot from the one reserved for the high school students in an instant. The lot with the newer, more expensive models? Students.

on-one. Your first opportunity will probably be at the parent-teacher conference. These meetings are usually brief, between twelve and twenty minutes, so come prepared.

- If a progress report has already been sent out, bring it along so you can refer to it.
- If you are unsure how you can best help your child with any problems he may be having, ask the teacher for clarification.
- If your child is or will be facing emotional challenges, let the teacher know. Without over-sharing, put frankness before personal privacy or embarrassment. Tell the teacher you'd be grateful if she would alert you to any changes she sees in your child's behavior or mood. This provides her with more evidence of your "I can take it" attitude. Common issues that affect children's behavior include parents who are separating, a parent who is ill, a sibling who is having a problem, a new baby on the way, or a beloved nanny who is leaving the family.
- Tell the teacher if your child has a previously diagnosed emotional or learning issue. I know you may not want to do this. *We want to protect him from negative expectations or labeling! A new teacher and classroom offers us an opportunity to test out whether the problem was environmentally induced.* But by not alerting the teacher to these challenges, you're violating the spirit of an open partnership and depriving your child of her sensitivity and expertise.
- Some schools have adopted a model of parent-teacher conferences that includes the student. There are benefits to everyone hearing the same feedback and joining together to appreciate a child's growth (parents tend to remember any reported weaknesses better than even a long and enthusiastic list of his strengths). If a child is going through a rough patch, it can help to have everyone put their heads together to set goals. But some topics are best explored initially without the student

present, for instance, concerns about your child's mental health or possible learning disorders. After the conference, contact the teacher to ask for an additional appointment and inquire whether she feels it would be useful for the school counselor to observe your child in the classroom and on the play yard before your next meeting.

TAKING TEACHER RELATIONS UP A NOTCH

During the parent-teacher conference you'll want to stress your support for the teacher and avoid words or deeds that will cause her to feel defensive. Within this framework you can still voice concerns, and the teacher will be more open to them because you've shown that you respect her work and commitment. To that end:

Know your occupational hazard.

A parent who was an FBI agent told me, "My job is to look for clues and figure out who the perp is, so it's hard for me as a mother because I'm always assuming my daughter is hiding something." Parents do the same thing with teachers and other trustees. The attorney moms will cross-examine the teacher. The therapist father will psychoanalyze her. Marketing managers try to flatter and seduce; CEOs try to intimidate. We all have occupational hazards, so try to identify yours. If you have a hard time avoiding that behavior, issue a friendly self-deprecating warning up front. For example: "I'm an attorney, so let me know if I slip into cross-examination mode. I so value your input." Or let the other parent do the talking. I often tell parents who are preparing for a meeting where some topics they wish to broach may cause the teacher to become defensive to let the more intense, in-the-know parent prepare a list of talking points in advance of the meeting but let the more affable, less fretful parent do the talking in the room. If you're a single parent concerned about any touchy issues coming up, role-play the meeting with a friend. Focus on style of delivery, content, and tone.

Build an alliance with the teacher.

If you agree with the teacher, say so. For example, if she comments on the value of getting students to school on time: "I know it's important, so we're figuring out a new plan for the mornings. We're moving *everyone's* wake-up time up by fifteen minutes. We're also considering switching to a new car pool." Or in response to feedback about your child, "Wow, this is such an eye-opener for me. I'm so close to the situation that it's hard to get perspective."

Begin parent conferences with a flattering remark. Repeat word for word one true thing your child said about the teacher.

The teacher is looking for validation. Just as she will scour her memory and the thesaurus for something positive to say about your child, you want to start the conference with appreciation. Although teachers care what you think of the job they're doing, a compliment from your child means more. Kids typically have a lot to say about their teachers. If your son or daughter hasn't shared much or actively dislikes the teacher, try to draw him out by asking open-ended questions about things like field trips, activities, room decorations, or anything specific they've enjoyed. One detail is all it takes:

> "Mariah said, 'Long division is actually really easy. Ms. Garza explained it to us perfectly.'"
> "Andrew said you told the class you went zip-lining over the break. He was impressed!"
> "Gabrielle is obsessed with your plant-propagation display. It really sparked something in her."

Present your concerns not as criticism but as a desire to understand the teacher's approach and help your child.

If you're learning about a problem from your child, you're only getting half of the story. Don't confront the teacher with, "Daniel said you told the class the test would only cover chapter four, but it covered four and five. He wasn't prepared." Instead say, "Can you offer me some guidance? Daniel often misunderstands what will be covered on the tests. Any advice on how he might improve? Is the problem getting him to listen?" Your underlying attitude is that the teacher is the expert: "This is my first eight-year-old, and you've had experience with so many of them."

If the teacher says something that upsets you, keep your reaction in check.

Telling parents their child is or has a problem is not something teachers take lightly. Typically they wait until they're confident the problem is more than a small bump in development that will resolve itself without intervention. Assume the teacher is being guided by intuition, experience, and goodwill. If she recommends that your child get special help—an IEP (individualized education program) or a professional assessment—assume her intention is not to make her job easier but to help your child. Have faith that she'll be discreet and will not spread the news around the community.

If she suggests therapy or testing, ask her (or the division head or principal) for a referral. You don't have to make an appointment that day, and it's wise to talk over the teacher's suggestions with your pediatrician or a sensible friend or colleague. If you decide to proceed, recommendations from the school have a special value: these professionals are familiar with one another and accustomed to communicating about students' progress. In school psychology parlance we call it a "child study team."

A BRIEF BUT VITAL LIST OF DON'TS

Self-control is the trait you're after when navigating your conversations with the teacher. One shortcut to self-control: don't complain. Not even in a way you think is humorous or breaking the ice. At the parent conference in particular, don't mention:

- The little chairs.
- The fifteen-minute wait because she was talking to other parents for longer than the scheduled time.
- The time spent on state-mandated testing.
- The school using three different math curricula in three years.
- The "unclear" assignments (as explained to you by your child).
- Anything beyond the teacher's domain, regardless of how valid the issue. The teacher has no control over the administration, state or federal laws, funding and disbursements, or the academic arms race.

Whether at the conference or in less formal settings, there are behaviors that cause teachers to become apprehensive about dealing with a parent.

Don't show up clutching a fistful of your child's papers.

It's like you're serving the teacher a summons. If you must discuss a test or assignment, keep the papers in your bag or briefcase and bring out Exhibit A only if it seems appropriate after you've diplomatically broached the topic during the conference.

Don't arrive for a conference early or late. Be on time.

The teacher may run late with the previous set of parents, but by the same token she may take extra long with you. Allow yourself enough time to be flexible.

Don't look at your phone or leave it on the table.

Mute it and keep it out of sight for the duration of the conversation.

Don't scapegoat other students.

"It's not my son. He's never uncooperative at home. [She knows that's a fib!]. It's Max's influence. If you would only keep them apart, I know you'd see a difference." If this were true, don't you think the

259

teacher would have separated them long ago? When a teacher feels the need to talk to you about your child's behavior or other difficulties, she's already considered the obvious solutions. Scapegoating arises from an urge to protect your child, so monitor yourself for this natural reflex.

Don't gossip about other parents.

In an effort to bond with the teacher, you may be tempted to pass along a rumor or two ("Did you hear that Gordon's parents are splitting up?"). That puts the teacher in an awkward position. Only share news about yourself and your own family.

Don't ask for an impromptu meeting at drop-off or pickup.

This most often happens after school, when the teacher is assembling her homework for the night (papers to grade, tests or reports to prepare). Her workday isn't over. Your surprise visit will only prolong it.

Don't treat the teacher as a friend and co-conspirator instead of a professional.

Parents often rely on the school for a sense of community, especially at private schools or if the parents moved to a neighborhood because of the school district. In these cases a culture of niceness sets in where everyone needs to like one another and therefore cannot be frank. If you want the benefit of the teacher's wisdom and skill, respect the boundary that allows her to be a professional.

Don't "drunk text" the teacher.

Charlotte tells you Logan tried to strangle her at recess. You inspect her neck for marks. None. And yet . . . better safe than terribly sorry. And wouldn't Ms. Harrison want to know before school starts tomorrow? A powerful twelve-step slogan is "WAIT." It stands for "Why am I talking?" In parent-teacher relations this translates to: *Why am I texting/e-mailing/voice-mailing during the teacher's respite from schoolyard drama?* Off-load your concerns too impulsively and too often, and you'll become the boy who cried wolf. The risk? Vital communication will be thrown into the teacher's mental bin marked *No big deal. Just Charlotte's mom again.* Recognize that the teacher needs time after hours and on weekends to replenish herself.

APPROACH WITH CARE: SCHOOL HEADS AND PRINCIPALS

The director at a prestigious private school told me that during an admissions interview one couple announced, "We'll be happy to send our daughter to your school as long as you don't offer a readmission contract to Kelsey H." *Readmission contract* is fancy-school speak for allowing the child to return to that school the following year rather than kicking her out.

I've heard dozens of stories like this. If parents are sometimes skeptical or dismissive of teachers, they tend to view school heads and principals as their equals, especially if the parents have deep pockets for donations. Once their child is admitted, maintaining boundaries is a daily challenge for administrators. To increase their odds of admitting students whose parents are somewhat level-headed, directors and admissions officers look for the following signs.

Are the parents at war with each other?

The body language and nonverbal clues are fairly obvious when parents (whether married or not) are at odds. These disagreements often get played out at school or projected onto the teacher. Many parents are divorced, and it's not that the schools are biased against those families. They just don't want to get caught in the middle of an ongoing battle.

Are they on the same page about the child?

Even if the parents' relationship is sturdy, they may have very different takes on their child's capabilities or temperament. This generally means that one parent is somewhat pragmatic and the other has fastened onto a rosier view of the child's potential. Where the truth lies is less important to the school than the possibility that conflicting perceptions of the student will lead the parents to hold unrealistic expectations of the school.

Are they pushy from the very beginning?

Administrators encourage parents to ask questions about the school's curriculum, culture, and mission. But think carefully before posing challenging hypotheticals during an initial interview: "If my child misses a test or assignment, does the faculty allow extra credit to make up for lost points?" "We take three weeks off every spring to travel. At Riley's lower school he was given a work packet so he didn't miss any material. Will the teachers here be able to provide this for him?" Remember, schools that have the option of being selective accept *families*, not just individual students. Introducing yourself in an arrogant way, posing challenges, or signaling that you believe extending an offer of acceptance to your child will raise the status of the school can easily backfire. It's like putting a "Difficult!" sticker on your forehead.

Do they seem to trust the school?

Directors are looking for clues that the parents believe the school knows what it's doing and has their child's best interest at heart. They want reassurance that the parents will generally stay out of the teacher's way and let her do her job.

Have they thought about how this school would fit with their individual child, regardless of its brand name?

Everyone wants to get in, but will it be the right environment for the child? Academic pressure from the parents and high reliance on tutors can mask a child's emotional or cognitive readiness for a given institution. Even with admission test scores inflated by lots of prep, and even in schools that don't do their own testing or formal evaluations on site, seasoned admissions officers have well-developed sensors for the match between a student's capacity and motivation and the demands of the curriculum. Admitting students who aren't prepared for the workload is inviting possible failure for the child.

Principals at public schools don't have the luxury of rejecting students whose parents are setting off alarms. But just like in any intimate community—your office, your place of worship—those in positions of authority assess every member for their team spirit and adjust their flexibility and generosity accordingly. In terms of accessibility, the general rule is that unless it's a special event or there's a crisis with your child, you should not expect hand-holding from these administrators.

SMART PARENTS DON'T TATTLE ON TEACHER

Parents are told at the beginning of the year, in the handbook that nobody reads, and in myriad other ways, to go to the teacher first if their child is having a problem. Yet many fail to understand or respect the accepted hierarchy of complaint. Some feel more comfortable talking to the top dog. Others don't want to sully the friendship they think they have with the teacher: "We've got such a great rapport! I just couldn't go to her about this." So they avoid difficult conversations and make an end run to the principal.

Parental entitlement and urgency are also at play. "I would've gone to the teacher, but what she did is so awful! My child told me . . ." Children are experts at weaving tales that make them look like innocent victims of coldhearted teachers. As in any game of Telephone, the story gets distorted by the time the parent tells the administrator what the child said about the teacher.

This is a form of tattling—exactly what you're training your child not to do. You want him to develop the courage to confront the friend who's doing something that's hurting him or someone else.

When is it appropriate to go to the principal or director? If you've been wrangling with the teacher for so long that you're considering withdrawing your child from the school. I can hear parents protesting, "That's ridiculous! It's just that this teacher is so inept [prejudiced, young, old, mean]. And she yells at the kids! I have to go to the head, especially since the quality of the school system is the whole reason we moved to this town."

But school is like your workplace. If you're having a disagreement with your boss, you go to her and try to assess the problem and brainstorm solutions. Only when the situation is dire do you go around your superior to the head of the organization, because that person is going to go right back to your boss or the teacher and say, "Katy's parent told me that you isolated Katy, mocked her, and left her outside the classroom for two hours without allowing her to use the restroom." And after this brouhaha your child will still be in the same class, only now the problem will be compounded by the teacher's loss of trust in you.

WHEN TO WORRY

Regardless of the tuition you're paying or your school district, teachers will range from the phenomenally talented to the well-meaning but mediocre to, rarely, the truly bad or psychologically abusive. I've often said and written that it's good for children to have one mediocre elementary school teacher because this is how they become resilient. I stand by that. But if your son or daughter is suffering because of an abusive teacher, it's time to shift into mother-lion mode and demand that the child be moved to another class.

Very infrequently, you'll encounter a teacher with long tenure and lots of allies on the faculty, or a newbie rushed in to fill an emergency opening, who is extraordinarily insensitive, experiencing emotional issues that make her unqualified to be in a classroom, or is so lacking in zeal and zest that she spreads fear, misery, or extreme ennui among her students. Young children just starting out in school don't have the experience to know what to expect. When a teacher's behavior is consistently unpleasant, unkind, or out of bounds, they may not

264

realize they are entitled to a better experience. Some may not have developed the language skills needed to describe what goes on in a grim or tense classroom. For parents, this presents a challenge: How to discriminate between normal slow adjustment to the rigor of the school day (compared to the rhythm of life at home or in day care or preschool) and the suffering caused by a bad elementary school teacher?

To start, do an honest accounting of other causes of your child's distress or regression. Was there a recent move, illness, or family troubles? Did you have a gut feeling that he wasn't ready for a full day of kindergarten? If nothing like this comes to mind, the first piece of evidence to consider is school refusal. "I don't want to get up. I don't want to go. I hate school. My teacher's mean and she hates kids." More subtle signs include a previously toilet-trained child wetting the bed at night, waking up complaining of nightmares, chewing on his shirt, or complaining of lots of stomachaches and headaches to avoid going to school.

If you notice signs of distress, ask an administrator or the school psychologist or counselor to observe your child's behavior with his classroom teacher and at lunch, on the playground, or with a specialist (for example in an art, music, or PE class not taught by the main teacher). The observer can tell you whether your child brightens soon after arriving at school or if he is withdrawn, irritable, or provocative with other children.

When an older student complains about an abusive teacher or one who "hates" him, first rule out a dynamic sometimes masked by family denial or lack of awareness: students who act up with teachers when the real issue is fear or anger at a parent or stepparent. Most teenagers are open and voluble about a bad teacher—you won't have to dig for clues. An exception is the student who has a history of problems with authority, especially teachers, and who may feel like his parents won't believe him if he complains about yet another bad egg. These struggling students deserve protection as much as the articulate student-council president.

The older student's grades, his report card narrative, and the consistency of his complaints and frustration about one particular teacher (not all of them or the institution of school itself) will give you more clues about when to step in and ask to have your child removed from a teacher's classroom.

NOT EVERYBODY'S GOT TALENT

When my father was in elementary school in Brighton Beach, Brooklyn, all students were given a singing test at the beginning of the school year. Each child was then placed in one of three groups: sopranos, altos, and listeners. The duties of the listeners? Learn the words to all the songs, attend all performances, and mouth silently.

Try that singing test now, and you'd find parents picketing outside the school with signs reading "Perfect pitch is relative" or "Solo parts discriminate!" Along with grade inflation has come talent delusion, leading to some interesting dilemmas. Drama teachers search for plays that have thirty-five parts of near-equal importance (hello again, *Annie*). An elementary school teacher in Baton Rouge told me she was mounting a production of *101 Dalmatians*. Every cast member needed not only a line of dialogue but also a name. The pressure was causing her to lose sleep: "Last night I woke up at two a.m. thinking, *Tic, Tac, and Toe! That's three right there!*"

Many parents behave like obsessive fans because they're convinced their child is remarkably talented or they're afraid she'll crumble if she realizes she's not. Others view sports, music, or any form of creative expression as potential résumé fodder to be pursued with determination but not necessarily joy. I always cheer inwardly when a parent says, "My son plays club basketball. He's not very good, but he loves it." They just saved themselves $3,000 on psychological testing—I know that's a healthy kid with a sensible mom and dad.

In terms of life lessons, extracurriculars are ideal. It's a blessing when you can leave the truth-telling to others. If the school informs your daughter that her dress is too sheer or the driving instructor chides your son for his scant attention to the rearview mirror, that means you don't have to do it. In the same spirit, you can sit back and be encouraging but not fanatical about your child's tryout for the football team or audition for *Legally Blonde: The Musical*. Let the coach or drama teacher call the shots, and then read lines with your child, go to the game, root or console within reason. What's reasonable? Consider that only about 2 percent of undergraduate students in bachelor's degree programs receive sports scholarships. That gives you a yardstick by which to measure a rational level of pressure to put on your high school running back.

Alas, teachers and coaches report that many parents are not able to contain themselves. A drama teacher recalled one parent's lament: "My daughter sings like Adele! How can she be playing a *saucer* in *Beauty and the Beast*? By the way, her schedule is too full of other extracurriculars to make it to all the rehearsals." A coach told me about a high school freshman who desperately wanted to get on the varsity baseball team. He was talented and made the team, but because he was the youngest, he naturally ended up spending a lot of time on the bench. His dad went straight to the coach, saying, "We both know Cameron is a phenomenal pitcher. So what's the problem? Why hold him back?"

Getting a minor role and warming the bench is how a child learns to tolerate frustration, study the skills of the more developed players, and push himself to practice on his own. It's also the only way he'll get to experience the surge of glory that comes when he lands a bigger role or better position. Without harassing the coach or inflaming your child's sense that he's been wronged, you can empathize. You do this not by focusing on the child's disappointment but by sharing your own setbacks, goals, and achievements.

I recently had a session with a mother who is a successful artist. Her teenage daughter is an aspiring painter as well. Sighing, the woman geared up to tell me some news.

"Well, I had entered my latest pieces in the biannual—"

I interrupted her and said in an encouraging tone, "And you were rejected."

"Um, yes. And you're glad about it?"

"For your daughter's sake. Now you can talk to her about how you feel, what you do to boost your morale when you're disappointed, and how you plan to improve your skills so you'll have a better chance of getting accepted next time."

When we try to shield our children from failure and disappointment, we send the message that it's unbearable. Pleading their case to the teacher or coach sends the additional signal that the child is too weak to handle this terrible trauma on her own. By sharing your own experiences, you're treating your child like an equal, and that show of respect is a powerful salve. You're also teaching her how to survive life's inevitable letdowns.

When is it appropriate to talk to your child's coach, drama teacher, or the leader of the debate team? After they enter middle school, never, unless the child is too ill to cancel a rehearsal or meeting herself. Otherwise, such conversations are your child's business. If you step in to advocate, you're depriving her of an opportunity to practice an essential skill that is more valuable than the issue you're managing on her behalf.

A TRUSTEE MAY NOTICE WHAT YOU'RE TOO CLOSE TO SEE

The parents sat stiffly on the couch for their first session. "We're here about our daughter," the mother began. "The teacher told us she broke down in class sobbing over a test. She's only ten!"

As a psychologist, I feel my antenna go up if a child is having emotional outbursts at school but not at home. That's a reversal of the norm.

"Do you have a photo of your daughter?"

The mom pulled out her phone and showed me a young girl in a baggy Swarthmore sweatshirt.

"Did one of you go to Swarthmore?"

"We both did," said Mom.

"We met there," said Dad

"So she's a double legacy?"

They nodded.

"Is she already worried about whether or not she's going to get in?"

"Oh maybe, but it's fine. We told her she doesn't even have to apply there if she doesn't want to," the mother said.

"She just better not go to State," muttered the dad. Mom shot him a critical look.

I reminded them, "Children don't see nuances. They have a very different level of cognitive ability than adults. Your daughter doesn't understand the concept of applying to multiple colleges or that even though you gave her that sweatshirt you won't be disappointed if she doesn't go to your alma mater. You can try to mend this by saying, the good thing about being in fifth grade is that you don't need to think about college for even a second now. You've got years and years to figure out where you want to be. So you can wear the sweatshirt if you want, or not. Either way is totally fine with us.'"

This girl's teacher was alert enough to notice her tears and call the parents right away, perhaps sparing the child years of anguish. Teachers and other trustees can act as a firewall between a child and her parents' expectations, projections, and unintended mixed messages.

SHINING A DIFFERENT LIGHT ON YOUR CHILD

One day a shy and studious seven-year-old arrived at her classroom early and slid into her seat. Her teacher, "a brawny woman" named Ms. Ward, was the only other person in the room. In her memoir, *Born Bright: A Young Girl's Journey from Nothing to Something in America*, C. Nicole Mason recalls Ms. Ward glancing up from her desk and commanding, "Come here."

> She continued to write in her grade book as I stood fully prepared to answer any question she threw my way. . . . She dropped her pen and looked up at me.

"You're smart. Do you know that? What do you want to be when you grow up?" Her unblinking eyes were trained on mine. She wanted me to understand what she was saying.

I shrugged. No one had ever asked me that question before and I did not have an answer.

"It doesn't matter if you don't know now. You're a smart little girl and you can go far, just keep it up."

I stood there, feet glued to the floor, waiting for her to say more, but she did not. She returned to her grade book. After a few moments, I retreated back to my desk. What did she mean by "keep it up" or that I could "go far," I wondered. Go where?

For Mason, the exchange sparked a flame of curiosity and self-awareness that led to a career as a professor, author, commentator, and public policy expert.

The benevolent trustee is a precious resource in every child's life. When a new patient tells me that *neither* of her parents made the grade—they were too angry, gloomy, preoccupied, or self-destructive to provide loving care—I always ask, "Who cherished you? Because it's clear to me that you were loved." Not one person has ever had to ponder this question for long. It was Auntie Louisa! Or a neighbor, coach, teacher, Grandma, the librarian at the elementary school. There was always one person who was able to connect with the child and somehow make it known, *I see you and I like what I see.*

Trustees have a wealth of gifts to offer. Sometimes it's uncritical and abiding love. Sometimes it's a dose of much-needed reality. They can recognize a talent or break the news to a parent that despite a child's aptitude for the oboe, she hates playing it. The teacher, the tutor, the camp counselor, the nanny—to get the best out of the trustees, simply assume the best of them. You'll usually be right.

Epilogue

Throughout this book I've called on you to take the role of cultural anthropologist, silent steward, or armchair traveler. I've asked you to view your child the way you would a visiting niece from a distant state, an exchange student from Kazakhstan, a discerning fashionista, a dog. Why? Because every day I see parents and children locked in such a tight embrace that there's no room for conversation. What I've shared here are the shifts of mind, practices, and incantations that work best to get parents to loosen the embrace and take a few steps back.

In a letter to a student, the poet Rainer Maria Rilke wrote about how separation leads to understanding and affection:

> Once the realization is accepted that even between the closest human beings infinite distances continue, a wonderful living side by side can grow, if they succeed in loving the distance between them which makes it possible for each to see the other whole against the sky.

To love the distance between you and your child, you need only honor what nature requires: the normal development of children as separate beings from their parents. With your words and actions you'll teach your child how to comprehend the world, locate himself in it, and explain it all to you. His universe will be different from any you have known; that's its beauty. But a young child lacks the vocabulary to paint the full picture. Small children are overwhelmed by all they sense and see; they need an alert, patient, and lively translator.

The minds of older children are already stuffed with words. They need a parent who strides in step while walking the dog and listening to a son's musings; who asks astute questions about the favorite TV show and not a daughter's private life; who waits without interrupting when a teenager is moved to share his pride or pain. It's not a stretch to say that the most valuable voice lesson is knowing when to keep quiet.

Your child is a new person every day: more cells, more wonder, more variations of anguish and delight. When you slow down, when you put down your phone and turn up your curiosity and enthusiasm, you deepen your connection. You serve as an escort out of technology's magnetic field and into the "great cathedral space" of childhood. In that wide and sacred place, children will speak from their heart. Listening to you, they'll learn empathy for themselves and others. Your world and theirs will be richer and more magical. You'll see each other whole against the sky.

Acknowledgments

This book would not exist without the editorial talent and support of Lynette Padwa. She keeps me on course and on topic. Also, she's funny. And patient. And calm. Instead of sending long e-mails, Lynette picks up the phone *to talk* or suggests we get together and do our work *in person*. Voice lessons personified.

Thank you to the Scribner team: my editor, Kara Watson, for her accessibility, warmth, gentle hand, and deft pivots toward clarity and style; publisher Nan Graham for her distinguished stewardship; editorial assistant Emily Greenwald, who kept our outlook fresh and up-to-date; Jaya Miceli for a playful and inventive jacket design; Kyle Kabel for an inviting interior design; and Mary Beth Constant for dexterous copyediting.

Gratitude to my agents, Suzanne Gluck (literary) and Debbie Greene (lecture), two women whose communication style I try to channel in any situation that calls for a particular magic: the ability to fuse laser-sharp business savvy with relaxed "best friendliness."

Thank you to Kara Wall, my assistant for more than a decade, for good humor, good sense, and a sharp eye; speedy interview transcriber Amanda Buckner; Liz Newstadt and Erica Lutrell of Chevalier's Books (Los Angeles's oldest independent bookstore!) for cheerleading authors and books; and the librarians of the lovely Pio Pico Koreatown branch

Acknowledgments

of the Los Angeles Public Library, the only place where I keep myself device-free and write in longhand.

I'm indebted to the National Association of Independent Schools for making the "View From the Nurse's Office" research project possible and to the nurses who so generously shared their insights into the changing world of students and parents, even as they applied Band-Aids and soothing words to their small charges.

How could I write a book about conversation without having good ones? Special thanks to my husband, Michael Tolkin, for his voice—deep, droll, and enlightening—and to my adult daughters, Susanna and Emma, for expanding my knowledge with the lexicons of their very modern lives. And to colleagues and friends: child and adolescent psychiatrist Kal Maniktala—enduring supporter for thirty-five years—for the pleasure of sharing the stories of our own passages and that of our families' stage after stage after stage; Dr. Gary Emery, longtime guru and guide; and Laurie Goodman, the playful, wise, and good, a fast walker and fun talker.

I've dedicated this book to my parents, aged eighty-nine and ninety-five as of this writing. Each provided voice lessons of merit from the start. Thank you, Mom, for taking my opinions seriously as soon as I started opining, for enrolling me in drama school, buying the puppets that led to the shows, that led to the lectures, that led to my travels, that led me to see the importance of preserving and protecting the art of conversation, particularly with people who assume they are too different to find a connection. And thank you for remaining open-minded about every twist and bend in human cultural expression.

Thank you, Dad, for the conversations that flowed as you walked me to school on your way to work each day and for remembering every one of my friends' names. But thanks especially for being a master storyteller. You see the humor in everything and see everything as material: growing up in Brighton Beach, your army years in India and Burma, entering dance contests in Harlem, the trials of publishing the *National Lampoon* and *Weight Watchers Magazine* in the same office. Your tales are sprinkled throughout everything I write.

Recommended Reading

This is a selective list of my current favorites, categorized, then alphabetically by author. I've left off big names and popular classics and included lesser-known titles that prop open the door to those conversations that leave parents tongue-tied and those that provide a portal to shared enchantment.

Books for Children

Ellis, Carson. *Du Iz Tak?* Somerville, MA: Candlewick Press, 2016. Beautiful and whimsical creatures speak in a made-up language. This friendly picture book for children ages seven and up covers a broad spectrum of modern family formation, including adoption, same sex, single, and step-parenthood.

Harris, Robie H., and Michael Emberley. *It's So Amazing!: A Book about Eggs, Sperm, Birth, Babies, and Families.* Somerville, MA: Candlewick Press, 2014.

Schaefer, Valorie Lee, and Josée Masse. *The Care & Keeping of You: The Body Book for Younger Girls.* Middleton, WI: American Girl, 2012.

Tarshis, Lauren. *I Survived Hurricane Katrina, 2005.* New York: Scholastic, 2011. The thrilling and historically accurate books of the *I Survived* book series feature children alone—at Pearl Harbor, during the attacks of September 11, during the invasion of the Nazis. Making you nervous? As is always a sensible strategy, check commonsensemedia.org for ratings based on educational value, positive messages, positive role models, violence and scariness, and language.

Waber, Bernard, and Suzy Lee. *Ask Me.* Boston: Houghton Mifflin Harcourt, 2015. A father and daughter walk and talk on an autumn day. The sparse words and lovely rhythm of their conversation serves as a surprisingly practical guide to the delicate art of parent-child call-and-response.

Books for Teens

Harris, Robie H., and Michael Emberley. *It's Perfectly Normal: Changing Bodies, Growing Up, Sex, and Sexual Health.* Somerville, MA: Candlewick Press, 2014.

Hoxie, W. J. *How Girls Can Help Their Country: Handbook for Girl Scouts.* Carlisle, MA: Applewood Books, 1913. The book was written by the organization's founder, Juliette Gordon Low. Applewood Books, a Massachusetts-based publisher devoted to "reprints of America's lively classics—books from the past that are still of interest to modern readers," released a hundredth-anniversary edition. Read it and learn how a girl can secure a burglar using just six inches of cord!

Natterson, Cara, and Josée Masse. *The Care & Keeping of You 2: The Body Book for Older Girls.* Middleton, WI: American Girl, 2012.

Silverberg, Cory, and Fiona Smyth. *Sex Is a Funny Word: A Book about Bodies, Feelings, and YOU.* New York: Triangle Square, 2015.

Books for You

Biddulph, Steve. *Raising Boys: Why Boys Are Different—and How to Help Them Become Happy and Well-Balanced Men.* Berkeley, CA: Ten Speed Press, 2013. An Australian author. A terrific, accessible, sensible book.

Damour, Lisa. *Untangled: Guiding Teenage Girls through the Seven Transitions into Adulthood.* New York: Ballantine Books, 2016. I recommend this gem to all the parents of teens in my practice.

Gnaulati, Enrico. *Back to Normal: Why Ordinary Childhood Behavior Is Mistaken for ADHD, Bipolar Disorder, and Autism Spectrum Disorder.* Boston: Beacon Press, 2013.

Isay, Jane. *Unconditional Love: A Guide to Navigating the Joys and Challenges of Being a Grandparent Today.* New York: HarperCollins, 2018.

Kobliner, Beth. *Make Your Kid a Money Genius (Even If You're Not).* New York: Simon & Schuster, 2017.

Lancy, David. *The Anthropology of Childhood: Cherubs, Chattel, Changelings.* Second Edition. New York: Cambridge University Press, 2015.

Laureau, Annette. *Unequal Childhoods: Class, Race, and Family Life.* Berkeley: University of California Press, 2011.

Recommended Reading

Leitman, Margot. *Long Story Short: The Only Storytelling Guide You'll Ever Need.* Seattle, WA: Sasquatch Books, 2015.

Lieber, Ron. *The Opposite of Spoiled: Raising Kids Who Are Grounded, Generous, and Smart About Money.* New York: HarperCollins, 2015.

Lythcott-Haims, Julie. *How to Raise an Adult: Break Free of the Overparenting Trap and Prepare Your Kid for Success.* New York: Henry Holt, 2015.

Nash, Jennie. *Raising a Reader: A Mother's Tale of Desperation and Delight.* New York: St. Martin's Press, 2003.

Olive, John. *Tell Me a Story in the Dark: A Guide to Creating Magical Bedtime Stories for Young Children.* Sanger, CA: Familius, 2015.

Ripley, Amanda. *The Smartest Kids in the World: And How They Got That Way.* New York: Simon & Schuster, 2013.

Roffman, Deborah. *Talk to Me First: Everything You Need to Know to Become Your Kids' "Go-To" Person about Sex.* Boston: Da Capo, 2012.

Shatkin, Jess. *Born to Be Wild: Why Teens Take Risks, and How We Can Help Keep Them Safe.* New York: Penguin Random House, 2017. Teenaged mice choose to drink more alcohol when in the presence of their peers. Adult mice? Same amount. There you go.

A Book for All

Fisher, Dorothy Canfield. *Understood Betsy.* First published in 1916.

My mom told me I loved this book as a child. I read it again recently and still do. The novel features a protagonist with a host of modern problems. At the start, nine-year-old Elizabeth Ann is a most pathetic creature: scrawny, pale, and self-absorbed, she suffers from math phobia, chronic digestive disorders, generalized anxiety, and nightmares. When she is sent to live with relatives on a farm in rural Vermont, an uncle picks her up at the train station and matter-of-factly hands her the reins of the horses and of a new life.

Understood Betsy is Canfield's best-known book. "A mother is not a person to lean on, but a person to make leaning unnecessary" is her best-known quotation.

Appendix

RELATIVE DIFFERENCES BETWEEN BOYS AND GIRLS IN BRAIN DEVELOPMENT AND FUNCTION, EXPANDED	
Boys	**Girls**
The inferior parietal lobe of the brain is generally larger in males; this area is involved in spatial and mathematical reasoning. The areas of the brain devoted to language develop more slowly in boys than in girls. Boys primarily use the left side of the brain when speaking and listening.	Girls have more neurons in the Broca's and Wernicke's areas of the brain, where language is produced and interpreted. The corpus callosum, the nerve tissue connecting the two hemispheres of the brain, is thicker in girls' brains, which facilitates communication. Girls use both sides of the brain when speaking and listening.
Boys are better at three-dimensional reasoning (for example, the ability to imagine how an object will look when rotated) and better able to separate emotion from reason.	Girls more automatically integrate emotion and reason.
Boys can more easily hyperfocus but are less adept at shifting from one task to another.	Girls' thicker corpus callosum enables them to multitask better than boys because they are able to process stimuli using both sides of the brain simultaneously.
Areas of the brain involved in spatial memory mature four years earlier in boys than in girls.	Areas involved in language and fine motor skills mature up to six years earlier in girls than in boys.

Appendix

Boys	Girls
Nearly all of boys' speech is comprehensible by age four and a half. On average, they utter fewer words per day than girls and speak more slowly.	Nearly all of girls' speech is comprehensible by age three. On average, girls utter two to three times as many words per day as boys and speak twice as fast.
Boys learn to read at a slower rate than girls.	Girls learn to read one year to eighteen months earlier than boys.
Body secretes less serotonin, making boys more impulsive, fidgety; also secretes less oxytocin and vasopressin, making them less sensitive to signs of pain or distress in others.	Body secretes more serotonin, making it easier for girls to modulate their moods and regulate emotional expression; also secretes more oxytocin and vasopressin, making girls quick to respond to signs of pain or distress in others.
To comfortably hear a speaker, boys require the person's voice to be six to eight decibels louder than girls require. Boys have a higher tolerance for background noise.	Neural connectors that create listening skills are more developed in the female brain. Girls can discern voices at lower decibels and also can discriminate nuances of tone better than boys. Girls hear better at higher frequencies. They are more easily annoyed or distracted by background noise.
Boys process visual cues differently than girls; they are drawn to cool colors and motion, are better at seeing in bright light.	Girls are drawn to warm colors, faces, textures. During the first three months of life, baby girls will increase eye contact and mutual gazing by 400 percent; boys' gazing does not increase. Girls remain more attuned to facial expressions and body language than boys. Girls are superior at seeing in low light.
Autonomic nervous system in males (which regulates internal organ functions like heart rate, blood pressure, and digestion) causes them to react to stress or confrontation with excitement. Their senses are sharpened and they feel exhilarated.	Autonomic nervous system in females causes them to respond to extreme stress by freezing in place and/or feeling sick, dizzy, nauseated, fearful.

Appendix

Boys	Girls
Boys have higher levels of testosterone; however, levels vary widely. Testosterone leads boys to express social energy through aggression and attempts at dominance.	Girls have higher levels of estrogen and progesterone, the "bonding" hormone. Girls use social energy to form attachments and alliances with peers and adults. They also experience stronger and more rapid fluctuations of mood.
Boys take longer to process emotional stimulation; they are more emotionally fragile than girls and harder to soothe.	Girls process emotions via more senses than do boys and are able to articulate and process emotionally evocative experiences more effectively. Their wider informational stream (for example, the ability to read others' facial expressions) can cause girls to take things more personally.
Boys do not seek out eye contact as often as do girls and are more verbally communicative when seated beside someone who seeks their attention and during shared physical activity.	Girls seek out and react positively to eye contact, face-to-face verbal communication, nodding, and smiling.

Notes

Author's Note

xv *the work has begun.* Russo, Francine, "Is There Something Unique About the Transgender Brain?" *Scientific American*, January 1, 2016. https://www.sci entificamerican.com/article/is-there-something-unique-about-the-trans gender-brain/.

Chapter 1. The Audience Is Listening

8 *brain development is indeed linked to social interaction.* Catherine Saint-Georges et al., "Motherese in Interaction: At the Cross-Road of Emotion and Cognition? (A Systematic Review)," *PLOS One* 8, no. 10 (2013). http://www .ncbi.nlm.nih.gov/pmc/articles/PMC3800080/.

10 *reduces their perception of pain during medical tests.* Joanne Loewy et al., "The Effects of Music Therapy on Vital Signs, Feeding, and Sleep in Premature Infants," *Pediatrics* 131, no. 5 (May 2013), http://pediatrics.aap publications.org/content/early/2013/04/10/peds.2012-1367.abstract.

11 *Her voice and heartbeat have literally caused the baby's brain to grow larger.* Douglas Quenqua, "Mothers' Sounds Are Building Block for Babies' Brains," *New York Times*, February 23, 2014, https://well.blogs.nytimes.com /2015/02/23/mothers-sounds-are-building-block-for-babies-brains.

12 *vocabulary-rich verbal input between birth and age five.* "Frequently Asked Questions about Brain Development," *Zero to Three*, https://www.zero tothree.org/resources/series/frequently-asked-questions-about-brain -development.

12 *children who hear a plentiful assortment of words and those who don't.* Margaret Talbot, "The Talking Cure," *New Yorker*, January 12, 2015, http://www.new yorker.com/magazine/2015/01/12/talking-cure.

14 *more advanced expressive language development at thirty-six months.* Nadya Pancsofar and Lynne Vernon-Feagans, "Fathers' Early Contributions to Children's Language Development in Families from Low-Income Rural Communities," *Early Childhood Research Quarterly* 25, no. 4 (October 2010), http://www.ncbi.nlm.nih.gov/pmc/articles/PMC2967789/.

16 *she responded with an emphatic "Yes!"* Personal conversation with Los Angeles–based early childhood educator Beth Weisman.

16 *enables baby to properly enunciate her words.* Renee Bevis, RN, "Why Kids Need to Learn to Eat (not just suck) and Hungry Babies Must Be Fed (even if their parents are afraid they'll get fat)," *Child Care Health Solutions* newsletter, January 2014.

18 *"Caregivers absorbed in devices . . ."* Jenny Radesky et al., "Patterns of Mobile Device Use by Caregivers and Children During Meals in Fast Food Restaurants," *Pediatrics* 113, no. 4 (April 2014), http://pediatrics.aap publications.org/content/pediatrics/133/4/e843.full.pdf.

20 *than a parent who is using his phone.* Leah Todd, "Parents Who Use Cell Phones on Playgrounds Feel Guilty, Study Finds," Phys.org, May 21, 2015, http://phys.org/news/2015-05-parents-cell phones-playgrounds-guilty .html.

20 *"How far am I going, they might reasonably worry . . ."* Susan Dominus, "Motherhood, Screened Off," *New York Times Magazine*, September 24, 2015, http://www.nytimes.com/2015/09/24/magazine/motherhood -screened-off.html.

21 *The seek-and-find pleasure is intensified.* Susan Weinsehenk, "Why We're All Addicted to Texts, Twitter and Google," *Psychology Today*, September 11, 2012, https://www.psychologytoday.com/blog/brain-wise/201209/why -were-all-addicted-texts-twitter-and-google.

22 *"Many Internet companies are learning what the tobacco industry . . ."* Bill Davidow, "Exploiting the Neuroscience of Internet Addiction," *Atlantic*, July 18, 2012, http://www.theatlantic.com/health/archive/2012/07 /exploiting-the-neuroscience-of-internet-addiction/259820/sh.

22 *"We may think that kids have a natural fascination with phones."* Linda Stone, interview by James Fallows, "The Art of Staying Focused in a Distracting World," *Atlantic*, June 2013, http://www.theatlantic.com /magazine/archive/2013/06/the-art-of-paying-attention/309312/.

22 *"very young children learn best via two-way communication."* Ari Brown,

Donald L. Shifrin, and David L. Hill, "Beyond 'Turn It Off': How to Advise Families on Media Use," *AAP News*, September 28, 2015, http://www.aappublications.org/content/36/10/54.full.

22 *"can also harm the amount and quality of sleep."* American Academy of Pediatrics, "American Academy of Pediatrics Announces New Recommendations for Children's Media Use," news release, October 21, 2016.

23 *"the number of schoolchildren needing expert help . . ."* Laura Clark, "Gadgets Blamed for 70 Per Cent Leap in Child Speech Problems in Just Six Years," *Daily Mail*, December 27, 2012.

26 *"they'll only know how to be lonely."* Nick Bilton, "The Child, the Tablet and the Developing Mind," *New York Times*, March 31, 2013, http://bits.blogs.nytimes.com/2013/03/31/disruptions-what-does-a-tablet-do-to-the-childs-mind/.

Chapter 2. The Great Cathedral Space of Childhood

50 *"The fairy tale is suggestive."* Bruno Bettelheim, *The Uses of Enchantment: The Meaning and Importance of Fairy Tales* (New York: Vintage, 1989).

Chapter 3. The Biggest, Strongest, Fastest

59 *If denied the opportunity, trouble awaits.* David Lancy, *The Anthropology of Childhood: Cherubs, Chattel, Changlings* (New York: Cambridge University Press, 2008).

60 *when girls and boys speak, do puzzles, or are presented with visual distractions.* David Walsh, PhD, *Smart Parenting, Smarter Kids* (New York: Simon & Schuster, 2011).

60 *areas that affect language, spatial memory, and motor coordination.* Virginia Bonomo, "Gender Matters in Elementary Education: Research-Based Strategies to Meet the Distinctive Learning Needs of Boys and Girls," *Educational Horizons* 88, no. 4 (Summer 2010), 257–64.

61 *"is less likely to annoy a boy."* Leonard Sax, "Sex Differences in Hearing: Implications for Best Practice in the Classroom," *Advances in Gender and Education* 2 (2010), 13–21. Full text online at www.mcread.org.

62 *"in the front row than he was in the back row."* Ibid.

62 *Relative Differences between Boys and Girls.* Chart information compiled and adapted from: Walsh, *Smart Parenting, Smarter Kids*; Sax, "Sex Differences in Hearing"; Bonomo, "Gender Matters in Elementary Education"; and Michael Gurian, *Boys and Girls Learn Differently!: A Guide for Teachers and Parents* (San Francisco: Jossey-Bass, 2001).

Notes

64 *something that happened two days ago, not that afternoon.* Gurian, *Boys and Girls Learn Differently!*

64 *slower to respond to the emotional or physical pain of others.* Ibid.

76 *"increasing the odds that they will suffer from anxiety, depression, and other disorders."* Peter Gray, "The Decline of Play and the Rise of Psychopathology in Children and Adults," *American Journal of Play* 3, no. 4 (Spring 2011), http://www.journalofplay.org/issues/3/4/article/decline-play-and-rise-psychopathology-children-and-adolescents.

81 *"smoke a FRESH cigarette!"* "10 Creepy Vintage Ads of Doctors Endorsing Cigarettes," *Ghost Diaries*, July 2015, http://theghostdiaries.com/10-creepy-vintage-ads-of-doctors-endorsing-cigarettes/.

81 *"symptoms of withdrawal when kept from gaming."* American Psychiatric Association, *Diagnostic and Statistical Manual of Mental Disorders* (Washington, DC: American Psychiatric Association, 2013).

82 *about 8 percent of gamers between the ages of eight and eighteen meet that criteria.* Daphne Bavelier, "Brains on Video Games," *Nature Reviews Neuroscience* 12 (December 2011), http://www.nature.com/nrn/journal/v12/n12/full/nrn3135.html.

82 *"feelings of happy connection."* Amanda Lenhart, "Teens, Technology and Friendships," Pew Research Center, August 6, 2015, http://www.pewinternet.org/2015/08/06/teens-technology-and-friendships/.

82 *more than three hours of daily play.* Andrew K. Przybylski, PhD, "Electronic Gaming and Psychosocial Adjustment," *Pediatrics* 134, no. 3 (September 2014), http://pediatrics.aappublications.org/content/pediatrics/early/2014/07/29/peds.2013-4021.full.pdf.

Chapter 4. The Boss, the Bestie, the High Priestess of Pretend

92 *are more likely to be prematurely sexually active.* B. J. Ellis et al., "A Longitudinal Study: Does Father Absence Place Daughters at Special Risk for Early Sexual Activity?," *Journal of Child Development* 74, no. 3 (May–June 2003), 801–821.

104 *the same conclusion: don't do it.* Brian Wansink, Lara A. Latimer, and Lizzy Pope, "'Don't Eat So Much': How Parent Comments Relate to Female Weight Satisfaction," *Eating and Weight Disorders*, June 6, 2016.

113 *"Say a sentence or ask a question in a variety of tones."* Peggy Post and Cindy Post Senning, *Emily Post's The Gift of Good Manners: A Parent's Guide to Raising Respectful, Kind, Considerate Children* (New York: William Morrow, 2005).

Notes

Chapter 5. Hard Topics

132 *"Other words have many different meanings (like play)."* Cory Silverberg and Fiona Smyth, *Sex Is a Funny Word: A Book about Bodies, Feelings, and YOU* (New York: Triangle Square, 2015).

138 *tailor the vocabulary to a level the child is sure to understand.* Betsy Brown Braun, *Just Tell Me What to Say: Sensible Tips and Scripts for Perplexed Parents* (New York: HarperCollins, 2008).

Chapter 6. Spirit Guides in Disguise

161 *attraction to risk helps teens separate.* Agnieszka Tymula, "Adolescents' Risk-Taking Behavior Is Driven by Tolerance to Ambiguity," *Proceedings of the National Academy of Sciences of the United States of America* 109, no. 42 (October 16, 2012), http://www.pnas.org/content/109/42/17135.

164 *emotionally loaded situations and images.* National Institute of Mental Health (NIMH), *The Teen Brain: Still Under Construction* (Bethesda, MD: 2011).

164 *anger and disgust.* Kate Lawrence, Ruth Campbell, and David Skuse, "Age, Gender and Puberty Influence the Development of Facial Emotion Recognition," *Frontiers in Psychology*, June 16, 2015, https://www.ncbi.nlm.nih.gov/pmc/articles/PMC4468868/.

164 *impact their response to stress.* NIMH, *The Teen Brain: Still Under Construction.*

176 *nine to ten hours a night.* Mary A. Carskadon, PhD, "Sleep and Teens—Biology and Behavior," National Sleep Foundation, Spring 2006, https://sleepfoundation.org/ask-the-expert/sleep-and-teens-biology-and-behavior.

176 *anxiety, depression, and impulsive behavior . . .* NIMH, *The Teen Brain.*

177 *absorb new information the following day.* Gary Stix, "Sleep Hits the Reset Button for Individual Neurons," *Scientific American*, March 22, 2013, https://blogs.scientificamerican.com/talking-back/sleep-hits-the-reset-button-for-individual-neurons/.

177 *". . . we lose touch with how impaired we are."* Camille Peri, "10 Things to Hate About Sleep Loss," *WebMD*, last modified February 13, 2014, http://www.webmd.com/sleep-disorders/features/10-results-sleep-loss.

178 *her techniques for talking suicidal people off ledges.* Jaime Lowe, "How to Talk to a Stranger in Despair," *New York Times Magazine*, January 13,

2017, https://www.nytimes.com/2017/01/13/magazine/how-to-talk-to-a-stranger-in-despair.html.

Chapter 8. The Visiting Niece from a Distant State

200 *"children have grown into adulthood."* Lucia Ciciolla and Suniya Luthar, "Why Mothers of Tweens—Not Babies—Are the Most Depressed," *Aeon*, April 4, 2016, https://aeon.co/ideas/why-mothers-of-tweens-not-babies-are-the-most-depressed.

203 *". . . mobile phone use among young people has been linked to depressed mood."* Ramin Mojtabai, Mark Olfson, and Beth Han, "National Trends in the Prevalence and Treatment of Depression in Adolescents and Young Adults," *Pediatrics* 138, no. 6 (December 2016), http://pediatrics.aappublications.org/content/early/2016/11/10/peds.2016-1878.

204 *winning money or eating chocolate.* Association for Psychological Science, "Social Media 'Likes' Impact Teens' Brains and Behavior," news release, May 31, 2016, https://www.psychologicalscience.org/news/releases/social-media-likes-impact-teens-brains-and-behavior.html#.WKIXCYWR-Kz.

Chapter 9. The Opinionators

231 *steal fresh tortellini.* "Massimo Bottura," *Chef's Table*, season 1, episode 1, directed by David Gelb (Netflix, 2015).

Chapter 10. The Trustees

267 *2 percent of undergraduate students in bachelor's degree programs receive sports scholarships.* "NCAA Recruiting Facts," National Collegiate Athletic Association, July 2016, https://www.ncaa.org/sites/default/files/Recruiting%20Fact%20Sheet%20WEB.pdf

Appendix

279 *Relative Differences between Boys and Girls.* Chart information compiled and adapted from: Walsh, *Smart Parenting, Smarter Kids*; Gurian, *Boys and Girls Learn Differently!*; Sax, "Sex Differences in Hearing"; and Bonomo, "Gender Matters in Elementary Education."

Index

Page numbers in *italics* refer to charts.

Index

Index